THE WORKS OF SRI CHINMOY

POETRY
VOLUME VII

THE WORKS OF SRI CHINMOY
POETRY
VOLUME VII

★

DISOBEDIENCE, TIME IS UP! • MATTER AND SPIRIT
MY PERFECTION-PROMISE TO GOD
I AM MY LIFE'S GOD-HUNGER-HEART
FAST, FASTER, FASTEST PROGRESS
GOD'S COMPASSION-EYE AND MY HAPPINESS-HEART
MY LIFE'S SIXTY-THREE HEART-BLOSSOMS • MY SOUL IS FREE
NO RETURN ON MY GOD-DESTINATION ROAD
COMMAND FROM GOD THE JUSTICE, WHISPER FROM GOD THE COMPASSION
GOD'S HEART I DESIRE, GOD'S FEET I CHOOSE
TAKE YOUR GOD-SEARCH SERIOUSLY • HEAVEN'S ECSTASY-FLAMES
IDLENESS: THE LONELIEST EXISTENCE IN THE ENTIRE WORLD
IMPURITY: THE MAD ELEPHANT MENTAL ASYLUM
MY JEALOUSY IS MY MADNESS-BURDEN
NO UNREACHABLE GOAL
SAY A FINAL FAREWELL TO YOUR MIND'S BONDAGE-LIFE
SUCCESS-JUMPS, PROGRESS-SONGS
PEACE: GOD'S HEART-HOME
MY EVENING DESCENDS • MY MORNING BEGINS
POWER AND LOVE • SCIENCE AND NATURE
A TRUE DISCIPLE • I CLIMB UP, I FALL DOWN

LYON · OXFORD
GANAPATI PRESS
XCI

THE WORKS OF SRI CHINMOY
POETRY
VOLUME VII

★

(CONTINUED)

THE DIFFERENCE BETWEEN GOD AND ME
GOD'S GREATNESS AND GOD'S GOODNESS
I AM FLYING AND FLYING AND FLYING
RETIREMENT NOT GRANTED • A HEART OF ONENESS-PEACE
GOD WAS SIMPLY SHOCKED • MY LORD READS MY LETTERS
THE DIFFERENCE BETWEEN A FALSE MASTER AND A TRUE MASTER
TWO DIVINE QUALITIES: CONFIDENCE AND SINCERITY
EMPEROR-SMILES. ORPHAN-TEARS
THE MOMENT I PLEASE GOD IN GOD'S OWN WAY
MY SUNRISE-HEART, PART I
YES, I CAN! I CERTAINLY CAN!!
GREAT PEOPLE AND GOOD PEOPLE • HERE AND NOW
IF I COULD START MY LIFE ONCE MORE
MY LIFE'S EVERY DAY HOPE-BLOSSOMS AND PROMISE-TREES
MY MASTER • TO-DAY IS THE DAY
THE STREET BEGGAR

LYON · OXFORD
GANAPATI PRESS
XCI

© 2022 THE SRI CHINMOY CENTRE

ISBN 978-1-911319-40-5

See appendix for notice regarding this edition.

FIRST EDITION WENT TO PRESS ON 13 JANUARY 2022

POETRY

VOLUME VII

PART I

DISOBEDIENCE, TIME IS UP!

DISOBEDIENCE, TIME IS UP!

1

Disobedience,
Time is up!
Now, you shut up,
Pack up
And go away!

2

Disobedience,
You have destroyed
My life's beauty
And my heart's fragrance.

3

There is no such thing
As negligible disobedience.

4

Disobedience,
You are always intolerable,
But you are never, never
Invincible.

5

Disobedience-thoughts
Are responsible
For the total loss
Of my heart-beauty's eyes.

6

Sleeplessly and breathlessly
Protect yourself
From disobedience-dragon,
O God-lover.

7

Today's disobedience
Is
Tomorrow's
Calamity-thunderstorm.

8

Disobedience unlimited
Is
Your stupidity-hunger.

9

This world of ours
Is full of disobedient people.
Can you not try
To be an exception?
Try!
Certainly you can succeed.

10

With hope
God built this world.
With disobedience
Man is building his world.

11

A disobedience-seeker
Is doomed to enter early
Into his spirituality-empty
    grave.

12

Disobedience,
God may come to you
With His Forgiveness,
But never, never with His
    Pride.

13

Obedience says to God,
"Father, please tell me
How I can please You more,
Infinitely more."

Disobedience says to God,
"God, if You are really
The Possessor
Of infinite Compassion,
How is it that You cannot
Make me happy
In my own way?"

14

In the inner world,
The seeker's disobedience
Is dangerous.
In the outer world,
The seeker's disobedience
Is contagious.

15

Poor God!
I feel sorry for You.
I am sure You never even
    dreamt
Of my disobedience.

16

Disobedience,
Look what you have done to me!
You have turned
My aspiration-flame-dreams
Into my frustration-ashes.

17

My Lord, I beg of You,
Do give me the capacity
To end my long acquaintance
And association
With disobedience.

18

Disobedience,
Do you not realise
That you make my Lord cry?
Can you not see
That you have devoured
God's Mountain-Hopes for me?

19

O my mind's disobedience,
O my heart's ingratitude,
Do tell me,
Who instigated whom first
To displease God?

20

Alas, my life-boat plies
Between
My life's disobedience
And
My soul's embarrassment.

21

Obedience prayerfully
Cares to see
God's Happiness-Heart.
Disobedience proudly
Dares to see
God's Volcano-Eye.

22

God-disobedience
Is
The universal ignorance-sleep.

23

Obedience is
Earth-heart-evolution.
Disobedience is
Earth-life-revolution.

24

My Compassion-Lord
Has promised me
That He will hold my hand,
Even in my disobedience-hell.

25

I was a fleeting dreamer
Of God-disobedience-force.
But now I am
A permanent dweller
In God-obedience-delight.

26

Disobedience,
God is infinitely more displeased
With you
Than you can ever dare
To imagine!

27

Disobedience,
What you want is constant
Attention-appreciation
From God,
But what you need is constant
Illumination-perfection
From God.

28

Disobedience
Is
To make extravagant demands
Upon God.

29

Disobedience,
Shame on you!
You are
The worst possible
 extremist
In God-rejection.

30

Disobedience of my mind-sword,
I do not want you.
Obedience of my heart-flute,
I love you and I need you.

31

Disobedience,
You have deserted spirituality.
Disobedience,
You have discarded integrity.

32

Disobedience-pride, hide!
My frustration-anger is all ready
To chide you ruthlessly.

33

Disobedience means
The mind's bold refusal
To bow to the illumined heart.

34

Disobedience means
The mind's shameless
 tug-of-war
With the blameless God.

35

Disobedience means
The heart's
Universal oneness-promise-
 destruction.

36

Disobedience
Is
A hardliner God-doubter.

37

Disobedience enjoys
Self-imposed exile
From God.

38

Disobedience,
You are blind!
Can you not see
That you are heading towards
An uncharted wilderness?

39

In the spiritual life,
Two real beasts:
Disobedience, the mad elephant,
And
Suspicion, the hungry wolf.

40

Disobedience
Is
Negativity's
Supreme authority in action.

41

Disobedience
Is
Spirituality's
Completely paralysing fall.

42

Disobedience
Is
A barking God-doubt-dog.

43

Disobedience,
You are more than
An aspiration-starvation.
You are more than
An aspiration-death.
You are indeed
An aspiration-grave.

44

Disobedience,
You teach me
How to dislike God
And
How to reject God.
But I clearly see
That your days are numbered,
For God's
Compassion-Illumination-
  Satisfaction
Will ultimately be victorious
In and through my life.

45

Disobedience,
Are you not lucky?
God has not given up,
Even on you.

46

Disobedience,
I am telling you once and for all,
Do the right thing:
Look at God's
Compassion-flooded Eye.
Be the right thing:
God's Forgiveness-seeker
And
God's Fulfilment-lover.

47

Disobedience,
God the Compassion whispered.
You did not care to respond.
Now God the Justice thunders:
"Surrender you must!
No escape! No escape!"

48

Disobedience,
Yesterday God stood
In front of you
As a street beggar.
Today the same God stands
In front of you
As the Absolute Lord
  Commander Supreme.

49

Disobedience,
God's rival you are.
Do you know what God does?
In spite of knowing
Who you are –
Destruction-dreamer,
Destruction-lover,
Destruction-enjoyer –
He claims you as His own,
Very own.

50

Disobedience,
Can you not try to be
God's worthy rival
By offering Him your
Ignorance-mountain
And
Ignorance-ocean?
Can you not try to become
His Eternity's choicest
　instrument,
Him to love,
Him to fulfil in
　His own Way?
Do not forget
That you are of God.
Do not forget
That you are for God
ONLY.

PART II

MATTER AND SPIRIT

MATTER AND SPIRIT

1

What is the difference
Between matter and Spirit?

Matter says:
"I have."

Spirit says:
"I am."

2

Matter
Cries for success-sky.

Spirit
Longs for progress-sun.

3

Matter challenges death
Only to lose.

Spirit ignores death
Only to conquer.

4

Matter
Is
Imagination-thought.

Spirit
Is
Aspiration-will.

5

Matter says to me:
"Look what I have."

Spirit says to me:
"Just feel what I am."

6

Matter
Is
Humanity's noise.

Spirit
Is
Divinity's Poise.

7

Matter serves
The divine in me.

Spirit feeds
The human in me.

8

Matter
Is
Ignorance-monster.

Spirit
Is
Wisdom-mountain.

9

Man entertains
Matter.

Man ascertains
Spirit.

10

Matter
Is
Evolution-joy.

Spirit
Is
Involution-peace.

11

With matter
I grow.

With Spirit
I glow.

12

Matter
Is
Dormant strength solid.

Spirit
Is
The all-awakening
Clarion-Call.

13

Matter
Is
Capacity unexpressed.

Spirit
Is
Quality revealed.

14

Matter
Is
A giant house.

Spirit
Is
A fruitful home.

15

Matter
Is
A very slow walker.

Spirit
Is
The fastest sprinter.

MATTER AND SPIRIT

16

Matter
Needs ambition-push.

Spirit
Needs satisfaction-pull.

17

Matter
Dampens and flattens
My enthusiasm.

Spirit
Quickens and enlightens
My enthusiasm.

18

Matter says:
"I can,
But
I don't want to!"

Spirit says:
"I can.
Look!
I have already done."

19

When I live in matter,
I at once become
My own funeral and burial.

When I live in Spirit,
I at once become
My journey's start
And
My journey's goal.

20

Matter
Is
Sleeping beauty.

Spirit
Is
Daring responsibility.

21

Matter tells me:
"Go back.
You have walked
Farther than you needed."

Spirit tells me:
"Go forward,
Go forward.
Indeed, you are meant
For the Call of the Beyond."

22

Matter
Is
Eternity's patience-exercise.

Spirit
Is
Infinity's radiance-
　distribution.

23

Every day
I am forced to listen
To matter's self-doubt-
　stories.

Every day
I enter into life's battlefield
To watch Spirit's
Self-conquest-power.

24

Matter and desire-life
Are inseparable.

Spirit and aspiration-breath
Are inseparable.

25

May my God-prayers
Envelop my matter-
　desire-life.

May my God-meditations
Satisfy the Spirit
In my aspiration-breath.

26

Matter is not cognisant
Of fear.

Spirit is cognisant
Of wisdom,
Birthless and deathless.

27

Matter and frustration
Like to live together.

Spirit and illumination
Love to live together.

28

Matter and I
Are good talkers.

Spirit and I
Are sleepless doers.

29

Matter
Is
My energy-stealer.

Spirit
Is
My energy-multiplier.

30

Matter
Is
My mind's sealed room.

Spirit
Is
My heart's wide-open door.

31

I am ashamed
Of my matter-life.

I am proud
Of my Spirit-breath.

32

Matter
Is stubborn.

Spirit
Is ever-born.

33

I implore matter
To care for me.

I implore Spirit
To share with me.

34

Matter's hobby:
Evolution-stories.

Spirit's hobby:
Involution-songs.

35

Matter needs
God-concentration
For matter's fastest
  progress.

Spirit needs
God-manifestation
For Spirit's fastest progress.

36

Greatness is sufficient
For matter's satisfaction.

Greatness is not sufficient,
Even goodness
Is not sufficient;
Beyond greatness and
  goodness,
Only oneness –
Absolute self-transcendence-
  oneness –
Is sufficient
For Spirit's satisfaction.

37

Matter
Has tremendous admiration
For the dignity of the mind.

Spirit
Has tremendous love
For the purity of the heart.

38

Matter's giant body
I admire.

Spirit's immortal
  heart-breath
I implore.

39

As I do not listen
To matter's continuous
  demands,
Even so, alas,
I do not listen
To Spirit's precious
  requests.

40

The moment I think
Of matter,
I see my mind's sky overcast.

The moment I think
Of Spirit,
I see rainbow-smiles
Within and without.

41

Matter
Is
Self-confinement.

Spirit
Is
Self-enlargement.

42

When I am matter-bound,
I feel that I am
An anxiety-thorn.

When I am Spirit-free,
I feel that I am
The flower-fragrance.

43

When I am matter-bound,
I feel that I am
A doubt-wolf.

When I am Spirit-free,
I feel that I am
A confidence-lion.

44

When I am matter-bound,
My world within is chaotic
And
My world without is chaotic.

When I am Spirit-free,
My world within
Is harmony-song
And
My world without
Is harmony-dance.

45

When matter moves
It really moves.

When Spirit moves
It moves,
   yet
It moves not.

46

Matter is not conscious
Of the existence-reality
Of Eternity's Silence
Or Infinity's Sound.

Eternity's Silence
And
Infinity's Sound
Spirit consciously embodies,
Reveals and manifests.

47

Matter
Is
Self-unawareness.

Spirit
Is
Self-quest and self-conquest.

48

Matter
Is
Self-doubt-confusion.

Spirit
Is
Self-faith-illumination.

49

Matter
Is my mind's
Trouble-preserver.

Spirit
Is my mind's
Trouble-shooter.

50

Matter
Is
Quantity's giant pride.

Spirit
Is
Quality's loftiest height.

PART III

MY PERFECTION-PROMISE TO GOD

MY PERFECTION-PROMISE TO GOD

1

My prayer
Is my perfection-promise
To God.
My meditation
Is my God-satisfaction
In God's own Way.

2

The stupidity-expert
Will eventually be exposed.
The wisdom-expert
Will eternally be adored.

3

My mind does not want
To remember
God's powerful Eye.
My heart tries
To remember
God's blissful Heart.

4

My desire-tour-cancellation
Has made God
Immensely happy.
My aspiration-journey-inception
Has made God
Universally happy.

5

God has revoked
My desire-car-license.
God has given me
A free aspiration-plane-ticket
To fly all over the world.

6

My mind pointedly reminds me
Of all the things
That God has not done for me.
My heart lovingly reminds me
Of all the things
That God has unconditionally
Done for me.

7

I see a new world
Of peace and bliss
Emerging from my age-old
Mind-hallucinations.
This is what
My compassion-heart
Has done for me.

8

Put your aspiring heart
Inside your boasting mouth.
Lo, you are on your way
To arriving at
Your God-Destination.

9

When I soulfully cry,
I see my Lord's
Smiling Eyes.
When I powerfully smile,
I see my Lord's
Fulfilled Dreams.

10

When I live inside
My Lord's Heart-Garden,
I feel that each time
I breathe in and breathe out
A new
God-realisation-hope
And a new
God-manifestation-promise
Have become
My two real friends.

11

My old friend
Was a thought-life.
My new friend
Is a will-fulfilled breath.

12

My Lord Supreme shows me
His Compassion-Power
To make me happy.
My Lord Supreme gives me
His Hope-Power
To make me perfect.

13

I see today
My self-giving gratitude-heart
Standing at the top of God's
Compassion-Distribution-List.

14

I need only one friend,
And my Lord Supreme
Has already given me
That particular friend:
His Compassion-Eye.

15

Alas,
Why do I not cheerfully,
Gratefully and sleeplessly
Allow God's Compassion-Light
To enter into my heart-room
Faster than the fastest
To turn me into
His peace-blossoming tree?

16

When I sleeplessly
Offer myself to God,
He tells me
I have now become
A true member of
His intimate and inner Circle.

17

Mine is the sound-life
That God uses to produce
His Victory here on earth.
Mine is the silence-heart
That God uses to transcend
His own Infinity's
Self-Transcendence-Dreams.

18

My searching mind
Is sincerely looking
For the heart-garden
Of the God-seekers.
My aspiring heart
Is selflessly looking
For the full manifestation
Of the sleepless God-dreamers.

19

My earth-responsibilities
Are my Heaven-sent
Opportunities
To bring to the fore
My divinity's prosperity
And offer it
To the heart of humanity
For the manifestation
Of God's Peace,
God's Bliss
And God's Satisfaction
On earth.

20

Not easy to find,
A purity-heart-temple.
But impurity-mind-debris
Is easily everywhere found.

21

God asks my clever mind
To shut up immediately.
God asks my torpor-heart
To wake up smilingly.

22

God and I every day
Play various games.
I play to win.
I play to prove
That I am a better player.
God plays to improve
His Game.
God plays to transcend
His Capacities.

23

Of all the Limbs of God,
I choose
God's Protection-Feet.

24

For him, either to love
The farthest soul
Or to love
The nearest man
Is an extremely difficult task.

25

From now on
I shall discount the things
That my soul does not need.
I want to make my soul happy
In my soul's way.

26

I came into the world
To enjoy the infinite Love
Of my Lord Supreme
And not to be employed
By the pleasures
Of ignorance-night.

27

Alas,
The narrowness of the mind,
The loneliness of the vital
And the idleness of the body
Have made me what I am now.

28

My heart's actions
And not my life's positions
Can and do please
My Lord Supreme.

29

My seeker-friend,
You can count
How many times
You have fallen.
I shall count only
How many times
You have bravely
And cheerfully arisen.

30

My seeker-friend, I love you,
Not because
You think well of me,
Not because
You always do good things,
But because
You are pleasing
Our Lord Supreme
In His own Way.

31

Most convincing,
Most satisfactory progress
We make in the spiritual life
Only after we have stopped
The mind's
Whirlwind-thought-speed.

32

The heart's faith
Chases the mind-car
And also silences
The mind's doubt-storms.

33

How can God
Have any confidence
In your spiritual life
If you do not want
To come out of
Your mind's desire-forest?

34

There cannot be a single mind
That has not suffered from
Ignorance-bound thoughts.

35

The mind loves
To stay indefinitely
In the ignorance-ego-hotel.

36

After a long time,
Today I am so happy
To watch inspiration-flames
Lighting my mind.

37

Every morning
I am awakened by my Lord's
Delight-Compassion-Whisper.

38

My soul has already told
My aspiration-heart
That there is no U-turn
On its realisation-road.

39

God loves me,
God loves my crying heart,
God loves my smiling soul.

40

A life of surrender
Strikingly lengthens
The heart's aspiration-strides.

41

My devotion
Purifies my heart.
My surrender
Satisfies my Lord.

42

My heart's sincerity-flames
God transforms
Into His Divinity-Sun.

43

A mind of peace
Expands and expands
And becomes a citizen
Of oneness-aspiration-land.

44

Show, show
Your surrender-life.
God will stop
Your desire-train.

45

An impurity-mind
Is a heart-sinking
Experience.

PART IV

I AM MY LIFE'S GOD-HUNGER-HEART
PART 1-4

I AM MY LIFE'S GOD-HUNGER-HEART

Part I

1

I am
My life's
God-hunger-heart.

2

Mind
Is by nature bitter.
Heart
Is by nature sweet.

3

The unknowable God
May be honoured,
But the knowable God
Must be loved.

4

Just because my soul's love
For me is unimaginable,
My soul has the right
To chastise and punish me
For my life's
Perfection-dream-fulfilment.

5

A division-mind
Is not only to be doubted
But discarded.
A oneness-heart
Is not only to be loved
But treasured.

6

"Morning shows the day."
There is much truth in it.
A God-seeker
Must be an early bird
If he wants to proceed
In his inner life of aspiration
And if he wants to succeed
In his outer life of dedication.

7

Expectation does not want
To converse with frustration.
Frustration is always tempted
To converse with expectation –
And sometimes it succeeds.
I want my mind to be as wise
As my heart is.
Therefore, I command my mind
To keep out of
The expectation-frustration-
Conversation.

8

My seeker-friend,
Pray and meditate soulfully
Every day, without fail,
So that in this lifetime
You can realise God.
Even so,
God does not expect you
To be in a hurry.
At God's choice Hour,
You will definitely realise God.
Rest assured,
There is no deadline.

9

Do you believe in
The existence of your soul,
Who is the direct representative
   of God
In your life?
If so,
Then do try to make your soul
   happy.
How will you do that?
It is by cheerfully acting in
   obedience
To the orders of your own
   inner Pilot.

10

I came into the world to prove
That our soul's powers
Are next to God's only,
And no other power
Can ever dare to equal
The powers of the soul,
The God-representative on earth.

11

I came into the world
Sleeplessly to produce
God-Smiles.

12

My Beloved Lord Supreme,
I wish to become an eternal
   traveller
In distant galaxies.
Will You help me, my Lord?
"My child,
I shall help you.
I am asking your ageless
And deathless soul-bird
To do the needful."

13

My Lord Beloved Supreme,
Although I do not obey You,
Do You have any specific advice
For me today?

"My child, your conscious and deliberate
Refusal to comply
With My Compassion-Request
Will unmistakably destroy
Your aspiration-hunger
And dedication-thirst."

14

My Lord Beloved Supreme,
I am completely lost
Between Your Justice-Light
And Your Indifference-Might.
Do forgive me.
Do give me the capacity to please You
In Your own Way.

15

My Lord Beloved Supreme,
I am not praying to You
To shorten my road.
I am praying to You
To strengthen my heart.
I am praying to You
To grant me liberation.
I am praying to You
To grant me Compassion.

16

My Lord Beloved Supreme,
I am not praying to You
To give me what You have
And what You are.
I am praying to You
To take what I have
And what I am.

17

My Lord Beloved Supreme,
I am not praying to You to bless me
With a larger than the largest home.
I am praying to You to bless me
With a oneness-heart-home
Where Your Infinity's Peace
And Immortality's Bliss
Together sing, together play
And together dance.

18

My Lord, I bow to You,
O God the Creator.
My Lord, I bow to You,
O God the creation.
My Lord, I bow to You,
O today's God the man.
My Lord, I bow to You,
O tomorrow's man the God.

19

If your love of God is not enough,
If your devotion to God is not
  enough,
If your surrender to God is not
  enough,
Then employ your gratitude-tears
To increase your love, devotion
And surrender.
Your gratitude-tears can and will
  be
Of immediate help.

20

Short is the forgiveness-supply
The world receives from my mind.
Abundant is the forgiveness-
  supply
The world receives from my heart.
Unlimited is the forgiveness-
  supply
The world receives from my soul.

21

Alas, I am totally lost
Between my mind's ego-volcano
And my heart's oneness-fountain.

22

As long as man
Just thinks of God,
No life will be a failure.

23

Alas,
The insecurity-guest
That I love so much
Is my real enemy.

24

I vehemently ignore
My decision-making mind.
I self-givingly implore the
  presence
Of my direction-giving soul.

25

Doubt is something we acquire
But do not require.
Fear is something we acquire
But do not require.
Impurity is something we acquire
But do not require.
Ignorance is something we
  acquire
But do not require.
Divinity is something
We not only require
But also acquire
Only on the strength
Of God's Willingness to give
And our willingness to receive.

26

Every day my compassion-flooded
 soul
Feeds my Heaven-climbing heart
And silences my cyclonic
 questions.

27

My soul knows
My mind's room number.
It comes to my mind-room
To be of help,
But my mind vehemently rejects
My soul's unconditional help.

My soul knows
My heart's room number.
It comes to my heart-room
To be of help.
My heart not only receives
Unconditional help
But also offers ceaseless
Gratitude-tears in return.

28

My sleepless faith-heart
Is my peerless
Confidence-life-builder.

29

My Lord,
I am ready to wait,
Wait for Your Eternity's
Compassion-flooded Call.
"My child, cry,
Cry only one more time
For My Arrival.
This time I will definitely come."

30

God was waiting,
God is waiting
And God will always wait
For my life's
Perfection-satisfaction-sunrise.

31

The mind's obedience-necessity
Has no limit.
The heart's compassion-capacity
Has no limit.

32

God tells me that because
I am a true God-lover,
He will never allow me
To go my own way.

33

God-obedience has to be
The strongest point in my life
If I want my heart to be hungry
For God's Compassion-Eye-
   Favours.

34

God wants me to have
A very special fondness
For my oneness-heart-sky
And not for my vastness-mind-
   desert.

35

God
Is God-Eternity's
Forgiveness-Sweetness.

36

The most sacred duty
Of a God-server
Is his desireless and sleepless
Self-offering.

37

I am supremely happy
Because my heart-master
Is always exceptionally kind to
   me.

38

The path of God-obedience
Is the only path
That I sleeplessly and breathlessly
   need.

39

Each pure thought
Embodies the beauty and
   sweetness
Of paradise.

40

When I become a soulful lover
Of God's Dream,
God becomes a fruitful Fulfiller
Of my reality.

41

What am I doing?
I am exploring my own
Aspiration-surrender-gratitude-
   selves.

42

May I grow in the silence
Of Eternity's Heart.
May I glow on Infinity's Face.

43

Start, start, start!
Delay not
Your God-dedication-day.

44

There is no difference between
My surrender-heart
And
My happiness-life.

45

Finally I have convicted
My doubting mind,
Which is not only usually
But constantly guilty.

46

My Lord of Compassion whispers,
But, alas,
I am always talking and talking
With my stupid mind.

47

When my heart makes
Innumerable mistakes,
My compassionate Lord Supreme
May leave my heart for a short
   time.
But like a traveller
Who covers some distance
And comes back,
My Lord Supreme also comes back
To my heart-home.

48

Is there any human being on earth
Who has never suffered
From expectation-headache?

49

Each soulful meditation
Has the capacity to show me
Where God is hiding.

50

My sweet Lord Supreme,
My mind is too old.
Do give me a new mind.

My sweet Lord Supreme,
My heart is too weak.
Do give me a strong heart.

My sweet Lord Supreme,
My life is too useless.
Do give me a useful life.

Part II

51

I am
My life's
God-hunger-heart.

52

Nothing is more important
Than my heart's sleepless
  cry
For God's Compassion-Eye,
His Protection-Feet
And His Forgiveness-Heart.

53

My Lord, my Lord, my Lord,
From today on
I shall not cry anymore for Your
  attention;
No, not even for Your Compassion.
I shall cry only for my perfection.

54

My Lord, my Lord, my Lord,
I know that unless I satisfy You
In Your own Way,
My own satisfaction will always
  remain
A far cry.

55

Each time my mind cherishes
A divine thought,
God drops a Compassion-Drop
From His Fountain-Delight-Eye.

56

No more shall I climb up
My hope-mountain-heights.
From now on I shall live
Inside the heart of faith-fountain
And inside the breath of
  promise-sky.

57

I sail with perfection-oneness
And satisfaction-peace
Only when I unconditionally love
My Lord Beloved Supreme.

58

God has provided my mind
With a thousand exits
To leave doubt-prison.
Alas, my mind simply does not
　want
To avail itself
Of this golden opportunity.

59

Spiritual awakening, spiritual
　feelings
And spiritual self-giving
Must be natural and spontaneous
And can never be forced.

60

The heart's love for God
And the mind's obedience to God
Can and must go together.

61

My soul's promise
And my heart's satisfaction
Walk, march and run together
Along the same road
To reach the Heart of the
　Unknowable.

62

Spirituality is not
　self-forgetfulness.
Spirituality is
　self-awareness.
Spirituality is God-fulness.

63

My Lord Beloved Supreme loves
Even my abysmal abyss Godless
　days
And my abysmal abyss Godless
　nights!

64

O my tormented mind,
I am my lover-heart.
Your days are numbered.
My protector-soul
Is fast approaching my
　lover-heart.

65

I always choose God's Needs
Over my needs.
This is the only real way
To make myself and keep myself
  happy.

66

I never want to count
My heart's aspiration-moments.
I just want to multiply
My life's dedication-hours.

67

My Lord Supreme,
May I always be found
Between my prayer-life-beauty
And my aspiration-heart-
  fragrance.

68

Ambition kills spirituality.
Aspiration not only revives
  spirituality
But also energises and
  immortalises
Spirituality.

69

My life's insecurity
And my heart's satisfaction
Always love to remain
Strangers to each other.

70

May my prayer-heart-power
Silence every day
My desire-mind-sound.

71

I am so happy
That I now have the capacity
To compel my life to surrender
To my heart's
Secret and sacred God-hunger.

72

God wants me to be the owner
Of God's Smile-Beauty-Heart.
He does not want me to be the
  owner
Of my self-pity-tears.

73

O seeker,
You want to know what
Your insecurity, jealousy and
   impurity
Have done to you?
Your insecurity, jealousy and
   impurity
Have spread death-seeds
In your inner life of aspiration
And your outer life of dedication.

74

I am divinely proud
Of my mind
Because it is sleeplessly obedient
To God.

I am supremely proud
Of my heart
Because it is breathlessly grateful
To God.

75

My mind thinks that nothing
Has to change.
My heart feels that everything
Has to change.
My soul knows that everything
Is already changed in the inner
   world
And now is in the process of being
   changed
In the outer world.

76

I need God's Compassion only,
I need God's Affection only,
I need God's Love only
To be really, divinely
And supremely fulfilled.

77

Even the very thought of
   gratitude
Clears my mind,
Purifies my heart
And satisfies my life.

78

Every day
I keep my heart's door open
To impossibility's
Highest and brightest galaxies.

79

My prayer-mind
Is my miracle-power.
My meditation-heart
Is my satisfaction-tower.

80

Each human life
Has only two supreme necessities:
The God-foundation within
And the God-illumination
 without.

81

Short, shorter and shortest
Is the span of my earthly fame.
Long, longer and longest –
Nay, birthless and deathless –
Is my soul's Heavenly
 God-oneness-game.

82

While my soul is in this body,
I must learn the proper way
To love God, serve God and
 fulfil God
Here on earth and there in
 Heaven.

83

O my suspicious mind,
I shall not allow you
To destroy the most precious
Faith-fragrance of my heart.

84

True love lives
Inside the life-garden.
True devotion lives
Inside the heart-flower.
True surrender lives
Inside the soul-fragrance.

85

I am not self-indulgent
Only when I choose
God's Compassion-
 Protection-Feet.
Otherwise,
I am always self-indulgent.

86

I want to be God's
Constant willingness-slave.
God wants me to be
His sleepless, breathless
Oneness and fulness-child.

87

Every morning
My compassionate Lord Supreme
Tells me the same thing:
"My child, become an
   aspiration-grower
And not an expectation-collector.
I shall give you everything that
   I have
And that I am
At My choice Hour."

88

Who can reverse the course of my
   life-river
So that I may reach the Golden
   Shore?
God the Compassion-Eye
And
God the Forgiveness-Heart.

89

One God-realisation-hero
Absolutely can challenge and
   destroy
The pride of the world-ignorance-
   army.

90

I have definitely two goals:
My very short-term goal is
   self-giving.
My very long-term goal is
   God-becoming.

91

Birthless is the heart-beauty
Of my love
For my Lord Beloved Supreme.
Deathless is the soul-fragrance
Of my surrender
To my Lord Beloved Supreme.

92

God loses faith in us
Only when our enthusiasm-mind
And eagerness-heart
Deliberately start limping.

93

When I was in the desire-world,
I was forced by the undivine forces
To live in an abyss of nothingness.
Now that I am in the
   aspiration-world,
The divine forces are helping me
Climb up my
   realisation-pinnacles.

94

God laughs and laughs
When I doubt Him to my
　heart's content.
God cries and swims in a sea
　of despair
When I cherish even an iota
　of doubt
About myself.

95

God loves me unconditionally
Not because I have a great mind
And not because I have a good
　heart
But because, unlike human
　beings,
He simply does not know
And does not want to know
How to do anything else.

96

It is never too late to seek newness.
It is never too late to achieve
　fulness.
What we need are
The heart's eagerness-tears
And the mind's enthusiasm-
　smiles.

97

May my faith-heart
Run faster than lightning speed
To arrive at my God-destination.

98

God wants me to simplify
My life-story,
God wants me to purify
My heart-breath,
And God Himself wants to glorify
My soul-song.

99

At least in my case,
I am absolutely sure that
My endless fountain of creativity
Comes from only one Source
And that Source is
The unconditional
　Compassion-Eye
Of my Beloved Supreme.

100

Only my heart's streaming tears
Can and shall expedite
My Lord's Compassion-flooded
　Arrival.

Part III

101

I am
My life's
God-hunger-heart.

102

My soul's highest promise
And my Lord's deepest
   Satisfaction
Are two immortal travellers,
Walking side by side
Along Eternity's Road.

103

A perfect Truth-seeker and
   God-lover
Is not Heaven-born.
He is earth-born
From earth's sleepless and
   breathless
Tears and cries.

104

Each and every God-thought
In my mind
Comes from the peace-fragrance
Of my heart.

105

Ignorance-night invades us
Only when our hearts
Are empty of devotion.

106

Aspiration
Is how I breathlessly feel
And not
What I ceaselessly talk about.

107

My mind's fog and clouds
Cannot hide
The sunlit path of my heart.

108

My aspiration-heart dearly
   loves me
Because I love God only.
My God-realisation-soul
   proudly loves me
Because God is my All.

109

Today my mind's desire-night
Is over.
My heart's aspiration-dawn
Is blossoming.

110

God cannot help feeling shocked
When He hears from me
That I am an utter failure.

111

Peace-seed
Is my heart's inner name.
Bliss-harvest
Is my life's outer name.

112

Each and every pure thought
  of mine
Is a direct and perfect
  representative
Of God's purest Dream
Here on earth.

113

My Lord, I do so many things for
  You.
How many things do You do
For me?
"My child, since I am an old man,
I do only one thing for you.
Every day, for twenty-four hours,
I cradle you inside
  My Compassion-Eye
And Forgiveness-Heart."

114

Our oneness-inspired actions
Are the only actions
That God treasures.

115

May the beauty, purity and
  fragrance
Of my heart
Fly beyond time and space.

116

During the day I amuse my Lord
With my life-stories.
At night I feed my Lord
With my soul-songs.

117

God will tell the whole world
That I am a supremely choice
  instrument
Of His
Only when my eyes are filled
With the beauty of silence
And my heart
With the divinity of peace.

118

I can clearly see that each time
I shake hands with desire,
The beauty of my aspiration-life
Is immediately marred.

119

My aspiring heart is immortalised
By God Himself
Just because I am no longer
Victimised by my doubting mind.

120

I was born of hope-seed
To fly
In Infinity's Promise-Sky.

121

The farther I move away
From my own expectation-prison,
The closer my Lord Beloved
   Supreme
Comes to me
With His immortality's Joy, Love
And Pride.

122

My Lord Beloved Supreme,
When You bless me with Your
Heart's Compassion-Ocean,
What can I give You in return
To make You happy?
"My child, only a gratitude-drop
From your heart-cup."

123

My Lord,
Is there any single piece of advice
You can give me
That will immediately illumine
   me
And satisfy me completely?
"Yes, My child, I have one.
At every moment listen
To your dreaming heart-whispers
And never listen
To your roaming mind-roar."

124

I pray to sit
At God's Compassion-Feet.
I meditate to see
God's Illumination-Heart.

125

Humanity's most deplorable
   audacity
Is its declaration:
"No oneness-heart-exercise!"

126

Since you know that your mind
Is conscience-guilty,
Why do you hesitate
To correct your mind?

127

As the desire-mind-attack is
   severe,
Even so is
The aspiration-starvation-attack.

128

May my soul's rainbow-beauty
Brighten my heart-sky
Every day.

129

Mine is the heart
That feeds on gratitude-blossoms.
Mine is the life
That feeds on surrender-blooms.

130

The mind that thirsts
For the Newness-God-Beauty
I have.
The heart that hungers
For the Oneness-God-Fragrance
I am.

131

My desire-mind wants to bind
God's powerful Hands.
My aspiration-heart wishes to
   touch
God's beautiful Feet.

132

O my mind,
Stop broadcasting your
   ego-balloon-news!
God wants to hear
My heart's sweetness-
   oneness-flute-melody.

133

God Himself has brought me
To the path of spirituality.
Therefore, it is my bounden duty
To love Him, please Him and
   fulfil Him
Only in His own Way.

134

Each time I dive deep within,
My Lord Supreme blesses me
With the paradise-fragrance
Of the ever-transcending Beyond.

135

Each man
Is a helpless victim-slave
To his own self-importance.

136

Today I am a supreme enjoyer
Of two realities:
My fast-decaying doubt-mind
And my fast-blossoming
   faith-heart.

137

Your progress-delight
Is guaranteed
The moment your heart can sing
A prayerful and tearful God-song.

138

Beauty incarnate
Is a God-lover.
Delight incarnate
Is a God-server.

139

A twenty-four-hour God-lover
Can never have a vulnerable point:
So says God.

140

My mind is happy because
My mind is choosing
   God's Victory
Over my mind's victory.

My heart is happy because
My heart is choosing
   God's Needs
Over my heart's needs.

141

Desire-mind-tragedy
I was.
Aspiration-heart-melody
I am.

142

A stubborn unwillingness-mind
I was.
A docile willingness-heart
I am.

143

Spirituality without purity
Is like
A boat without the boatman.

144

Only a peace-bird-heart
Can fly
In God's own Rainbow-Sky.

145

Only a peace-bird-heart
Can dance
To God's universal
   Oneness-Melody.

146

Eagerness-sincerity
And aspiration-intensity
Always love to be
In each other's company.

147

Forgiveness
And
Happiness
Are twins.

148

Choose we must!
Desire's destruction-dance
Or
Aspiration's liberation-song.

149

God Himself nurtures
My heart's fondest hopes
And
My life's bravest promises.

150

No one told me;
I just know that God's Eye
And His Compassion-Heart
Will help me hold
His flaming universal
   Peace-Torch.

I AM MY LIFE'S GOD-HUNGER-HEART

Part IV

151

I am
My life's
God-hunger-heart.

152

Only by bringing the positive
   qualities,
And not even one negative quality,
Of human beings to the fore
Will this world be able to make
Abiding progress.

153

In the long run
It is the haters of mankind,
Not the lovers of mankind,
Who will be the really miserable
   losers.

154

When I sincerely pray
And soulfully meditate,
I feel that I am only
A mere instrument.
There is a higher Power
That is coming to help me,
And that higher Power
Is God's Grace.

155

When we pray and meditate,
We are not taking away
God's Strength;
Only we are establishing
A free access
To everything God has and is.

156

We have so many friends
Within us and around us.
It is we who have to accept
   the world,
Not as our enemy
But as our true, illumining
And fulfilling friend.

157

Look only at the bright side.
The bright side means
To have implicit faith in ourselves
And in others
And to feel oneness-light
And fulness-delight.

158

The answer to the problems
Of this world
Is for every one of us
To go far beyond
Our present capacity-boundary
And become better citizens
Of the world.

159

Contemplation is something
Far beyond the vastness
Of meditation.
Contemplation is God-oneness
　itself.

160

In your absolutely best
　meditation,
Your entire being offers itself
To the Supreme –
Your soul with its illumination,
Your heart with its aspiration,
Your mind with its clarity,
Your vital with its determination,
Your body with its alertness.

161

Once we have peace,
We feel that
We have everything
In the outer world
And we have become everything
In the inner world.

162

We have to gratefully help
The inner world –
The world that wants to
　supply us
With the light, joy, peace
　and oneness
Of the Beyond –
To come to the fore.

163

In this world we are all
Running after satisfaction.
He gets satisfaction
By doubting me.
I get satisfaction
Because God's Grace is acting
In and through me.

164

If I become a better person,
Mother-Earth will be so happy
Since She will be blessed
With one less undivine
And unproductive soul.

165

When we allow the doubting
   mind
To come forward,
Our imagination-bird's wings
Are clipped
And its flight is all over.

166

At your journey's start,
Have a pure mind,
A receptive heart
And a willing life
To surrender to God's Will
To expedite your journey.

167

Every day we have to go
To our heart-garden
To see a beautiful
   inspiration-rose –
Not yesterday's rose-beauty
But today's rose-divinity.

168

Your heart and your life
Must know
What prayer and meditation are.
Prayer and meditation
Are the Life-Breath of God.

169

We have to believe in a higher
   Power.
Only by believing in a higher
   Power
Can we go beyond and beyond
Our limited, human capacity.

170

In my case,
It is not a matter of decision;
It is a matter of obedience.
I simply listen to the dictates
Of my Inner Pilot.

171

Just a little
Of the soul's illumination
Washes away
All the undivine things you have
   done
Over an untold period of time.

172

In the spiritual life
There is no rest.
Either we have to go forward
Or nature will force our
   unaspiring life
To go backwards.

173

Do not allow your mind
To take your heart
Out of the soul's faith-garden
Into the mind's doubt-forest.

174

Dive deep within.
What more do you need to
  accomplish,
As long as God is inside your heart
And you are inside God's Heart?

175

Your cheerful joy
Is the expression
Of your gratitude-heart
To your Inner Pilot.

176

Gratitude is something very sweet
That makes you feel
Your whole existence has offered
Something great and precious to
  God.

177

Many will come and many will go.
But why do you have to be
One of those who leave God?
Can you not be one with your
  heart
For God-embodiment and
God-fulfilment?

178

Cultivate your heart's oneness
  with God
And you will see:
Life is not a mere dream;
Life is not a tragic error;
Life is a touch of magic –
Miracle after miracle.

179

Do not reject the doubting mind.
Make your mind clear and pure;
Teach it to think positively.
Your mind will eventually become
A real help to you.

180

Peace will take you
Closer to God.
Bliss will keep you
In God.

181

Because of our wild human
 nature,
We need God's Forgiveness
At every moment.
We cannot move an inch forward
Without having
God's Forgiveness-Heart.

182

Heaven is around us
When we meditate.
And when we do not meditate,
Everywhere is hell.

183

Outwardly
He barks and barks
At his spiritual children.
But inwardly
They see a fountain of peace
And an ocean of love.

184

You are not valuing
Your Heavenly Father's
 spiritual wealth.
What are you valuing?
Your lethargy-idleness-
 ignorance-tree.

185

Life is expectation,
And expectation can be either
Illumination or frustration.
There is practically no difference
In the eyes of a God-realised soul.

186

Feel at every moment
That you have a few new names:
Cheerfulness, soulfulness,
 devotedness,
Closeness and oneness.
These names will satisfy God
Far beyond your imagination.

187

A new wave of opportunity,
A new wave of determination,
A new wave of satisfaction
God wishes to see
In each of His seeker-children.

188

While practising meditation
 soulfully,
Remember that
The heart of regularity-joy
Makes us perfect.

189

O seeker, dive deep within.
Inside peace
Is our Perfection-Lord Supreme.
Inside oneness
Is our Satisfaction-Lord Supreme.

190

I will always prefer my inner
   school,
For the Teacher is none other than
My Lord Supreme.

191

Who says
Meditation is a lack of activity?
On the contrary,
Meditation intensifies activity
In a divine way.

192

Meditation
Increases life's intensity
And shows us life's true purpose.

193

When we meditate before we act,
We get satisfaction
Because we know we are working
Not for ourselves,
But for our Inner Pilot.

194

Not to value God's
   Compassion-Light
And God's Justice-Height
Equally
Is to make a serious blunder.

195

Every day try to sing
At least one obedience-song
To love and please God
In His own Way.

196

The life-breath
Of spirituality-hunger
Is obedience.

197

My Beloved Lord Supreme,
So many of your choice
    instruments
Have failed, failed badly.
Why? Why?

"My child,
There is only one answer
And that answer is disobedience,
Inner and outer disobedience."

198

To transcend
Our heart-capacities
Means to transcend
Our life-qualities.
Capacity and quality must go
    together.

199

For many years, my Beloved
    Supreme,
You have brought into my
    inner life
Your boundless Compassion,
    Concern,
Affection, Love and Blessings.
Yet far beyond my own
    imagination,
I continue to disappoint You.

200

Call it obedience
Or call it oneness,
But try to feel the necessity
Of listening to your own
    highest self.

PART V

FAST, FASTER, FASTEST PROGRESS

FAST, FASTER, FASTEST PROGRESS

1

I make progress fast
When I am
A professor of peace.

I make progress faster
When I am
A teacher of peace.

I make progress fastest
When I am
A student of peace.

2

I make progress fast
When I see a flower.

I make progress faster
When I feel the beauty
Of a flower.

I make progress fastest
When I breathe the fragrance
Of a flower.

3

I make progress fast
When my mind
Cheerfully loves God.

I make progress faster
When my heart
Soulfully serves God.

I make progress fastest
When my life
Unconditionally obeys God.

4

To make progress fast
I uproot my heart's ego-plant.

To make progress faster
I cut down my mind's ego-tree.

To make progress fastest
I destroy my life's ego-seed.

5

O my insecurity-heart,
Leave me alone!
I want to make progress fast.

O my impurity-mind,
Leave me alone!
I want to make progress faster.

O my complexity-life,
Leave me alone!
I want to make progress fastest.

6

I make progress fast
When I do not expect
Compassion from God.

I make progress faster
When I do not expect
Love from God.

I make progress fastest
When I do not expect
Concern from God.

7

With my mind's faith-flames
I make progress fast.

With my heart's love-lamp
I make progress faster.

With my life's surrender-sun
I make progress fastest.

8

Ego no more!
Therefore,
I am making progress fast.

Unwillingness no more!
Therefore,
I am making progress faster.

Expectation no more!
Therefore,
I am making progress fastest.

FAST, FASTER, FASTEST PROGRESS

9

God has given me
A newness-mind
To make progress fast.

God has given me
A soulfulness-heart
To make progress faster.

God has given me
A oneness-life
To make progress fastest.

10

God has given me
A certitude-mind
To make progress fast.

God has given me
A gratitude-heart
To make progress faster.

God has given me
A beatitude-life
To make progress fastest.

11

I have given God
My nectar-dreams
To make progress fast.

I have given God
My bitterness-reality
To make progress faster.

I have given God
My surrender-smiles
To make progress fastest.

12

Good-bye, my self-imposition!
I want to make progress fast.

Good-bye, my self-deception!
I want to make progress faster.

Good-bye, my self-glorification!
I want to make progress fastest.

13

When I do not confine God.
I make progress fast.

When I do not define God,
I make progress faster.

When I do not entwine God,
I make progress fastest.

14

To make progress fast,
I live a doubt-free day.

To make progress faster,
I live a complaint-free day.

To make progress fastest,
I live a temptation-free day.

15

I make progress fast
When I do not look down
On those who do not aspire.

I make progress faster
When I pray to God
To forgive them.

I make progress fastest
When I compassionately,
Soulfully and lovingly
Inspire them to aspire.

16

I do not enter into
My mind's hesitation-room.
Therefore, I make progress fast.

I do not enter into
My heart's expectation-room.
Therefore, I make progress faster.

But I do enter into
My soul's satisfaction-room.
Therefore, I make progress
   fastest.

17

When I pray to God
To increase my love for Him,
I make progress fast.

When I meditate on God
To increase my devotion to Him,
I make progress faster.

When I contemplate on God
To increase my surrender to Him,
I make progress fastest.

18

When my mind
Looks at God's Eye,
I make progress fast.

When my heart
Looks at God's Heart,
I make progress faster.

When my soul
Looks at God's Feet,
I make progress fastest.

19

Doubt is no longer my boss.
Therefore, I make progress fast.

Jealousy is no longer my boss.
Therefore, I make progress faster.

Insecurity is no longer my boss.
Therefore, I make progress fastest.

20

When God thinks of me
Compassionately,
I make progress fast.

When I meditate on God
Soulfully,
I make progress faster.

When I serve God sleeplessly
And tell Him that
Although I serve Him sleeplessly,
I shall not mind
If He wants to think of others,
Meditate on others,
Love others,
And fulfil others in His own Way,
I make progress fastest.

21

Only when I am in
A very high consciousness,
I come to learn why
My Lord Supreme does not listen
To my mind-demand-prayers
And why He treasures
My heart-surrender-meditations.

22

Alas, will there be a time
When my Supreme Lord
Will find my mind-line free
So that He can compassionately
And affectionately
Instruct my mind
About soulful aspiration
And fruitful dedication?

23

My dear Supreme,
My sweet Supreme,
My Lord Supreme,
My Beloved Supreme and I
Are most eagerly looking for
The return
Of my long-lost aspiration.

24

This morning my sweet Supreme
Not only blessed me
With His Heart-Clock
But also struck powerfully
My heart's aspiration-hour.

25

O my disobedience-mind,
Be careful!
I am telling you once and for all
That soon you will have to stand
Before God's Absolute
Justice-Light.

26

My Lord's
Oneness-Heart-Smile
And my heart's
Insecurity-blindness
Can never establish
Even a fleeting friendship.

27

My Lord of Compassion infinite,
Please grant me the capacity
To take every morning
The gratitude-short-cut
To Your Satisfaction-Highway.

28

Every morning
There is a serious battle
Between my heart's eagerness
And my mind's unwillingness.
To my extreme joy,
Every single day
My heart's eagerness wins.

29

God does not ask us
To do many things for Him.
He asks us to do only one thing:
To demolish completely
Our mind-made ignorance-fort.

30

My Lord asks me not to be afraid
Of my desire-nights.
He asks me only to increase
My heart's burning
Aspiration-flames.
He tells me that
My heart's burning
Aspiration-flames
Will soon be able to devour
All my desire-nights.

31

I am so happy
That even my doubting mind
Is struggling hard to reach
My heart's faith-oasis.

32

Every day I need
A new wave of enthusiasm-light
To speed up my purity-heart's
Heavenward aspiration-journey.

33

Every day I must strengthen
My aspiration-heart
With a new supply
Of confidence-delight
So that my heart does not suffer
From security-shortage.

34

This morning
My heart's aspiration-boxer
Has knocked out
Easily and permanently
My confusion-mind.

35

Not from any human being
But from God Himself
I have learned how to throw
My mind's unwillingness-insects
Into my heart's eagerness-fire.

36

My Lord tells me
That it is only
My complete satisfaction-heart
That has the divine right
To kindle my life's
Self-transcendence-flames.

37

Alas, why am I so helpless
That I am compelled to hear
My mind's nothingness-story
Every day?

38

Slowly, steadily
But unmistakably
I have unloaded
My mind's doubt-excess.

39

Just yesterday I gave away
All my old ignorance-toys.
Today my Lord Supreme
Has given me His own
Ever-new and ever-beautiful
Love, Joy and Peace-Toys.

40

Alas, there are so many
Burning hope-heart-countries
In this world,
But where
Is the peace-ambassador,
Where?

41

My God-fulfilment-
    Confidence-promise-heart
Is from my sleeplessly
Faith-trained hero-life.

42

Only my soul's promise-eye
Has the God-commissioned right
To light
My God-manifestation-torch.

43

Beautiful, supremely beautiful,
Was my aspiration-journey's start.
Powerful, unimaginably powerful,
Was my Supreme Lord's
    Compassion-Blessing-Rain.

44

Every morning without fail
My Beloved Supreme asks
My gratitude-heart
To read out His own
Transcendental Victory-Speech.

FAST, FASTER, FASTEST PROGRESS

45

I simply do not know
And certainly do not want to
   know
When and how
I cut off completely
All my uncomely and powerful
Bondage-thought-chains.

46

Mine is the life
That will never surrender
To ignorance-tyranny.
Mine is the mind
That will never surrender
To agitation-turmoil.

47

Each purity-thought of mine
Is a silver-moon-beauty
Of my Lord's Heart.

48

My outer life succeeds
And my inner life proceeds
Precisely because
My Beloved Supreme
Has kept my aspiration-heart
In between
His own Compassion-Heart
And His own
   Encouragement-Eye.

49

Because He enjoys
His own Silence-Delight,
My Lord Supreme
Gets tremendous satisfaction
When my body, vital, mind
And heart
Monopolise their conversation
With Him.

50

Divinity's transcendental peak
You are bound to ascend
If you have become a sleepless
Existence-Consciousness-
   Bliss-climber.

51

When I live in the very depths
Of my Lord's Compassion-Eye,
My life's success-speed
And my heart's progress-speed
Are so fast
That not even the cosmic gods
Can adequately time them.

52

My concentration-warrior-eye
Is sleeplessly and breathlessly
Determined to dethrone
My confusion-mind-king.

53

O my seeker-heart,
Sincerity-flames are calling you.
Arise, awake!

54

This morning,
With each soulful breath,
My aspiration-heart accepted
My Lord's blessingful Invitation.

55

Peace-fulfilment-songs
Are sung only
By the God-singing souls.

56

Every morning I make a solemn promise
That I shall not answer
My mind-desire-phone.
Alas,
Every day I badly fail.

57

Be not afraid
Of your desire-nightmares.
Your heart's aspiration-fire
Can and shall devour them
At God's choice Hour.

58

Each aspiration-heart
Is bound to live
In a progress-paradise.

59

The temptation-disaster
May challenge
The meditation-protector,
But it will always lose.

60

My heart's aspiration-morning
Never sees
A hesitation-day.

61

My God-meditation-captain
Puts my soul, my heart, my mind,
My vital and my body
Every day in line
Before they receive
Transcendental Blessings
From my Beloved Supreme.

62

"My child, my child,
Do not be afraid of your mind's
Volcano-confusion.
My Compassion-Eye
At My choice Hour will devour
Your mind's volcano-confusion."

63

"My child, my child,
Every morning you must wake up
When I ring My Heart's
Universal Oneness-Bell."

PART VI

GOD'S COMPASSION-EYE AND
MY HAPPINESS-HEART

GOD'S COMPASSION-EYE AND MY HAPPINESS-HEART

1

God's Compassion-Eye
Makes me a millionaire.
My happiness-heart
Makes God a multi-millionaire.

2

My Lord Supreme,
Every day do inundate
My heart, my mind, my vital
   and my body
With a new and record-breaking
Obedience-ecstasy-sea.

3

I came into the world to prove
That my Lord is always right
And I am always wrong.
I am right only when
I am with Him, in Him and for
   Him.

4

My prayer-mind
Expects my Beloved Lord
   Supreme
To make me happy.
My meditation-heart
Expects me to make
My Beloved Lord Supreme happy.

5

My Beloved Lord Supreme,
It is getting so late.
When are You going to bind me
With Your Oneness-Heart-Chains?

6

My Beloved Lord Supreme,
May each and every breath of
   mine
Become a gratitude-prayer-
   fragrance
To love You and please You always
In Your own Way.

7

My Lord Beloved Supreme,
What happens when I obey You
And when I don't obey You?
"My child,
When you obey Me,
You think that I gain much
   from you,
But I gain nothing, absolutely
   nothing.
But when you disobey Me,
You lose everything that you have
And you are in the inner world
Where real reality abides.
In the inner world
You are not even a match
For a street beggar."

8

My Lord Beloved Supreme,
I do not have love-garden for
    You today.
I do not have devotion-flower for
    You today.
I do not have surrender-fragrance
    for You today.
I do not have gratitude-tears and
    smiles
For You today.
But will You not give me another
    chance,
Another day,
To give You all these and anything
    more
That I have deep within
And I am not aware of?
My Lord,
No matter what I say,
No matter what I do,
I know that You are all mine,
Only mine,
And I am Yours, only Yours.

9

There is no holiday for a
    God-lover
Who longs to love God
In God's own Way.
There is no holiday for a
    God-server
Who longs to serve God
In God's own Way.
Why?
Because God Himself does not
    want them
To have holidays.
God says:
"Each holiday can easily
Become a prey to a new
Temptation-frustration-
    destruction-day."

10

Not God's Sound-Mouth
But God's Silence-Eye
Has silenced my big mouth
And tall pride.

GOD'S COMPASSION-EYE AND MY HAPPINESS-HEART

11

My Lord,
At times You smile at me;
I wonder why.
My Lord,
At times You cry for me;
I wonder why.
"My child,
I smile when your heart
Is only for Me.
I cry when I do not find
Your heart inside My Heart."

12

I pray to God for God to bless me
With His Protection-Feet.
I meditate on God for God to bless me
With His Satisfaction-Heart.

13

It is good to be compassionate,
But to whom?
To the one who is still trying
And not to the one who has
   given up.

14

Sincerity expands my mind.
Purity expands my heart.
Humility expands my life.
Divinity expands my entire being.

15

My prayers
Are my heart's tears.
My meditations
Are my soul's smiles.

16

My Lord cares infinitely more
For my presence
Than for my excellence.

17

Where do I live?
I live inside
My Lord's Forgiveness-Smiles
And my heart's gratitude-tears.

18

By God's Measure,
I want my heart
To be always pure and good.
By God's Measure,
I want my life
To be always self-giving and
   perfect.

19

I shall succeed,
I must succeed,
Because my outer and visible
   partner
Is faith.
I shall proceed,
I must proceed,
Because my inner and invisible
   Partner
Is God Himself.

20

A self-giving heart
Everywhere sees
God's Hope-Blossoms
And God's Promise-Blooms.

21

My Lord Beloved Supreme,
Please save me, save me,
From insecurity's constantly
False alarms.

22

My heart goes
Wherever my heart is needed.
My soul goes
Wherever my soul is needed.
My Supreme goes
Even unheeded and unneeded
To so many places.

23

God wants my aspiration to
   grow into
The Smile of His Transcendental
Self.
God wants my dedication to
   blossom into
The Throb of His Universal Heart.

24

Am I not fooling myself?
How can I be a God-dreamer
If I am not already a God-believer?
How can I be a God-lover
If I am not already a God-listener?
How can I be a God-fulfiller
If I am not already a God-server?

25

There was a time when I was
My mind-centred bitterness.
But now I am
My God-centred sweetness.

26

God-disobedience-seekers
Will bury themselves
Long before the actual arrival
Of their death.

GOD'S COMPASSION-EYE AND MY HAPPINESS-HEART

27

Peace
Is not mutual agreement.
Peace
Is oneness-achievement.

28

So many God-Secrets are being hidden
Inside my heart's secret tears
And inside my soul's sacred smiles.

29

O my Absolute Lord Supreme,
I never thought
That there would come a time
When all my desires
Would be desireless.

30

I do not speak to God
When my mind is angry with Him.
God does not speak to me
When my heart is not hungry for Him.

31

My Lord Supreme,
Do make me my soul-bird's
Rose-fragrance.

32

A God-readiness-mind
I have.
A God-willingness-heart
I am.

33

I am divinely happy
Because my mind-master
Has lost his job.

34

Mine is not the life
Of God-disappointment-tears.
Mine is the life
Of God-fulfilment-smiles.

35

The power of silence
Is the only power
That can and shall
Transform the world.

36

We can run away
From God's Compassion-Heart,
But we cannot hide
From God's Justice-Eye.

37

My Lord Beloved Supreme,
I have given up completely.
Do whatever You want to do
With my doubtful mind,
Tearful heart and fearful life.

38

God wants me to please Him
With my heart's tears,
Not with my mind's fears.

39

My Lord, my Lord, my Lord,
If You really love me,
Then do not allow me
To miss even one single
Obedience-opportunity.

40

My Lord, my Lord, my Lord,
I am trying to touch Your Eye
For Power.
You are trying to touch my heart
For love.
Alas, both of us are unsuccessful.

41

My self-acceptance
Is making me brave.
My God-dependence
Is making me perfect.

42

When I tell God
That I love Him only
And I need Him only,
He secretly tells me
How He wishes He could hear it
Again and again.

43

I am proud
Of my mind-glory-palace.
God is not only proud
But also fond
Of my peace-heart-cottage.

GOD'S COMPASSION-EYE AND MY HAPPINESS-HEART

44

God's Compassion-Eye
And man's insecurity-heart
Are inseparable.

45

Alas, I am totally lost.
I want to conquer
God's world.
God wants me to conquer
His Heart.

46

My Lord, not Your seething Eyes
But Your streaming Tears
Are killing me.

47

The beaming smiles
From my Master's eyes
Are making me happy beyond
   measure.
The streaming tears
From my Master's heart
Are making me perfect —
Far, far and far beyond
My imagination-flights.

48

God's Compassion-Eye
Had chosen me
Long before I chose
God's Protection-Feet.

49

When I give my mind to God,
He says to me,
"My child, I gladly accept
Your mind."
When I give my heart to God,
He says to me,
"My child, I desperately need
Your heart."

50

When I give God what I have,
God says to me,
"You are such a nice
And beautiful child."
When I give God what I am,
God says to me,
"You are such a perfect
And indispensable child."

51

May my God-realisation-hope
Every day rise
Like the exquisite beauty
Of the morning sun.

52

My mind
Does not dare to challenge
My heart's
Confidence-sunrise.

53

Yesterday
My name was desire-despair.
Today
My name is aspiration-ecstasy.

54

Even though I never answer
God's Calls,
His Heart of Compassion
Keeps calling me
Day in and day out.

55

There was a time
When God lived
Inside my surrender-heart.
Now God lives
Inside my gratitude-breath.

56

O my mind,
Please do me a big favour:
Start shining.
O my heart,
Please do me a big favour:
Start meditating.
O my life,
Please do me a big favour:
Start serving.
O my soul,
Please do me a big favour:
Start whispering.
O my Lord,
Please do me a big favour:
Start smiling at me!

57

My Beloved Lord Supreme,
When I do not obey You,
I am absolutely sure
That it deeply hurts You.
Now tell me which method You prefer:
To force me to obey You
With Your absolute Power,
Or to descend into my heart
With infinitely more Love
To obey You?
"My child, I have only one Way,
And I will always have one Way.
That Way is the Way of My Love—
My Eternity's Love, My Infinity's Love
And My Immortality's Love."

58

My Lord Beloved Supreme,
What is the difference
Between human pride
And divine pride?
"Human pride is
   destruction-dance
Before possession-smile.
Divine pride is when you claim
Me
As your own, very own,
And I claim you
As My own Eternity's Dream
And My own Immortality's
   Reality."

59

Desire life
We acquire.
Aspiration-heart
We require.

60

Compassion-Village
Is my Lord's Birthplace.
Satisfaction-Cottage
Is my Lord's Village-Home.

61

God's Confidence blossoms
Inside my aspiration-heart.
God's Assurance blooms
Inside my inspiration-eyes.

62

My mind-experiment tells me
That God is a very old Man.
My heart-experience tells me
That God is the most beautiful
   Child.

63

A sincere God-lover
Conquers insecurity.
A false God-lover
Surrenders to insecurity.

64

A newness-searching mind
Gladdens me.
A oneness-starving heart
Enlightens me.

65

God comes to me
With His endless Smile-Dreams.
I go to God
With my helpless reality-tears.

66

My desire-mind travels
Through fantasy's
  frustration-lands.
My aspiration-heart flies
In ecstasy's illumination-skies.

67

My Lord Beloved Supreme
Every day
Gives me the same
Single piece of advice:
"My child,
Smile, smile, smile."

68

When my mind prays,
I hear the sweet melody
Of the unseen Beyond.
When my heart meditates,
I hear the soul-stirring melody
Of the ever-transcending Beyond.

69

Each good thought
Helps me gloriously return
To my universal oneness-
  heart-home.

70

May each prayer-beauty
Of my mind
Add my soul's fragrance-delight
To the peace-bird
Of my heart.

71

God's Compassion-Eye-Smile
Looks out for me.
My aspiration-heart-cry
Looks out for God.
Successful is God's Eye –
So is my heart.

72

In all the years I have known God,
Not even once has He asked me
Why I am so shamelessly
  unaspiring.
But He has asked me repeatedly
Why I am not more aspiring.

73

My real inner name is my heart's
Climbing aspiration-mountain.
My real outer name is my life's
Spreading dedication-fountain.

GOD'S COMPASSION-EYE AND MY HAPPINESS-HEART

74

Behold!
I am no longer
In my mind's doubt-prison.
I am now in my heart's
Faith-kingdom.

75

May my aspiration-life
Be found between
The blessingful dictates
Of the inner world
And the cheerful and full
Acceptance
Of the outer world.

76

Every day without fail
From Heaven my heart imports
God's Forgiveness
And from earth my heart exports
My gratitude.

77

My Lord,
Every day do give me the capacity
To offer a new promise
In my obedience-life to You
And my surrender-heart to You.

78

My mind feasts
On the newspapers.
My heart feasts
On the Bible.

79

God cries
When I run away from Him.
God laughs and laughs
When I try to hide from Him.

PART VII

MY LIFE'S SIXTY-THREE HEART-BLOSSOMS

MY LIFE'S SIXTY-THREE HEART-BLOSSOMS

1. One

My Lord Beloved Supreme,
On my birthday I am praying to
   You
To make me a member
Of Your inner Circle.

2. Two

My Lord Beloved Supreme,
On my birthday I am praying to
   You
To make me realise
That my Master is my soul-heart-
   life-lover
And not my soul-heart-life-
   dictator.

3. Three

My Lord Beloved Supreme,
On my birthday I am praying to
   You
To make me realise
That I am Your Heart's golden
   Dream,
That You are my life's only Reality.

4. Four

My Lord Beloved Supreme,
On my birthday I am praying to
   You
To grant me the capacity
To keep my mind-telephone-line
Open only to You.

5. Five

My Lord Beloved Supreme,
On my birthday I am praying to
   You
To make me realise
That my life is not a false hope's
   dead end
But a true, illumining and
   fulfilling hope's
Continuous journey.

6. Six

My Lord Beloved Supreme,
On my birthday I am praying to
   You
To give me the capacity
To stop broadcasting
My mind's giant-ego-news
Once and for all.

7. Seven

My Lord Beloved Supreme,
On my birthday I am praying to You
To compel my fighting mind
To completely surrender
To my embracing heart.

8. Eight

My Lord Beloved Supreme,
On my birthday I am praying to You
To torture me, to punish me
In the forest
Of my disobedience-repentance-tears.

9. Nine

On my birthday
My Lord Beloved Supreme
Is commanding me
Not to underestimate
My God-manifestation-capacity.

10. Ten

On my birthday
My Lord Beloved Supreme
Is telling me
That although He is omnipotent,
Although He is the Possessor
Of infinite Power,
He is my heart-happiness-Beggar
And my life-smile-Dreamer.

11. Eleven

On my birthday
My Lord Beloved Supreme
Wants me to answer
A few Compassion-questions:
"My child, who told you
To swim in the sea of stupidity?
Who prevented your life
From progressing?
Who gave you the capacity
To decide your fate?
Who compelled you to sing
Your life's failure-song?
And who compelled you to stop dancing
Your life's victory-dances?"

12. Twelve

I am thirsty
For my Lord's Compassion-Eye.
My Lord is hungry
For my satisfaction-heart.

13. Thirteen

I call it
My great concentration.
God calls it
My indomitable will.

14. Fourteen

Alas,
My mind's fatal frustration
Has eclipsed
My heart's sunlit smile.

15. Fifteen

Alas,
I do not know who has stolen
My heart's fountain-hope
And my soul's mountain-promise.

16. Sixteen

I do not want to thrive
On my desire-greatness-
  splendour.
I want to thrive
Only on my aspiration-goodness-
  candour.

17. Seventeen

Impurity, you destroy
The beauty of my eyes,
The sincerity of my mind,
The purity of my heart
And the simplicity of my life.

18. Eighteen

God smiles at my readiness.
God sings for my willingness.
God dances in my eagerness.

19. Nineteen

The desiring mind
Loves division-campaign.
The aspiring heart
Loves union-refrain.

20. Twenty

The God-intensity-heart
Purifies
The man-impurity-mind.

21. Twenty-one

The mind that longs for light
Consciously
Can never be caught
In jealousy-current.

22. Twenty-two

Where do I live?
I live in between
My receptivity-heart-tears
And God's Infinity-Heart-Smiles.

23. Twenty-three

My willingness-heart
And God's Availability-Heart
Inseparably live.

24. Twenty-four

I am so happy that at long last
My heart-faith-friend
Is challenging
My mind-doubt-intruder.

25. Twenty-five

There was a time
When I was my mind's
Unwillingness-lethargy,
But now I am my heart's
Enthusiasm-energy.

26. Twenty-six

The mind-grandeur
Is a sleeping breath.
The heart-surrender
Is an everlasting life.

27. Twenty-seven

My real love of God
And my God-disobedience
Can never be together.

28. Twenty-eight

When I get up early to meditate,
My Lord says to me:
"You are My Victory-Crown!"

29. Twenty-nine

If You at all love me, my Lord,
Then keep me away from
My mind's desire-jungle.

30. Thirty

God's Signature is always glowing
Inside the life
Of an unconditional
   surrender-heart.

31. Thirty-one

One must look for
Only one thing:
The Smile of God's Heart
In God's Eye.

32. Thirty-two

Two things I have
To make me happy:
The hope that soars beyond
And the promise that touches
Earth-life.

33. Thirty-three

Very few are those
Who recognise God,
And fewer still are those
Who are ready to welcome God.

34. Thirty-four

This morning I said farewell
To my suspicion-mind
And hesitation-heart.

35. Thirty-five

Sleeplessly God calls your name,
Expecting a prayerful
And grateful answer.

36. Thirty-six

What has earth given me?
Earth has given me
Its helpless sorrows.
What else has earth given me?
My dream-fulfilment-tomorrows.

37. Thirty-seven

I am proud of my mind
Because it is a sleepless
God-seeker.
I am proud of my heart
Because it is a breathless
God-lover.

38. Thirty-eight

The mind's insincerity
Has no friends.
The heart's purity
Has no enemies.

39. Thirty-nine

When you become
A God-ingratitude-heart,
You score a decisive goal
For your own worst enemy:
Ignorance.

40. Forty

Alas,
God-disobedience-drums
Are deafening
Mother-Earth's ears.

41. Forty-one

Each time I meditate well,
I become Heaven's
Flowering and illumining
Silence-joy.

42. Forty-two

Each suspicious thought,
No matter how small it is,
Has the capacity to eclipse
The seeker's heart-sun.

43. Forty-three

Only two times I am truly
　fulfilled:
Once
When I am an open heart
And once
When I am a closed mouth!

44. Forty-four

God is always beautiful,
But He is infinitely more beautiful
When He shows me His
　Compassion-Eye.

My heart is always beautiful,
But it is infinitely more beautiful
When it becomes a gratitude-
　heart.

45. Forty-five

If we do not appreciate
God's Appearance,
Why should God appreciate
Our performance?

46. Forty-six

Both are equally needed:
The astrology
Of the inner life
And the technology
Of the outer life.

47. Forty-seven

The mind loves to listen
To doubt-recordings.
The heart loves to listen
To faith-recordings.
The soul loves to listen
To promise-recordings.
God loves to listen
To perfection-recordings.

48. Forty-eight

When you reach your heart-home,
You will discover that your
　God-Guest
Has been waiting for you
For a long time.

49. Forty-nine

The pulse of a purity-heart
At every moment
Can see the universal Beauty
Of the Transcendental God.

50. Fifty

Be not late in sending
Your aspiration-application to
   God
If you really need God.

51. Fifty-one

Prayer
Is my heart-song.
Meditation
Is my soul-dance.

52. Fifty-two

My Lord Supreme
Openly admires me
When I secretly love Him.

53. Fifty-three

God does not want you to carry
The ashes of your old desires.
He wants you to carry with you
The fragrance of your heart's
Flower-beauty.

54. Fifty-four

The seeker's disobedience
Expedites his spiritual death
And also changes
God's opinion of him drastically.

55. Fifty-five

At long last
I have vehemently chased away
All my God-disobedience-
   thoughts!

56. Fifty-six

If you follow the mind's road,
Then you are bound to meet
With doubt-hooligans
On the way.

57. Fifty-seven

Slowly and secretly
The mind-thief enters
Into the heart's purity-room
To steal the faith-fragrance
Of the soul.

58. Fifty-eight

I must reject
What God has already
Rejected for me:
Ignorance-dream.

59. Fifty-nine

The mind's obedience-smile
Is beautiful.
The heart's oneness-dance
Is perfect.

60. Sixty

Yesterday's dream-flute
And today's reality-drum
Can awaken and illumine us
In God's own Way.

61. Sixty-one

Each undivine thought
Is nothing but
Useless dust
Of its own nothingness.

62. Sixty-two

The mind compiles
A complaint list.
The heart supplies
The aspiration-flames
To burn it.

63. Sixty-three

My Lord,
When I call others my own,
They invariably deface me.
But when I call You my own,
You invariably embrace me.

PART VIII

MY SOUL IS FREE

MY SOUL IS FREE

1

My soul is free to smile at
The beautiful God-dreamers.
My life is free to serve
The faithful God-servers.
My heart is free to love
The unconditional God-lovers.
And I am free to admire
The conscious God-owners.

2

My Lord does not want
My surrender-life
From my suffering heart-tears,
But He wants
My surrender-life
From my flying heart-smiles.

3

The rising sun says:
"O stupid seeker, wake up!
You have a long way to go,
Although the Goal is yours."
The setting sun says:
"O stupid seeker, can you not see
That you have badly
And sadly failed?
Perhaps my rising brother-sun
Will give you another chance
Tomorrow
To reach your destination.
If you fail this time,
Who knows?,
He may not give you
Another chance
In this God-realisation-
   promise-incarnation
Of yours."

4

For the prominence-cherishing
And gratification-nourishing
Aspirants,
Unprecedented inner failures!

5

Each time I lose a pound,
I fly a mile higher.
Each time I fly a mile higher,
I come nearer than the nearest
To God the Smiler.

6

The clever mind
Can and does give
Many things to the world
Without loving.
The pure heart
Will never and can never give
Even one thing to the world
Without loving.

7

Each and every
Self-giving God-lover
Is an absolutely perfect
Peace-discoverer on earth.

8

Man can satisfy God the Eternal,
God the Infinite
And God the Immortal.
But God cannot fully satisfy
Even one single desire-man
On earth.

9

My prayers
Are the ascending stairs
To God's transcendental
Compassion-Height.
My meditations
Are God's descending Stairs
To His universal
Manifestation-Delight.

10

Yesterday
The victory of my humility-mind
Was announced by the trumpets
Of the vastness-sky.
Today
The victory of my purity-heart
Will be announced by the organs
Of the fulness-sun.

11

When I offer my heart's
Gratitude-breath
To my Beloved Supreme,
He tells me that I am His only
Satisfaction-Empire-builder.

12

This morning I declared war
On my doubting mind.
Therefore, my Beloved Supreme
Is blessing me
With His unprecedented Dance
Inside my fully-blossomed
Heart-garden.

13

Each pure and soulful thought
Inside my mind
Is a series of my life's
Bondage-free successes.

14

Surrender is always mutual.
To God
I soulfully surrender
The darkness of my
   ignorance-life.
To me
God blessingfully surrenders
The Light and Delight
Of His Compassion-Heart.

15

The first God-Call awakens us
From centuries' ignorance-sleep.
The second God-Call illumines
Our unlit human nature.
The third God-Call inspires
The divine in us
To sing the God-manifestation-
   song
In God's own Way
Here on earth.

16

It is not an impossible task
To forgive and forget
One's failure-past
If one starts to live
For God and God alone.

17

My seeker-friend,
You want to know
Who gave me
God's Home Address.
My seeker-friend,
It is my spiritual heart
And not my intellectual mind
That has given me
God's Home Address.

18

Do you want to get close,
Very close, to God?
Then never for a second
Must you worry
About your earthly
Achievements
And your Heavenly
Accomplishments.

19

I must never forget
That each impure thought
In my mind
Is supported by troops
Of ignorance-night.

20

The moment I surrendered
My sadness-vital
To my Lord Supreme,
He immediately increased
My heart-hunger immensely
And placed His own
Victory-Crown
On my head.

21

"My sweet child,
My sweeter child,
My sweetest child,
When you come to see Me,
I never ask you to tell Me
What others are doing wrong.
I do not ask you to tell Me
Even what you are doing wrong.
I immediately ask you to tell Me
What you are doing right,
And in how many ways
You are trying to please Me.
My sweet child,
My sweeter child,
My sweetest child,
It does not become you
To see others'
Teeming imperfections.
I am constantly dreaming
In and through you
To make you My Eternity's
Absolutely perfect instrument.
Please fulfil My Dream,
My long-cherished Dream,
My only Dream!"

22

"My child, My child,
Do not disappoint Me,
Do not fail Me!
If you disappoint Me,
If you fail Me,
Then I shall lose
A very precious Dream
Of My ever-transcending
Vision-Eye."

23

This morning my Lord Supreme,
Out of His infinite
Compassion-Light,
Has given me the power
Of receptivity
To make a permanent contract
With gratitude-delight.

24

Today's headline:
My heart has made
Its unconditional surrender
To God's Will.
Tomorrow's footnote:
My mind is all ready
To welcome God soulfully.

25

No,
Not the annihilation of the mind
But the illumination of the mind;
No,
Not the renunciation of life
But the acceptance of life;
No,
Not the hesitation of the heart
But the expansion of the heart
We need in order to sign
A permanent contract
With world peace.

26

If God is your favourite subject,
Then who can object
To your immediate
God-realisation
And your ultimate
God-manifestation?

27

If your heart's aspiration
Is immense
And your life's dedication
Is intense,
Then your outer life
Is bound to succeed
Powerfully
And your inner life
Is bound to proceed
Dauntlessly.

28

What is unlit
And what is sunlit?
Unlit is when I say
That I can do it.
Sunlit is when I say
That my Lord Supreme
Has already done it for me.

29

The favourite question
Of a useless seeker is:
"My Lord God,
Do tell me when and how soon
I will be able to realise You."

The favourite statement
Of a faithful and soulful seeker is:
"My Lord Supreme,
I know that at Your choice Hour
You will make me realise You.
Therefore,
I am not at all in a hurry."

30

My spirituality is not
My timidity's turtle-pace.
My spirituality is
My purity's deer-speed.

31

Perfection is the freedom
From desire.
Satisfaction is the freedom
Of oneness.

32

Everything else in life
You may keep a supreme secret,
But not your love of God,
For your love of God alone
Will give you salvation from sin,
Illumination from darkness,
Liberation from bondage,
Realisation from imperfection
And Immortality from death.

33

My God-obedience is the seed
That I am offering
To God the man.
My God-discovery is the fruit
That I shall offer
To man the God.

34

I am now concentrating.
I know that
My Lord Beloved Supreme
Is right above my head.

35

I am now meditating.
I can feel
The blessingful Presence
Of my Lord Beloved Supreme
Right inside my heart.

36

I am now contemplating.
I can vividly see
My Lord Beloved Supreme
Right in front of my vision-eye,
And He is telling me
That He is eager to play
Hide-and-seek with me.

37

I must immediately shake off
My God-disappointment-past
So that my Lord Beloved Supreme
Can smilingly and proudly
Grow, glow, sing and dance
Inside my today's
Silver dreams
And my tomorrow's
Golden realities.

38

My inner Pilot is extremely
   pleased
With me,
For I no longer allow
Doubt-insects
To cling to my mind-walls.

39

My inner Pilot is extremely proud
Of me,
For I have finally caught
And defeated
My life's cleverest
Temptation-dealer:
Ignorance-demon.

40

My Inner Pilot is extremely fond
Of me,
For every morning I employ
His supremely choice
Ecstasy-pilots
To fly me in my own
Meditation-plane
To His Immortality's
Nectar-flooded Land.

41

Today I am inviting
The whole world
To come and see
My Lord Supreme
While He is illumining
The affection-flooded
  village-home
Of my heart's aspiration-cry.

42

My Lord Supreme,
Out of His infinite Compassion,
Affection, Love and Fondness,
Has given me a sleepless
Willingness-heart.
Alas, what have I done?
I have given my poor life
An obstinate unwillingness-mind!

43

Outwardly God may never
Expose and arrest
My false and insincere aspiration.
But inwardly every day
He detects and rejects
My false and insincere aspiration.

44

God's Sweetness-Eye
Inspires the soulful beginning
Of my life's journey.
God's Fulness-Heart
Immortalises the fruitful
  perfection
Of my self-transcendence-life.

45

The fragrance of my heart's purity
Goes far beyond
My mind's impurity-territory.

46

When I am in my desiring mind,
I offer a very painful prayer
To my Lord Supreme.
When I am in my aspiring heart,
My Beloved Supreme blesses me
Not only with a soulful meditation
But also with a fruitful satisfaction.

47

My self-searching mind
Is by far the best investment.
My self-giving heart
Is absolutely
The highest enlightenment.

48

My God-manifestation-promise
Will never be broken by me.
My God-satisfaction-hope
Will ever be spoken by me.

49

I call it
My cheerful willingness,
But God calls it
His complete Satisfaction
In my perfect aspiration.

50

When I tell Him
That He is my Father Supreme,
He loves me sleeplessly.

When I tell Him
That He is my only Friend,
He loves me sleeplessly,
Plus He even loves
My imperfections.

When I tell Him
That He is my All,
He immediately tells me
That He will immortalise
My outer dedication-life
On earth
And my inner aspiration-life
In Heaven.

PART IX

NO RETURN ON MY GOD-DESTINATION ROAD

NO RETURN ON MY GOD-DESTINATION ROAD

1

Nothing can be sweeter
Than my life's
Unconditional
God-surrender-sweetness.

2

God-love is the only love
That quenches
Our satisfaction-desperate thirst.

3

If you allow your mind
To blindfold you,
How can you ever see
God's Compassion-illumination-
 Footprints
On your aspiration-life-shore?

4

You are bound to miss God's Boat
Sailing to the Golden Shore
If your life is empty of
Smiling eagerness-surrender.

5

O my life's service-boat,
On you sail at the lightning-speed
Of your willingness-mind
And your eagerness-heart!

6

God protects me
From jumping out of His Boat
When I shun
My love of ignorance-choice.

7

You are a rank fool
If you want to love God
Only after waiting
For all other love
To fail you first.

8

The belief of the doubting mind
Is indeed bondage.
The belief of the self-giving heart
Is indeed oneness-freedom
And fulness-delight.

9

For my perfection-life
I need only the God
Who reprimands my mind
And commands my heart.

10

God wants me to tell Him
What I know about the
  world-heart
And not what I think of the
  world-mind.

11

If you are happy
With your fleeting moments,
Then God will make you happier
By blessing you
With His everlasting Day.

12

The courage to live *in* God
I have.
What I now need is the courage
To live *for* God.

13

If you cannot have implicit faith
First in God
And then in the spiritual life,
Sooner or later
You will collapse under the
  weight
Of worries and anxieties.

14

God does not know
The meaning of lending.
He knows only the meaning
Of giving, giving and giving.

15

I want to live between
My soul's blessings
And my heart's gratitude.

16

In the spiritual life
Every day what we need
Is the renewal of our
God-gratitude-fulness.

17

My Lord, the moment I look at
  You,
My desire-thoughts disappear
In Your Compassion-Light-Eye.

18

The human childhood
Does end,
But the divine childhood
Does not and cannot end.

19

Our desire-mind conceals
But our aspiration-heart reveals
The grandeur-face of our soul.

20

My Lord, my only prayer
Is to have You
In every heartbeat
Of my aspiration-breath.

21

When I please God in His own Way,
He brings to the fore
A million Smiles from His Heart
To bless me.

22

O my mind,
I want you to swim
Every day
In the sea of my life's
God-dedication-bliss.

23

O my seeker-friend,
You must realise
That your faith in God
Will definitely silence
Your mind's doubt-storms.

24

Nothing can pierce
The mind's happiness
As ruthlessly
As a negative thought!

25

If you are an obedient seeker,
Then God and God's Compassion
Will always remain
At your disposal.

26

Every day
God deposits His Compassion-Smiles
Inside my heart-bank,
And He never makes a withdrawal.

27

How can you expect
God's Compassion-Eye
And His Satisfaction-Heart
To play with you
If you do not care
To obey Him?

28

I am so happy
That I have reached at last
The point of no return
On my God-Destination-Road.

29

O pride,
Do you have anything
To be proud of
Except your shameless stupidity?

30

My heart says to my mind,
"O mind, tell me
All about your plans.
In how many ways are you
Preparing yourself
To break my Master's heart?"

31

I am fated to doom
The moment I think of
Desire-fulfilment.
I am destined to bloom
The moment I meditate on
God-manifestation.

32

God has Himself said
Many, many times
That His full manifestation on
　earth
Will definitely take place,
In spite of the blind unwillingness
Of unreceptive mankind.

33

Is there any human being
Who does not want
Complete fulfilment
Without having to meet
All of God's requirements?

34

When you have a free access
To God's Heart,
Everything that you say and do
Will be from your firsthand
Experience-light.

NO RETURN ON MY GOD-DESTINATION ROAD

35

If you reject yourself all the time,
How can you be fulfilled?
Again, if you respect yourself
  unduly,
How can you be happy?

36

God's blessingful Smiles
In our aspiration-life
Are always more numerous
Than we can ever imagine.

37

If you do not keep
Your heart's aspiration-flames
Alive every day,
Then your soul's soaring dreams
Will fade into oblivion.

38

O seeker, be careful!
If you want to continue
To please God in God's own Way,
Then never lose
Your aspiration-heart-door-key.

39

If you live inside
Your doubting mind
And strangling vital,
Your God-manifestation-dreams
Will be completely shattered.

40

No desire lives forever.
Therefore, do not surrender
To your desire-mind.
At God's choice Hour
Your own aspiration-heart
Will come to bless and embrace
  you.

41

O seeker,
God never wanted you to live
An unhappiness-attachment-life.
O seeker,
Since you are wallowing
In your weakness-enjoyment,
What right do you have
To criticise God?

42

My mind has given up
Its bitterness.
It has invited the sweetness
Of my aspiration-heart.

43

God's Smile does not want
To destroy our mind.
It wants only
To illumine our mind.

44

The most I can do for God
Is remain silent
When the outer world
Does not understand
My love for Him.

45

The self-giving goodness
Of the heart
Is the pure beauty
Of life.

46

The sooner you realise
That expectation is your true
  enemy,
The better for you.

47

O my stupid mind,
How can you ever be happy
If you long for happiness
On your own terms?

48

A God-searching mind
Needs sweetness.
A God-longing heart
Needs happiness.

49

God-necessity
Will always be fed
By fulfilment-capacity.

50

Do not forget to return
God's Compassion-Calls
If you really value
His Eternity's
Golden Boat-Journey.

PART X

COMMAND FROM GOD THE JUSTICE, WHISPER FROM GOD THE COMPASSION

COMMAND FROM GOD THE JUSTICE, WHISPER FROM GOD THE COMPASSION

1

God the Justice commanded:
"Wake up!"
God the Compassion whispers:
"Wake up.
Stand up.
Walk.
March.
Run
And sprint and sprint!"

2

Self-enjoyer
I was.
Self-giver
I am.

3

Desire-beggar
I was.
Aspiration-lover
I am.

4

Ingratitude-darkness-night
I was.
Gratitude-light-delight
I am.

5

The mind-patient
I was.
The mind-doctor
I am.

6

Newness-curiosity
I was.
Fulness-necessity
I am.

7

Desire-thorn
Punctured me.
Aspiration-rose
Nurtures me.

8

Desire-mind-hunger-frustration
I was.
Aspiration-heart-feast-
  illumination
I am.

9

My heavy past
I unhappily and unwillingly
   buried.
My light present
I lovingly and cheerfully carry.

10

Self-delusion
Was my mind's sole occupation.
Self-investigation
Is my mind's sole occupation.

11

The mind's
Separation-destruction-dream
I was.

The heart's
Oneness-fulness-reality
I am.

12

Hesitation-mind's
Slowness-uselessness
I was.
Readiness-heart's
Willingness-self-givingness
I am.

13

Yesterday
I asked God
Who I was to Him.
Today
I am asking God
How I can please Him.

14

Yesterday
The Greatness-God
Frightened my mind.

Today
The Goodness-God
Enlightens my heart.

15

Yesterday
God asked me
To be His one-pointed listener.

Today
God is asking me
To be His one-pointed
   coordinator.

16

Yesterday
I thought
I could confuse God
Easily.

Today
I think
I will be able to amuse God
Self-givingly.

17

Yesterday
My loudest mind-drum
I was.

Today
My sweetest heart-flute
I am.

18

Yesterday
I was
My impure ego-enjoyment.

Today
I am
My pure oneness-fulfilment.

19

Yesterday
I prayerfully thanked God
For allowing me to watch
His Cosmic Game.

Today
I am tearfully, gratefully
And self-givingly thanking God
For allowing me to participate
In His Cosmic Game.

20

Yesterday
God belonged
To my streaming
Heart-tears.

Today
I belong
To God's ever-brightening
Heart-Smiles.

21

Yesterday
I thought
That God created my enemy
To humiliate and destroy me.

Today
I clearly see
And strongly feel
That God created my enemies
To warn and perfect me.

22

Yesterday
My aspiration was enough
To please God.

Today
Even my realisation
Is not enough to please God.

Today
I will be able to please Him
Only if I can manifest Him.

23

Yesterday
My mind deeply enjoyed
World-confusion-chaos.

Today
My mind enjoys
God's Vision-blossoming Cosmos.

24

Yesterday
God drastically forced me
To give Him my secret mind.

Today
God is blessingfully asking me
To offer Him my sacred heart.

25

Yesterday
I was my impurity's
Audacity-mind.

Today
I am my divinity's
Immortality-heart.

26

Yesterday
I did not have a moment
For God-adoration.

Today
I have no moment
For God-dissatisfaction.

27

Yesterday
I magnified
My self-examination-life.

Today
God is magnifying
My self-dedication-life.

28

Yesterday
God took His
Compassion-Step.

Today
I take
My surrender-step.

29

Yesterday
I invoked God
To devour my mind's
Bitterness-frown.

Today
I invoke God
To feed my heart's
Climbing flames.

30

Yesterday
God's Compassion
Fed my heart.

Today
My gratitude
Is feeding God's Eye.

31

Yesterday
Unwillingness-mind and I
Travelled together.

Today
Willingness-heart and I
Are dreaming together,
Are running together,
Are swimming together
And are flying together.

32

Yesterday
My mind killed
My heart-fragrance.

Today
My soul revives
My heart-fragrance.

33

Yesterday
God melted
My dissatisfaction-mind.

Today
I melt
God's Compassion-Heart.

34

Yesterday
I was in the mind.
Therefore, God's Face
I saw
Nowhere.

Today
I am in my heart.
Therefore, God's Heart
I see,
I feel
And
I distribute
Everywhere.

35

Yesterday
I never thought
That God would
Appoint me.

Today
I never think
That God will ever
Disappoint me.

36

Yesterday
God's Compassion invited me
To be a passenger
In His Dream-Boat.

Today
God's Satisfaction
Is beckoning me
From His Reality-Shore.

37

Yesterday
God whispered to my mind
His Compassion-Message-Light.

Today
I am whispering to God
My gratitude-message-delight.

38

Yesterday
God examined my mind
To see its sincerity.

Today
God examines my heart
To treasure its divinity.

39

Possessor
Of a dissatisfaction-mind
I was.

Sharer
Of a dedication-life
I am.

40

God took care
Of my incapacity.
I look after
God's Necessity.

41

Furious I was
When I thought
That God was neglecting me.

Curious God is
To see if I am joining
My volcano-eyes.

42

Prayer-cries purified
My mind.
Meditation-smiles electrify
My heart.

43

Humanity's applause-beggar
I was.
Divinity's self-giver
I am.

44

My sound-teacher gave me
World-destruction-lessons.

My silence-teacher gives me
Life-transformation
And
World-perfection-lessons.

45

With disobedience and
  unwillingness
I jumped up and down.

With readiness and willingness
I sing and sing along the way
And at the destination as well.

46

Spirituality-bankrupt
Your inner heart was.
Spirituality-orphan
Your outer world is.

47

Just yesterday
Spirituality-infancy-heart
You were.

Today
Spirituality-adolescence-life
You are.

48

One-sided truth
My mind and vital enjoyed.
The complete truth
My soul and my heart enjoy.

49

I drowned my undivine thoughts
In a sea of light-delight.
I fly my divine will
In the sky of silence-freedom.

50

I wanted more
To satisfy my outer
Desire-life.

I need less
To satisfy my inner
Aspiration-heart.

51

All I wanted
Was
Freedom-autocracy.

All I need
Is
Peace-ecstasy.

52

I desired to be head
Of God's new creation.
I aspire to be a oneness-heart
Of God's old and eternal creation.

PART XI

GOD'S HEART I DESIRE,
GOD'S FEET I CHOOSE

GOD'S HEART I DESIRE, GOD'S FEET I CHOOSE

1

I desire God's Heart
To make God happy.
I choose God's Feet
To make me happy.

2

The untold miseries
Of a suspicious mind
Are never undeserved.

3

There is a constant battle
Between
Inevitability-dream
And
Possibility-reality.

4

God-Forgiveness-passport
And
God-Satisfaction-visa
We need to enter into
The highest Heaven of Bliss.

5

Eagerness-cries
Give birth
To fulness-smiles.

6

Searing jealousy
Is
The desiring mind's forte.

7

Forgiveness
Is God's Miracle-Power.
So is man's patience.

8

My Lord Supreme,
Let me just hear from You
That I am not alone.

9

A desiring mind
Is
A paralysing fear.

10

A desire-life is
An ill-fated dream
And
An ill-founded reality.

11

While the soul
Is in the body,
We must by all means
Do what we are supposed
To do for God.

12

God tells me
That it is up to me,
Not up to Him,
Whether I want to live
Inside my bitterness-mind
Or
Inside my sweetness-heart.

13

The mind swims not;
The mind sinks.
The heart sinks not;
The heart swims.

14

Inspiration
Is
The might of the mind.

Aspiration
Is
The Light of the heart.

15

Eagerness and determination
Are
Two winner-partners.

16

Become a saint.
Your uncomely past
Cannot and will not
Remain the same.

17

To me,
Mere mental renunciation
Is nothing short
Of mental hallucination.

18

Your ignorance-mind
Is infinitely stronger
Than you think.

Your purity-heart
Is infinitely more illumining
Than you can ever imagine.

19

A useless nothingness-mind
Is all I have.
A fruitful fulness-heart
Is all I need.

20

Hope
Is not a stranger
To my desiring mind.

21

Promise
Is not a stranger
To my aspiring heart.

22

Humility is not
Mind-hesitation.
Humility is
Wisdom-perfection.

23

Do not reject the mind.
Accept the mind
And transform it.

24

Do not avoid the mind.
Catch the mind
And control it.

25

O my mind,
Be wise.
How long are you
Going to keep yourself
Endlessly in a doubt-circle?

26

Imagination
Is the
Power of the mind.

Aspiration
Is the
Purity of the heart.

Realisation
Is the
Divinity of the soul.

27

An illumination-heart
And
A perfection-life
Always in each other live.

28

Desire yesterday
Unmistakably will be proved
To be meaningless,
Fruitless
And useless today.

29

Death
Is
Life's
Unwanted sleep.

30

My heart's inner silence-room,
You are the only one
To give me oneness-fulness-peace.

31

Because of your
God-surrender life,
The blossoming of your
Satisfaction-heart
Is immanent.

32

A life of singular discipline
Is
A mind of intensity.

33

A life of humility's purity
Is
A heart of vastness.

34

Aspiring to serve
God the Creator
Is itself its
God-service-satisfaction.

35

O self-importance,
Look what you have done!
Because of you
My entire being
Has crumbled into dust.

36

Aspiration is the only thing
That will illumine my heart.
Dedication is the only thing
That will transform my life.

37

You want
A frustration-free mind.
Then cancel
Your expectation-flight.

38

Alas,
My mind has compelled me
To develop a sea-deep hatred
For the things that remain
Unaccomplished.

39

When I feel
That God is my all,
I immediately see
That my ultimate success
Is speeding towards me.

40

There is only one thing
That satisfies me,
And that is the smile
From inner circle friends.

41

Alas, what was I doing?
I was doing two things:
Collecting world-complaints
And
Enjoying God-gossip.

42

Prayerfully cry
And
Soulfully smile.
Your inner breath
Will become one
With God's Fragrance-Heart.

43

True encouragement
Adorns my heart.
True encouragement expedites
My heavenward journey.

44

A purity-heart
Always lives
In a suspicion-free
Mind-neighbourhood.

45

God,
I am afraid
You and Your Compassion
Are always stuck
With me.

My child,
I am afraid
You and your stupidity
Are always stuck
With My Dream about you.

46

My God-reliance
Has made me
Happiness incarnate
And
Perfection consummate.

PART XII

TAKE YOUR GOD-SEARCH SERIOUSLY

TAKE YOUR GOD-SEARCH SERIOUSLY

1

The human in us quite often
Beats frustration-drums.
The divine in us always
Plays illumination-flute.

2

O seeker, do you not realise
What you are doing?
Every day, just because
You pray and meditate,
You feel that you have the right
To make extravagant demands
Upon God.

3

Only if you live in the heart
Can you expect to feel
The presence of your soul.
Otherwise, you will be nothing but
Your mind's insane
Hurry and worry.

4

Is there any mind
That does not think
It can easily be
A God-specialist?

5

When the mind lives
In its own negativity-cave,
The divine in us
Painfully hides.

6

Quite often expectation embodies
Bad news and sad news.
Therefore, we must be careful
Of our sundry expectations.

7

My Lord Supreme,
Help me, help me
To hurry home,
Where Your Love's
Ocean-Delight is.

8

Delight and self-giving
Were born at the same time
And will always live
Together.

9

No matter how negligible
And insignificant
Your ignorance-thoughts are,
They are bound to obstruct
 and delay
Your Heavenward march.

10

If we do not pray and meditate,
Then we are foolishly waiting
For help that will never arrive.

11

O seeker,
You have made tremendous
 progress
Now that you do not have
Even an iota of faith
In your mind-vital-train.

12

God does not mind
If you do not understand Him
When He speaks to you.
You can be sure
He is not going to make
His point clearer
Just because you want Him
To make you understand
What He is saying.
His Vision-Light is not
Something to understand
But something to love and love
And eventually grow into.

13

When my expectation rises
With the morning sun,
My frustration begins
With the setting sun.

14

If you allow your mind
To leave its door wide open
To doubt,
Then God-blossoming faith
You will never be able to claim
As your own.

15

O obedience,
How sweet is your smile!
O obedience,
How pure is your song!
O obedience,
How perfect is your breath!

16

If your life revolves around God,
Then only are you entitled
To prayerfully claim God's
   Vision-Eye
And His universal Heart
As your own.

17

The heart is always eager
To tell the world
That its excellence-life
Entirely belongs to
God's Compassion-Light.

18

Be not afraid
To think high thoughts.
Today's high thoughts
Will tomorrow blossom
Into an omnipotent Will.

19

Are you sure
That you are worshipping
Your Lord Supreme
At His Shrine?
See if perhaps by mistake
You have been all along
Worshipping yourself
At your mind-shrine.

20

The divine dignity
Of a seeker's sleepless obedience
Can give the seeker
Tremendous inspiration,
Tremendous enthusiasm
And tremendous delight.

21

Each good thought
Inside your silence-mind
Is indeed a peace-seed,
And before long these seeds
Will be able to enjoy
Their golden harvest.

22

An ordinary man is possessed
By his possessions.
A spiritual man fulfils himself
By being possessed by God alone.

23

The moment we accept desire-life
To please ourselves,
Our aspiration-death
Starts nearing us.

24

A true lover of peace
Eventually becomes
A perfect giver of peace.

25

You can be free
From worldly entanglement
If you can convince yourself
That Heavenly enlightenment
Is your sleepless and breathless
  choice.

26

There is not a single day
That God does not invite our heart
To meditate.
But at times our heart is
  dominated
By the unwillingness
Of the vital and the mind.

27

If surrender is not
The strongest point in your life,
How can you make
The fastest progress in
  spirituality?

28

When I look
Into each and every corner
Of my heart-room,
I see only one thing:
God's Compassion-Eye.

29

Ignorance does not know the way
To go forward, to dive deep within
Or to fly upward.
It only knows the way
To go backward.

30

My poor Lord, every day
When I enter into Your Heart,
I see nothing but countless
  wounds.

31

I struggle
For my world-supremacy.
God struggles
For my heart-intimacy.

32

My self-love
Always stands against
My Lord's Promise-Blossoms.

33

If I can become
An unconditionally surrendered
Instrument of God,
Temptation is bound to avoid me.

34

Doubt, suspicion and arrogance –
These are the three
Almost incurable diseases
Of the mind.

35

A genuine aspiration-heart
Can definitely free itself
From ever-mounting desires.

36

Are you looking for God?
God is coming.
I hope you will be ready
To receive God in God's own Way.
If not, frustration will eclipse
Your hope-sun.

37

No yesterday and no tomorrow
For those who love
God-manifestation!
God-manifestation has to take place
Here and now.

38

Who is ruling your life?
If you are aspiring,
Then God Himself is ruling
  your life.
But if you are in the desire-world,
Then your mind
Is definitely ruling your life.

39

Free yourself
From your self-chosen bondage!
God wants you to enjoy
The beauty and fragrance
Of universal freedom.

40

The reason you fail to see God
Is simple:
You have lost your hunger
For God's Heart-manifestation
On earth.

41

If you listen to temptation-songs,
How can you expect God
To dance His Illumination-Dance
For you?

42

Every day I love and treasure
God's Forgiveness-Footsteps
Inside my aspiration-heart.

43

God does not mind
If you imitate Him,
But He does mind
If you doubt Him.

44

Just one unguarded moment
Can create lifelong suffering
For us.

45

My doubting mind,
I am determined to irritate you.
My loving heart,
I am determined to please you
Above everything.

46

God did give you
The first chance,
But your desire-bound mind
Ruined everything!

47

A heart of devotion
And a life of gratitude
Know no parallel.

48

The beauty of surrender
Blesses us
With a perfection-bliss-life.

49

Humility is not
A world-conquering reality
But a world-elevating
And world-transforming reality.

50

Take your God-search seriously
If you want to make your soul,
Your heart and your life
Happy eternally.

PART XIII

HEAVEN'S ECSTASY-FLAMES

HEAVEN'S ECSTASY-FLAMES

1

Heaven's ecstasy-flames
You can become
If you disperse
Your mind's jealousy-clouds.

2

When I am
My receptivity-heart,
God is
God's Sunrise-Smile.

3

There was a time
When I played
On my heart's
Hope-flute.
Now
I am playing
On my life's
Promise-drum.

4

Concentration-power
Is
The strongest power
That silences
Uncomely thoughts
And
Wandering mind.

5

A doubt-turbulence-free mind
Is
Unbelievably beautiful
And
Soulful.

6

The intensity of willingness
Marks the beginning
Of a divine fulness-heart.

7

Alas,
Everybody wants to be
A world-imperfection-
    perfectionist
And not
A world-transformation-
    optimist.

8

The mind-door is open
To hostile forces.
The heart-door is open
To God's Tears.

9

O my heart,
I want you only to love God.
O my mind,
I want you only to need God.
O my life,
I want you only to be of God
And for God.

10

If you love someone,
You will naturally have
  concern for them.
But love is infinitely more
  important
Than concern,
For love is oneness.

11

Concern gives
According to its limited
  willingness.
Love gives
According to its fullest capacity.

12

God is not asking you to be
  indifferent –
Far from it!
But your kindness has to be
  flooded
With the inner light.

13

Despite knowing perfectly well
That He is going to fail,
God still tries and tries
To console us and illumine us.

14

Feel that each day
Is the beginning of a new
  consciousness,
The beginning of a new hope,
The beginning of a new
  God-loving life
And God-manifesting life.

15

Claim your Master's achievements
As your very own.
You will make your Master
The happiest person on earth.

16

You did nothing
For God.
Yet
You expect everything
From Him.

17

Beautiful
Is
The God of Light.
Powerful
Is
The God of Compassion.
Delightful
Is
The God of Dream.

18

Willingness
Has
Intensity-speed.
Self-givingness
Is
The destination-arrival.

19

The heart of Heaven
Sweetly whispers.
The mind of earth
Ruthlessly roars.

20

You will be completely lost
Only when you ignore
The God-dreams
Of your aspiration-heart.

21

My Lord,
To love You is not only
The one thing,
But
The thing,
The only thing
I want to have
And
I want to be.

22

My silence-meditation-peace
Is
My Lord's Victory-Throne.

23

The mind is needed
To imagine
God-manifestation-possibilities.
The heart is needed
To explore
God-manifestation-possibilities.
The life is needed
To fulfil
God-manifestation-possibilities.

24

What is aspiration?
Aspiration is
The champion-transcendence-runner.

25

My aspiration-strength
And
God's Satisfaction-Length
Are always found
Together.

26

God the Justice
Is
My interviewer.
God the Compassion
Is
My interpreter.

27

O my mind,
Stop being a stranger to
Your soul's illumination-smiles
And
Your heart's aspiration-cries.

28

The heart-dreamer
We all are.
The mind-disbeliever
We equally are.

29

A constant satisfaction-heart
Is
The Heaven-ticket paid.

30

O doubt-infested mind,
From you I shall
Successfully hide.

31

As quantity-enormity
Is
A universal experience,
Even so, quality-rarity
Is
A universal experience.

32

When I pray
God blesses me
With an inspiration-boat.
When I meditate
God blesses me
By turning me into
The aspiration-boatman.

33

When I love God
For my sake,
My mind and I enjoy
Ignorance-darkness-feast.
When I love God
For God's sake,
My heart and I enjoy
His Wisdom-Light-Feast.

34

Be not seen inside
The ferocious pride
Of your mind
And
The voracious greed
Of your vital.

35

Friends will come
And
Friends will go.
Brothers and sisters will come
And
Brothers and sisters will go.
Who will remain with me
Forever?
My Eternity's God-lover.

36

The devotion-tears
Of the heart
Are the fastest
God-discoverers.

37

Many have done it
And I shall do it.
I shall break asunder
My mind's doubt-bondage-chains.

38

If you want to please God
In God's own Way,
Then the first thing
You have to do
Is
To shut down
Your impure mind's
Impure thought
Impurity-factory.

39

May my life's divinity
Be fully blossomed
Inside my heart's
Meditation-prosperity.

40

May I become my heart's
Enthusiasm-bird
With
Eagerness-wings
To fly in God's
Satisfaction-Sky.

41

May my self-giving
Oneness-business
Every day,
Every hour,
Every minute,
Every second prosper,
To please my Lord Beloved
    Supreme
In His own Way.

42

If your mind
Can derail
Your aspiration-train,
Then you can fix it
With your heart's
Sterling faith.

43

We are so fortunate
That
God the Compassion
And not
God the Justice
Examines our life's
Perfection-progress.

44

Is there any human mind
That does not want
To monopolise
God's Compassion-Smiles?

45

Your mind
May not have
Any respect for truth.
But your heart
Should have
Not only respect,
But also love for truth.

46

Alas,
We do not know why,
But we do allow hesitation
To hamper our heart's
Progress-speed.

47

All achievement-adventures
Are not only powerful,
But also
Beautiful and fruitful.

48

O my mind,
I will absolutely
No more allow you
To interfere
In my heart's
Hope-activities.

49

Enthusiasm
Is the fastest speed
Of the searching mind.
Eagerness
Is the fastest speed
Of the aspiring heart.
Oneness
Is the fastest speed
Of the serving life.

50

Beautiful I am
When I pray and sing
With the morning stars.
Peaceful I am
When I meditate and sing
With the evening stars.

PART XIV

IDLENESS: THE LONELIEST EXISTENCE
IN THE ENTIRE WORLD

IDLENESS: THE LONELIEST EXISTENCE IN THE ENTIRE WORLD

1

Idleness is
The lover of death.

2

Idleness is
The host of death.

3

Idleness is
The death-night-distributor.

4

O idleness,
You are evil
From the sole of your foot
To the crown of your head.

5

Idleness,
You torpedo
God's Dream-Boat.

6

Idleness,
You ruthlessly compel
Life-energy to starve.

7

Idleness,
You desire the stars in the sky
To be at your beck and call.

8

Idleness,
You are the mind-butcher,
You are the heart-puncher,
You are the vital-crusher,
You are the body-undertaker.

9

Idleness,
You are arrogant within,
Abhorrent without.

10

Idleness,
You do nothing for the world,
Yet you secretly and openly
 desire
World-attention,
 world-appreciation,
World-admiration and even
World-adoration!

11

Idleness,
You want everything
For the asking
Inside your empty
Body-hole.

12

Idleness,
Your inner life, if you have any,
Is all sadness.
Your outer life, if you have any,
Is all bitterness.

13

Idleness,
To our wide surprise,
Futility-luxury
You can always afford.

14

Idleness,
You constantly ask time
Not to look at you.

15

Idleness,
Time does not want
To be snubbed by you.
Therefore,
It does not approach you.

16

Idleness,
You are absolutely certain
That doomsday will never be able
To strike you.

17

Idleness,
Your eyes do not even
Try to hide
Their envy-look.

18

Idleness,
When are you going to realise
That yours is the loneliest
   existence
In the entire world?

19

Idleness,
In stupidity
Nobody can equal you.
You do not care
To cross the finish line.
Not only that,
You do not even care
To be at the starting line.

20

Idleness,
While voraciously eating,
You complacently hear
Others' victory-horn.

21

Idleness,
Your beyond-repair brain
Is adorning the abysmal abyss!

22

Idleness,
You are at once
Frustration-reservoir
And frustration-generator.

23

Idleness,
You are a slow
    poison-enjoyer.

24

Idleness,
You do not want to be
An aspiration-student,
But you do want to be
A God-realisation-professor!

25

Idleness,
You have taken the surrender-way
To self-annihilation
And not self-perfection.

26

Idleness,
In vain
The unconditional affection-
    world
Tries to please you.
In vain
The unconditional dedication-
    world
Tries to please you.

27

Idleness,
Secretly you treasure,
Openly you treasure
Displeasure-breath.

28

Idleness,
Yesterday I saw you mumbling.
Today I am seeing you fumbling.
Tomorrow I shall see you
   crumbling!

29

Idleness,
You want the whole world
To love you.
Without being loveable,
How can you be loved?
Can you not see that the world
Hesitates for a very long time
Before it condescends
To love you?

30

Idleness,
Unless and until
You seriously and fearlessly
Look at yourself,
Your happiness-dream
Will always remain
A far cry.

31

Idleness,
Can you not see
That your joyless and godless days
Have neither a beginning
Nor an end?

32

Idleness,
You do not value
God's Concern.
You do not value
God's Compassion.
You do not even value
God's Forgiveness.
You just value your mind's
Happiness-hallucination.

33

Idleness,
When will you be aware
Of the undeniable fact
That unawareness
Has befriended you,
Unwillingness
Has befriended you
And, in a broad sense,
Stupidity and futility both
Have inescapably
Befriended you?

34

Idleness,
Time is our master.
Our aspiration, dedication,
Self-giving – everything –
We have surrendered
To the eye of time.
But you want time
To helplessly surrender
To your every whim!

35

Idleness,
Who else is an inevitable victim
Of self-doubt,
If not you?

36

Idleness,
An insatiable hunger you have
For world-praise.
But you want to do nothing,
Absolutely nothing,
For the world.

37

Idleness,
Strangely enough,
Quite often you are enamoured
Of what you have
And what you are.
What you have
Is nothing short of stupidity,
And what you are
Is nothing short of futility.

38

Idleness,
A seeker devotedly enjoys
A full-time God-job.
You enjoy a full-time
Self-indulgence-job.

39

Idleness,
Never do you want
To please God.
Never do you want
To love God.
Never do you want
To serve and fulfil God
In God's own Way.
Therefore, it is no wonder
That your mind is bound by sin
And your heart is bound by guilt!

40

Idleness,
Are you not afraid of
God's Silence-Thunder-Eye,
As we all are?

41

Idleness,
When God asks you
To do something,
You always ask God
To show you how to do it.
While He is showing you
How to do it,
You purposely fall into
And enjoy
A deep and never-ending sleep.

42

Idleness,
How successfully you hide
Your outer aggression
And your inner retrogression
From us!

43

Idleness,
Ignorance-night
Is our partial possessor,
But your full possessor.

44

Idleness says to dynamism,
"For God's sake,
You don't have to shed tears
For me."

Dynamism says to idleness,
"My friend, it is too late!
I can't help it."

45

Idleness says to dynamism,
"Why do you so peculiarly
Look at me?
Do you think I am
Deplorably pathetic?"

Dynamism says to idleness,
"Unfortunately,
You are absolutely right.
But do not worry.
I am sleeplessly and
   unconditionally
Sympathetic."

46

Dynamism says to idleness,
"Wake up! Stand up!
Walk up and down!
When are you going to be wise?"

Idleness says to dynamism,
"Shut up, shut up!
Slow down, slow down!
When are you going to be
   careful?"

47

Idleness says to dynamism,
"Let us bury our past criticisms
Once and for all.
I do not want to remain
Shattered by my fate's blow
Any more."

48

Dynamism says to idleness,
"My friend, my dear friend,
My oneness-friend,
Do not build towers
Without a foundation
Any more.
Do not trust tomorrow.
Tomorrow is an old and expert
Deceiver.
It is high time for you
To leave the land
Of self-made fools.
Happily look every morning
At the rising sun.
Hope, without fail,
Will be your guardian angel.
God is showering upon you
His Heaven-Heart-
   Forgiveness-Blossoms.
Just place yourself at His Feet
With your mind's prayerful
   readiness,
Your heart's soulful willingness
And your life's cheerful
   eagerness."

PART XV

IMPURITY: THE MAD ELEPHANT MENTAL ASYLUM

IMPURITY: THE MAD ELEPHANT MENTAL ASYLUM

1

Impurity,
Where do you live?
Do you live inside my body?

"No!"

Do you live inside my vital?

"No, no!"

Do you live inside my mind?

"No, no, no!"

Do you live inside my heart?

"No, no, no, no!"

Do you live inside my soul?

"You stupid fellow!
I never thought
That you could be so stupid.
Of course, if your soul
Were made of charcoal,
I could live there.
But you must know
That your soul is made of
God's own Divinity."

In that case,
I will not dare to ask you
If you live inside God.

"Better not! Otherwise,
The elephant-pride of the
   mental asylum
Will immediately beckon you!"

Impurity, my dear friend,
Then do tell me
Where you actually live.

"I live inside the beauty
And fragrance
Of your incoming breath."

What about my outgoing breath?
Do you ever accompany
My outgoing breath?

"Yes, I do,
Only when I am forced to."

Impurity,
You are so powerful;
Who could ever dare
To force you?

"Although I am powerful,
Very powerful,
Extremely powerful,
Unimaginably powerful,
I am no match for
Your heart's streaming tears,
Your heart's climbing tears and
Your heart's falling tears,
Or for
Your soul's life-awakening smiles,
Your soul's world-illumining
   smiles and
Your soul's earth-transforming
   smiles."

2

Who is an impure seeker?

An impure seeker
Is the possessor of heart-sand.
An impure seeker
Is the possessor of mind-mud.
An impure seeker
Is the possessor of vital-clay.
An impure seeker
Is the possessor of body-filth.

3

What is impurity?

Impurity is
An atom bomb-explosion.
So says my purity-flooded
Consciousness.

4

Impurity says to the body:
"O body, where are you?"

The body says to impurity:
"Can you not see
That I am at your powerful feet?"

5

Impurity says to the vital:
"O vital, where are you?"

The vital says to impurity:
"Can you not see
That I am at your ruthless feet?"

6

Impurity says to the mind:
"O mind, where are you?"

The mind says to impurity:
"Can you not see
That I am at your inescapable
   feet?"

7

Impurity says to the heart:
"O heart, where are you?"

The heart says to impurity:
"Can you not see
That I am at your
   immeasurable feet?"

8

The body, vital, mind
And heart
Together say to impurity:
"Impurity, how we wish
We could see you
At the feet of somebody,
As we are always at your feet!"

Impurity says:
"O body, vital, mind and heart,
You four are really blind!
Can you not see
That I am at the feet
Of purity-thought-planters
And at the feet
Of Divinity-will-power-growers?"

9

Impurity,
In the abyss
Of inconscience-sleep,
You just descend
And
Descend.

10

Impurity
Is absolutely certain
That hell is another name
For Heaven.

11

Impurity
Is absolutely certain
That the hardest reality
Is another name for
The sweetest dream.

12

Impurity
Is absolutely certain
That emotional fantasy
Is another name for
Devotional ecstasy.

13

Impurity
Is absolutely certain
That negativity-forest
Is another name for
Positivity-garden.

14

Impurity and disobedience
Deeply enjoy
Their friendship.

15

Impurity,
You are my soul's
Disappointment.

16

Impurity,
You are my heart's
Failure.

17

Impurity,
You are my mind's
Backward march.

18

Impurity,
You are
Volcano-emotion-eruption
In disguise.

19

Impurity,
Purity-whisper
You ignore.

20

Impurity,
Callousness-drummer
You are.

21

Impurity,
I am consumed
With embittered memories
Of you.

22

Impurity,
At your mere presence,
The poor and helpless
   seeker's
Emotional temperature
Reaches its godless
Highest height.

23

Impurity,
Though I stumble often
On the way,
I am sure that
I shall ultimately succeed
In reaching God's
Golden Shore.

24

The seeker says to impurity:
"Impurity,
There shall come a time
In my life
When I shall swim and swim
In my heart's
Sleeplessly running
Purity-river
Towards the enlightenment-sea
Of my Lord Beloved Supreme.
And what you will do then?
You will be drowning
And drowning
And finally sinking
In the abysmal abyss
Of darkest inconscience-night!"

25

Impurity of the vital
And
Insecurity of the heart
Belong to the same family.

26

The seeker says to impurity:
"O impurity-hurricane,
I am facing you bravely;
I shall always face you
    bravely."

27

Impurity,
Like a pleasant host,
Slowly and smilingly,
Lovingly and charmingly,
Invites the seeker
Into its domain.

28

"Impurity,
You are overwhelmingly
Dangerous
And agonisingly
Contagious."
So says a seeker,
A highly advanced seeker.

29

Impurity,
No matter when
You place a call
To my heart's
Sleepless aspiration-phone,
You will always get
A busy signal.

30

Impurity,
You need a total
Transformation.
Therefore,
My soul's concern-circle
Does not exclude you.

31

Impurity,
Your very presence
Mutilates
My heart's oneness-happiness.

32

Impurity,
The moment I see you,
The human in me
Is immediately frightened
And the Divine in me
Is surprisingly amused.

33

Impurity,
Yours is a life
Bound for imminent
Or remote tragedy.

34

Impurity,
Desire-fire you are;
Aspiration-flame
You must needs be.

35

He who sets fire
To his mind's impurity-forest
Is blessingfully granted
An aspiration-garden
By God Himself.

36

Impurity,
To-day you are
An insurmountable obstacle;
To-morrow it is you
Who will be transformed
Into the heart's self-giving
Purity-fragrance-rose.

37

Impurity,
Are you ready to leave me?
Look!
I am tearing out the pages
Of your sordid past
In my life.

38

Impurity,
If you want to remain
Mischievous,
Then I can easily remain
Devious.

39

Impurity,
Can you not see
That God has dismissed
Your impertinent vital?

40

Impurity.
Can you not see
That God has revoked
Your indulgence-license?

41

Between an ungrateful person
And an impure person,
O seeker,
Whom do you prefer?

"I prefer an impure person
To an ungrateful person,
For I feel I will be able
To illumine and transform
An impure person,
But I will never be able
To transform
An ungrateful person.
Needless to say, I am saying this
From my personal experience."

PART XVI

MY JEALOUSY IS MY MADNESS-BURDEN

MY JEALOUSY IS MY MADNESS-BURDEN

1

My jealousy
Is my madness-burden.
My jealousy
Is God's sadness-burden.

2

Jealousy
Is an instant
Joy-killer.

3

Sooner than at once,
Jealousy brings to the fore
Its hidden sword.

4

Jealousy wants to unburden
Its miseries
Sleeplessly and breathlessly.

5

Jealousy
Is an ever-rising fever
Of man's ignorance-mind
And vital.

6

Jealousy
Is a fatal
Hatred-poison.

7

Jealousy
Is at once
Ferocious and atrocious.

8

Jealousy
Is at once
Rebellious and voracious.

9

Jealousy happily
Plies its boat
Between the inner tragedies
And outer tragedies
Of its rivals.

10

Jealousy
Is a deep-rooted
Love-rejection-life.

11

Jealousy
And supremacy
Are always fond
Of living together.

12

Unlike ours,
Jealousy's breath
Lives in its
Destruction-cherished vital.

13

Jealousy's phone
Rings and rings
Until it catches
The victim's ear.

14

Jealousy can live
Without a mind,
Without a heart,
Without a soul,
Even without God.

15

Human jealousy
And divine ecstasy
Are eternal strangers.

16

Jealousy
Is a one-way
Destruction-road.

17

Jealousy
Is an aggressive boxer,
A repulsive dancer,
A hopeless singer
And a useless storyteller.

18

In the desire-race,
Jealousy
Is always first.

19

Aspiration-plants
And dedication-leaves
Are ruthlessly destroyed
By the mad elephant:
Jealousy.

20

Jealousy
Is humanity's
Dream-boat-bomber.

MY JEALOUSY IS MY MADNESS-BURDEN

21

Jealousy has
Frightening eyes.
Jealousy has
Grinding teeth.
Jealousy has
A cunning face.

22

Jealousy's birth date
Everybody knows.
Jealousy's death date
Nobody knows,
For jealousy
Defies death.

23

The seeker says to jealousy,
"Jealousy, where are you?"
Jealousy says to the seeker,
"O seeker, are you blind?
I am everywhere!
Especially in the mind
And in the vital
Of every desire."

24

Jealousy comes from
The desire-life.
The desire-life comes from
The impurity-mind.
The impurity-mind comes from
The untouchability-night.

25

The unsuccessful jealousy
Surrenders
To the unmovable lethargy.
The unmovable lethargy
Surrenders
To the hurtful
Self-destruction.

26

Jealousy,
Before you entered
Into my life,
I was the world's
Richest prince.
Now that you are in me
And I am for you,
I have become
The poorest street-beggar.

27

Jealousy,
Before you entered
Into my life,
I was the possessor of
Two blue-vast eyes.
Now that you are in me
And I am for you,
I have become the possessor
Of two inferno-volcano-eyes.

28

Jealousy,
You are my mind's purity-stealer,
You are my heart's peace-intruder,
You are my life's divinity-invader.

29

Jealousy,
You may not know,
You may not even
Want to know,
But God's Compassion-Eye
Is beckoning you
And God's Forgiveness-Heart
Is ready for you.

30

Jealousy,
My God-searching mind knows
That you are malicious.
My God-aspiring heart feels
That you are treacherous.
My God-serving life knows
    and feels
That you are ferocious.

31

O my jealousy,
Your barking mouth
And biting eyes
Are equally and immediately
Destructive.

32

Jealousy,
You are my constant
Nightmare-mind.
You are my constant
Love-absence-heart.

33

Shortest is the distance
From jealousy to hell.

34

Jealousy says to fear,
"Out! out!
Get out of my vital,
Get out of my mind,
Get out of my very life!
I am on my way
To my enemy: destruction."

35

Jealousy,
You prefer
Ignorance-night-sleep
To illumination-perfection-
    dream.

36

Jealousy,
You do not come alone
To your victim.
You come with
Your darkest and wildest
Thunder-disaster.

37

Jealousy,
Matchless you are
As an insecurity-islander.

38

Jealousy,
You are your own
Ultimate
Self-destruction-indulgence.

39

Jealousy,
You are your own
Constant aggression.
Aggression and satisfaction
Live millions of miles apart.

40

Jealousy,
The sweetness of oneness-hope
And the fulness of God-promise
Will never befriend you.

41

Jealousy,
You are impossibly blind.
Therefore
God's descending Tears
You can neither
See nor feel.

42

Jealousy,
God is fast approaching you.
Do not ignore,
Do not even underestimate
His Compassion-flooded Arrival.

43

Jealousy,
Only because of you
My sweetest God-memories
Are fading fast,
Very fast.

44

Jealousy,
Are you not ashamed of
Thriving on world-suspicion
For such a long time?

45

Jealousy,
Can you not see
That every day you are running
Between ever-extending
And ever-disappearing goals?

46

Jealousy,
God is extremely happy
That finally
You are asking about Him.

47

Jealousy,
God is delighted to hear
That you feel the necessity
Of His Arrival
At your door.

48

Jealousy,
God is extremely proud of you
Because you want to demolish
Once and for all
Your huge ignorance-mansion.

49

Jealousy,
God will be extremely fond of you
If you take from Him
His unconditional Help
In your unprecedented adventure.

50

Jealousy,
Look how excited God is
To come and meet you!
You just say hello to God.
In no time
He will transform you
And make you
His Divinity's Life,
His Infinity's Heart
And His Immortality's Soul.

PART XVII

NO UNREACHABLE GOAL

NO UNREACHABLE GOAL

1

If we believe in our own
Self-transcendence-task
Then there can be
No unreachable goal.

2

The mind's expectation-danger
Destroys the heart's
Surrender-oneness-joy
To the Will of God.

3

Our goal is not to have
A problem-free life.
But to conquer all the problems
As they appear
Along our life-road.

4

We all must exterminate
The doubt-mind-insects
If we really want
True happiness in our life.

5

God does not mind
If you complain
Against God to humanity.
But God does mind
If you do not take proper care
Of your own inner life.

6

It is only
The oneness-heart-joy
That expands and grows
And becomes the vastness-sky.

7

The mind's thought-barrier
Is the source of impossibility.
Let us pray and meditate
To go far beyond
The extremities of the mind.

8

If we are not alive
To all our opportunities,
How can we ever proceed
In our God-loving aspiration-life?

9

To whom shall we give
Our stupidity-mind,
If not to God?

To whom shall we give
Our sincerity-heart.
If not to God?

10

If we are not hungry
For the Light Supreme,
We are bound to hanker after
Pleasure-illusion-life.

11

Each time My Lord Supreme
Fulfils my earth-bound desire,
I feel that my aspiration-heart
Enters deeper into
The jungle of despair.

12

O my sleeping body,
O my striving vital,
O my searching mind,
O my crying heart,
God has not forgotten you.
Before long He will bless you
With His complete
Satisfaction-Smiles.

13

I have betrayed my inner life.
My Lord of Compassion
Has forgiven me.
But I cannot and I must not
Forgive myself.

14

God gives Himself completely
To a seeker's surrender-life
And
To his gratitude-heart.

15

When God
Challenges ignorance-night
On my behalf,
Then only I am going to succeed.
Otherwise, never.

16

I love my heart's rainbow-dreams,
For they carry me
Lovingly and safely
To the Golden Shore.

17

Those who have
Astonishing capacities
For self-deception
Will need countless years
For self-perfection.

18

O my mind,
You are such a fool
That you are trying to rebuild
Your collapsing ego-building.

19

A seeker of the highest order
Has a silence-mind
To entertain him
All the time.

20

Earth-achievements
Are no match
Even for an iota
Of Heaven-enlightenment.

21

A doubtful and suspicious mind
Must carry a very heavy load
On a very long journey.

22

An aspiring heart
Every day must renew
Its contract
With God's Compassion-Eye.

23

We must vehemently and equally
Defy the pride of
Our mind's wrath
And
Our body's sloth.

24

O my mind,
God will be here in a minute.
Are you ready to receive God?

O my heart,
God will be here in a minute.
Are you willing to receive God?

O my life,
God will be here in a minute.
Are you eager to receive God?

25

God was not successful with
His Compassion-Height-
    approach.
He is now trying a new approach:
His Justice-Light.

26

The seekers who live
For the divine Cause
Will definitely receive
A thunderous applause
From the denizens
Of the higher world.

27

The day I expect
Nothing from the world,
I receive both
The heart-flower
And
The soul-fragrance
Of the world.

28

Our failure-life
Comes into being
From our own confusion-mind
And not from anything else.

29

The joy of a self-giving life
Can neither be measured
Nor be expounded.

30

He who thinks
That there is no room
For progress-delight
Is utterly mistaken.

31

The ups and downs
Of God-manifestation
Will entirely depend
On the seeker's
Sincerity-heart-aspiration
And
Simplicity-mind-inspiration.

32

He who serves God self-givingly
Will always remain close
To the Heart of God.

33

Faith is wisdom.
Faith is power.
Faith is heart-fragrance.
Faith is the sun-child
Of the Beyond.

NO UNREACHABLE GOAL

34

I shall plant
All my sufferings
In my soul's
Patience-light-field.

35

The wall on which
Humanity has to lean
Is
The wall of self-dedication
And not
The wall of self-admiration.

36

The world is growing
Worse and worse every day,
Precisely because
It has lost the fragrance
Of its God-surrender-heart.

37

True, we cannot reform
Our forefathers,
But we can and we must reform
Our own children
And their own children.

38

When I converse
With the ancient heart,
We always talk
About the goodness-depth
Of human beings.

When I converse
With the modern mind,
We only talk
About the greatness-length
Of human life.

39

We show ourselves
As we wish
To be seen.

God shows Himself
As we wish Him
To be seen.

40

O greatness,
You are the product
Of my transitory mind.

O goodness,
You are the product
Of my God-repository-heart.

41

The divine prosperity
Will come into existence
Only when sincerity-heart talks —
Here, there and everywhere.

42

Ignorance-sleep
Is universal.
Wisdom-delight
Is transcendental.

43

You will be happy
Only when you think
What God wants you to think
And not think of yourself
The way the whole world
Thinks about you.

44

If you are not ready
To endure sufferings
On your way to God's Palace,
How will you ever
Discover God,
The only Satisfaction?

45

If you do not disobey
Your doubting mind,
How can your aspiring heart
Ever carry you
To your Destination supreme?

46

If you do not sharpen
Your discrimination-sword,
Your mind-thorns
Will ruthlessly torture you.

47

We take pride
In our mind's mortal nest.
God wants us
To take pride
In our heart's immortal palace.

48

Because of aspiration-shortage,
Man is compelled
By God the Justice-Light
To have
A fearful heart
And
A tearful life.

49

Every day
The aspiring heart
Must dream a new
God-manifestation-dream.

50

O dreamers of peace, come.
Let us walk together.
O lovers of peace, come,
Let us run together.
O servers of peace, come.
Let us grow together.

PART XVIII

SAY A FINAL FAREWELL TO YOUR MIND'S BONDAGE-LIFE

SAY A FINAL FAREWELL TO YOUR MIND'S BONDAGE-LIFE

1

Stop your friendship
With your mind-fantasies
If you want to enjoy
Your heart-aspiration-ecstasies.

2

It is high time to revolt
Against the reign
Of your tyrannical and ferocious
Tiger-mind!

3

Every time I soulfully pray,
I see the blossoming Light
Of God's sacred Smile.

4

I am so grateful to my soul,
For it is helping me
So compassionately
To journey towards
Infinity's Peace.

5

O seeker,
What else is sheer stupidity
If not the greater love you have
For your mind
Than for your heart?

6

Each time I nourish a good
   thought,
I give a surprising victory
To my aspiration-heart.

7

Hesitation and indecision
Ruthlessly plague
Even sincere minds
And pure hearts.

8

Once we enter into the spiritual
   life,
Our possibility-fulfilment-life
Becomes infinitely easier.

9

My God-aspiration-hope
Can once more be rekindled
Only by God's Compassion-
   Eye-Smile.

10

I shall not allow my life
Anymore to remain
An undisciplined blunder.

11

I find no truth
In the curiosity
Of my mind's God-search.

12

O my mind, suspect nothing
If happiness is what you want.
O my heart, fear nothing
If happiness is what you want.

13

Idleness wants to be
A world-possessor
Without being
A self-mover.

14

Finally I have
The indomitable courage
To jump off my mind's
Jealousy-train.

15

If we ignore God the Pilot,
How will we be able to enjoy
His Boat Ride?

16

My heart flies
Higher than the highest
When I lose considerably
My mind's desire-pounds.

17

A disciplined life
Is the best freedom-enjoyer
In the inner world.

18

O my mind,
Why do you allow yourself
To suffer from
Desire-bound thought-disease?

19

How can we ever
Make God happy
If we do not feed
Our own God-hunger?

20

If you belittle
Others' gratitude-tears,
God-Satisfaction-Smiles
Will avoid you.

21

Be not satisfied
Only with your outer self.
Explore your teeming inner
   selves.
Only then can you ever
Be truly fulfilled.

22

My Lord,
I need Your very special Blessings
To cancel once and for all
All my world-complaints.

23

God wants
My life-surrender-sea
And not my surrender-drop
To satisfy Himself.

24

When you most powerfully
Say a final farewell
To your mind's bondage-life,
Your soul will treasure you
And utilise you
In God's own Way.

25

Every day I wash
My Lord's Compassion-Feet
With my heart's devotion-tears.

26

Is there anybody who does not
   think
That his problems are the worst
And that he is hopelessly
   drowning
In the sea of helplessness?

27

You cannot irritate God,
Even with your shameless
   impatience
And empty receptivity.
You just delay God's Arrival!

28

At every moment
God's Love grows and glows
Inside silence-hearts.

29

If you do not forgive and forget
The world's dreadful injustice,
You will not be able
To make the progress
That you want.

30

No more do I carry
My power-hungry past.
I live only in
My oneness-hungry present.

31

On the strength of
My unconditional surrender,
I feel that to please God
Every step of the way
Is not a difficult task.

32

Ignorance is obscure.
Ignorance is impure.
Ignorance is death-preparation.

33

If you live in the soul,
With the soul
And for the soul,
You have impeccable God-credentials.

34

A determination-mind
And an aspiration-heart
Are treasured by God's divine Pride.

35

Today you are
A disobedience-king.
Tomorrow you will be forced to be
The possessor of a flood of tears.

36

When I see God,
I always make the same request:
That He visit me
As often as possible.

37

From the outer world
You may at times escape.
But from the inner world
You can never escape,
Never!

38

My Lord Supreme comes
When He is prayerfully needed
And not when He is
Whimsically called.

39

Ignorance can neither
Know nor understand
Why it eventually becomes
A total failure.

40

May my love become a strong
　point,
My devotion a stronger point
And my surrender the strongest
　point
In my aspiration-life.

41

God looks into every corner
Of my heart-room
To see if there are
Aspiration-flames available.

42

Be proud of your patience.
Your patience will ultimately
　arrive
At the Goal
And make God exceedingly happy.

43

My heart knows
Only one way:
The way of unconditional
　surrender.

44

A desire-mind
Is
An obscurity-insincerity-slave.

45

O my mind, "No!"
A thousand times, "No!"
To your desire-hunger-fulfilment.

46

Self-worshippers eventually
Cry and cry.
God-worshippers unmistakably
Fly and fly.

47

Strength and tolerance
Must be eternal partners
To be victorious in life.

48

When we do something good
And when we love
The world of self-giving,
God is infinitely more pleased
Than we can ever imagine.

49

If you can dare to laugh at
Your hopeless helplessness,
God will bless you
With His most powerful
And most proud Smile.

50

With every child
God creates a new hope
And a new promise
For Himself.

PART XIX

SUCCESS-JUMPS, PROGRESS-SONGS

SUCCESS-JUMPS, PROGRESS-SONGS

1

Success-jumps
I jumped and jumped
At the Feet
Of my Lord Supreme.

Progress-songs
I sing and sing
Inside the Heart
Of my Beloved Supreme.

2

Obedience
Is the only identification
Needed to enter
Into God's Heart-Home.

3

Purity
Cares.
Impurity
Dares.

4

Sound,
Don't touch me.
You are untouchable.

5

Silence,
Let me touch you.
You are so loveable.

6

My mind proudly
Wants to interview God.
My heart devotedly
Longs to review God.

7

My Lord,
Will you not help me
To catch my mind-thief
Red-handed?

8

God's Pride in me
Means
My faith in action.

9

I am not at all curious
To know what God feels
Inside my heart.

I am all curious
To know what God thinks
Of my mind.

10

The mind
Is a voracious eater
Of doubt and disbelief.

11

Alas,
So often expectations
Are doomed
To dismal disappointments.

12

The limping doubt
And
The crawling despair
Never reach
The destination.

13

My Mother God
Protects my life.
My Father God
Perfects my heart.

14

The mind
Enjoys conspiracy.
The heart
Enjoys ecstasy.

15

I want to know
Where God is.
God wants me to know
Who I am.

16

God-reliance
Is
The perfect sail
Of my life-boat.

17

May each aspiration-heart-garden
Nowhere see
Impurity-weeds.

18

Impatience-tiger-mind,
I do not want you.
Never.
Patience-tortoise-heart,
I love you.
I need you.
Always.

19

God supremely enjoys
Watching my gratitude-heart-bird
Fly in my life-surrender-sky.

SUCCESS-JUMPS, PROGRESS-SONGS

20

May my mind
Think of God only.
May my heart
Love God only.
May my life
Need God only,
Until the final end of time.

21

In your mind-belief
Be not lukewarm
If success is what you want.

In your heart-faith,
Be not lukewarm
If progress is what you need.

22

O bumpy period of my life,
You have immensely increased
The immensity of my heart's
God-hunger-necessity.
Therefore, to you,
My heart is all gratitude.

23

God Himself removes
All disabilities,
Inner and outer,
From his supremely chosen
Self-giving children.

24

Dive deep within we must
To see God with a unique present
In His blessingful Hands
At every moment.

25

God is
God's Compassion-drill.
I am
My heart's devotion-thrill.

26

Peace-birds
Always fly
Carrying
My Soul's Silence-Fragrance.

27

As desire-disappointment
My mind is,
Even so,
Aspiration-enlightenment
My heart is.

28

Each human being
Is a helpless victim
To his own desire-shadow.

29

No heart
Can breathe
Without hope-flames.

30

Forgiveness
My mind needs
From God.

Fulness
My heart needs
From God.

31

If you never
Take God seriously,
How will you ever
Self-givingly please Him?

32

My soul,
If you do not teach me,
Who will?

My heart,
If you do not love me,
Who will?

33

There is no fixed hour
When you should unfurl
Your aspiration-sails.

34

I do not want to suffer
In my life
Only from one thing:
Aspiration-starvation.

35

Be careful of insecurity.
It spreads
Oneness-death-seeds
All-where.

36

Determination-famine
Announces
Death's arrival.

37

A desireless moment
Is
A faultless enlightenment.

SUCCESS-JUMPS, PROGRESS-SONGS

38

The inner thrill-fragrance
Is what my heart
Sleeplessly longs for.

39

God Himself
Cultivates
Our dream-heart-gardens.

40

Selflessness-life
You have
Because God-oneness-heart
You are.

41

Each mind has something
New to say.
Each heart has something
New to give.
Each life has something
New to become.

42

Our human life wants
Man-supremacy-foundation.
Our divine life needs
God-Ecstasy-Foundation.

43

Eagerness needs no visa
To enter into
The newness-kingdom.

44

Devotion-exhibition
I was.
Devotion-penetration
I am.

45

Man claps
When I quickly succeed.
God claps
When I unconditionally proceed.

46

My mind-slavery
I was.
My heart-bravery
I am.

47

The God-surrender-prayer
Is
The most powerful prayer.

48

I must never
Lose the beauty
Of my tearful eyes.

I must never
Lose the fragrance
Of my grateful heart.

49

Gratitude
Is the perfection
Of my heart-lotus-bloom.

50

Heart-power-shortage-seekers
Can never succeed
In pleasing God
In His own Way.

51

Self-doubt
Is a self-imposed
Torture-punishment.

52

Life-progress
Always depends on
Heart-receptivity.

53

O my mind,
You can make me happy
Only when you become
A mountain-majesty-poise.

54

A willingness-heart-seeker
Receives an inner
Olympic gold medal
From God Himself.

55

To self-doubt, yesterday,
"No," I said.
To self-importance, today,
"No," I say.

56

Fear dies
Only when you
Close the eyes
Of fear.

57

Doubt dies
Only when you
Punch the head
Of doubt.

58

Jealousy dies
Only when you
Twist the tail
Of jealousy.

59

Insecurity dies
Only when you
Burst open the heart
Of insecurity.

60

God takes a very long time
Before He hears
My mind-stories.

God in no time
Hears
My heart-songs.

61

Silence-tears,
How sweet you are.
Gratitude-smiles,
How beautiful you are.

62

O my heart's rainbow-dream-boat,
Stop not.
Sail on,
Sail on,
Sail on.

PART XX

PEACE: GOD'S HEART-HOME
PART 1 & 2

PEACE: GOD'S HEART-HOME

1

When everybody is
Everybody's equal,
The peace-heart blossoms.

2

Peace
Is the indispensable source
Of immortal Delight.

3

Without peace
The mind
Will eventually drown
And the heart
Will eventually die.

4

The mind counts
Troubles.
The heart measures
Peace.

5

A self-transcendence-mind
Has peace.
A oneness-heart
Is peace.

6

Peace reveals
The absolute excellence
Of human life.

7

Not only readily
But completely
I depend on my heart's peace.

8

Peace:
Our surrender-traveller's
Universal passport.

9

When I am
My peace-empty mind,
God becomes
His Joy-empty Heart.

10

Peace sleeplessly feels
God's Blessing-Touch
In everything.

11

Ignorance
Cannot enslave
A man of peace.

12

We must climb
The peace-tree
To pluck oneness-fruits.

13

God invites only
A heart of peace
To participate in
His Cosmic Game.

14

No man can receive
God's Peace-Abundance
Unless he can show God
His God-hunger-permanence.

15

Once you stop singing
Your self-interest-songs,
You will hear the melody
Of God's Peace-Manifestation.

16

No citadel
Is as strong
As our heart's peace eternal.

17

Faith embraces
God the Many.
Peace is
God the One.

18

The mind has no peace
Because it is swallowed
By the darkness of desire-night.

19

If we can simplify
Consciously and soulfully
Life's immediate complexities,
Then we are bound to have peace.

20

My Lord, I need peace.
Therefore, do keep my mind
Always in Your Presence
And my heart
Always at Your Feet.

21

When the divine attitude
Purifies the human attitude
Peace dawns in our aspiration-life.

22

There is only one way
To earn God's Smile
Every day,
And that way is
To have peace of heart.

23

Shun the very breath of
　negativity!
Lo, your mind has become
The possessor of peace.

24

It is not a better location
But a stronger motivation
That can definitely give us peace.

25

Expect not!
Suspect not!
Lo, peace is all yours.

26

God is so kind
And compassionate to me
Because I was introduced to Him
By my dearest friend,
Peace.

27

The mind that is empty
Of peace
Is always madly hurrying
Towards nowhere.

28

I have peace in abundance
Only when God speaks directly
To my aspiration-climbing heart.

29

The spirituality-student
Who is fluent
In God's Oneness-Language
Can swim in the sea of peace.

30

Of all our divine virtues,
Peace is the only virtue
That has the capacity to manifest
Our heart's limitless possibilities.

31

When we have peace,
We come to realise
That our faith in God
Is a direct and blessingful Gift
From God Himself.

32

Criticism takes away
The very life-breath
Of our peace-heart.

33

Every day I magnify my ego.
But if every day I can nullify my
  ego,
Peace is bound to befriend my
  heart.

34

When the mind loses peace,
The hope-heart-flower
Loses all its beauty and fragrance
Immediately.

35

How can you expect peace
When you serve God grudgingly
And not self-givingly?

36

To be a hero supreme,
Do not allow your mind
To be invaded by uncomely
  thoughts.
Lo, you will be the discoverer
Of peace.

37

Every day
Sing prayerfully and soulfully
Your God-surrender-song
That God Himself has taught you.
You will without fail have peace.

38

You can start your journey
Anywhere you want to,
Even in your emotional vital.
Once your emotional vital
Enters into your devotional
  heart-garden,
You will become the beauty
  and fragrance
Of peace-blossoms.

39

I feel peace in abundant measure
When I come to realise
That I belong
To God's Compassion-Smiles
And God belongs
To my aspiration-tears.

40

A man of peace
Has the capacity
To persuade the multitude
To cry for God's Light.

41

Peace
Is the only soil
In which humanity's perfection
Shall grow.

42

My heart knows
That it costs nothing
To be a dreamer and lover
Of peace.

43

My mind has to know
That it costs nothing
To be a seeker
Of peace.

44

Peace
Is the only end
That embodies
Humanity's
Goal supreme.

45

I do not need
An earth-shaking speech
I need
A peace-blossoming earth.

46

Peace
Has finally ended
The struggle between
My heart's faith
And my mind's doubt.

47

Yesterday
Peace gave me
The choice of freedom.

Today
Peace gives me
The voice of freedom.

48

My desire-mind sows
And counts worries.
My aspiration-heart grows
And collects peace.

49

God gives me
What I do not have:
Peace.
I give God
What He does not have:
Ingratitude.

50

Peace
My heart invoked
For my mind.
Now the reign of peace
Is beginning
In my mind.

51

A speaker-mind
Peace avoids.
A seeker-heart
Peace greets.

52

When I offered
My portfolio of earthly
  achievements
To my Lord Supreme,
He sighed and sighed,
For I did not include
My peace-achievement.

53

When you have
Peace of mind,
You realise that there can be
No unattainable heights.

54

Peace
Is easily available
In the morning light
Of sincerity.
Peace
Is always available
In the evening life
Of purity.

PEACE: GOD'S HEART-HOME

55

An austerity-mind
Cannot guarantee us peace,
But a purity-heart
Can definitely guarantee us peace.

56

Peace
Descends on earth
From the highest Home
Of God.

57

When we have peace of mind,
We shall start climbing upwards
From our untold miseries.

58

Peace
Is the only divine virtue of ours
That can summarise
Our heart's aspiration-cry
And our life's dedication-smile.

59

A man of peace
Is not afraid
Of losing his peace
To the thunderous applause
Of the multitude.

60

We can change the world,
But not improve it,
If we do not have peace.

61

If peace does not
Touch my heart,
Then I shall be compelled
To speak to God
With a heavy sigh.

62

Alas, we do not know
When humanity will be blessed
With peace
Between the cradle and the grave.

63

We get peace in abundance
Only when we are able
To run
Along life's perfection-path.

64

God asks me every morning,
"My child,
Is it such a difficult task
To say a prayer for world-peace?"

65

We cannot measure peace
By our flying years.
We can measure peace
Only with our streaming tears.

66

A heart of peace
Is made of God's
Own Sweetness-Smile.

67

My earth-bound desire
Cherishes
False peace-hopes.

68

My Heaven-free aspiration
Affirms
Genuine peace-promises.

69

God has His own secret Sorrows.
Alas, my peace-empty life
Is shamelessly adding to them.

70

World-peace
Can never be founded upon
Compromise and barter.

71

My heart of peace
Every morning and every evening
Is blessed by my Lord's
Paradise-Smile-Eye.

72

Speed
Is the success-thirsty
Runner in me.

Peace
Is the progress-hungry
Seeker in me.

73

Peace
Is not a rapid-growth
Plant.

74

Peace
Is a solid-growth
Tree.

75

God shares
His sweetest Peace-Breath
With my prayerful and cheerful
Obedience-life.

76

A peace-dreamer
Is a pilgrim
Of Infinity's Sky.

77

There is no
Real peace
In imaginary tomorrows.

78

Peace
Is not to be found
In self-pity-exercises.

79

Peace
Is a perfect stranger
To excitement.

80

Peace
And enlightenment
Are like flowers
And fragrance.

81

The path of peace
Is sunlit
For humanity's future.

82

Love illumines
My life.
Peace fulfils
My heart.

83

Peace and satisfaction
Are Eternity's
Friends.

84

A man of peace
Is incapable
Of world-indifference.

85

When self-doubt
Departs,
God-Peace
Arrives.

86

When we have peace of mind,
Attachment after attachment
Disappears from us.

87

A heart of peace
Hears
God's thunderous Applause.

88

When we have peace of mind,
We can ignore
Even major upheavals in life.

89

Peace never comes
From nothingness
But only from fulness.

90

As Truth
Is the greatest news,
Peace
Is the best news.

91

Cheerfully surrender
To the inevitable!
Peace will be all yours.

92

I am at peace
Not when my soul
Sees with my heart
But when my heart
Sees through my soul.

93

I become the possessor
Of peace-abundance
When I prayerfully adapt myself
To God's Ways.

PEACE: GOD'S HEART-HOME

94

Peace
Is not on your sickbed.
Peace
Is not in your grave.
Peace
Is inside your constant
God-obedience-heart.

95

Lethargy's peace
Is no peace.
Lethargy masquerades as peace.

96

The prayerful offering
Of one's life to God's Will
Is indeed peace.

97

Not the mind-forest-wanderer
But the heart-garden-lover
Has peace in abundance.

98

God and I get peace
When we can mutually whisper
Our heart's secrets
To each other.

99

When I pray to God,
Peace-power
Swiftly comes to me.

When I meditate on God,
Peace-shower
Slowly, steadily and unerringly
Comes to me.

100

Peace
Is the most reliable
And most expert charioteer
That carries our heart
To God's Heart-Home.

101

I get peace
Not when I have the courage
To look at God's Face
But when I have the eagerness
To embrace God's Feet.

102

My heart's burning tears
Give birth
To my life's blossoming peace.

103

God does not want us
To repay Him
For anything that He does for us.
Our peace is all that He needs
  from us.

104

If you do not see and feel
God's Blessing-Touch
At every moment,
It is impossible for you
To have peace.

105

Peace
Is the most nourishing fruit
Of my heart's solitude.

106

If we do not have
Peace of mind,
We may lose all our divine
  qualities
One after another.

107

O my heart's peace-fragrance,
I shall cherish you
To my life's last breath.

108

Even peace
Is not the final achievement.
The final achievement
Is constant oneness with God's
  Will.

109

May my peace-heart
Every day
Have the capacity
To jump over a thousand hurdles.

110

In the inner life,
Peace
Is God-obedience.

111

In the outer life,
Peace
Is God-surrender.

112

To peace
Even insurmountable obstacles
Surrender.

113

We want everything,
But peace already has
Everything.

114

Peace
Is all affirmation.

115

Peace
Knows no contradiction.

116

Peace
Is a life-game-player
Who always wins.

117

A man who has no peace
Often thinks
That the worst is going to happen,
Either in the immediate present
Or in the distant future.

118

A mind of peace
Is a reservoir
Of confidence.

119

A man of peace
Is always
Young at heart.

120

Peace
Invariably ascends
The fastest.

121

God can be displeased
With everything and everybody,
But never with His fondest child:
Peace.

122

Give God your peace-heart.
Lo, God has already given you
His Bliss-Eye.

123

The peace-dictionary
Does not include the word
"Subordinate".

124

My mind
Is an attention-hunger.
My heart
Is a peace-meal.

125

Peace
Is not in madness.
Peace
Is not in sadness.
Peace
Is only in selflessness.

126

Where is my peace?
Peace is in my hope's
Heart-temple.

127

Peace I feel
Only when
My mind is armed
With God-obedience.

128

My entire being
Is inundated with peace
Only when my heart sits
At the doorstep of
    Eternity's Beyond.

129

If you want peace-abundance,
Never disobey your conscience.

130

If you want peace-abundance,
Never contradict the
    wisdom-light
Of your soul.

131

When you have peace of mind,
You will become certain
That God is not only in Heaven
But also on earth.

132

My heart-cry embodies
Peace.
My soul-smiles reveal
Peace.

PEACE: GOD'S HEART-HOME

133

If my surrender to God
Does not become
One hundred per cent complete,
How can I, alas, have peace?

134

O my mind,
How can you ever have peace
If you are always racing
Through barren and fruitless
  days?

135

If God wants to bless you
With His Peace,
Then He can easily bring you
Out of the abyss
Of your mind's chaos.

136

God's Eye is misty
With Compassion-Tears
Because I do not value
His Heart's Oneness-Peace.

137

Peace
Is spirituality's
God-Pride-Crown.

138

The heart of God's Delight-Sky
Every day invites, without fail,
A man of peace.

139

Peace-dream
My earth-bound mind was.
Peace-reality
My Heaven-free heart is.

140

O my mind,
How can you have peace
When you deliberately betray
Your own inner life?

141

Every day I get peace
In abundant measure
From the sweetness
Of my heart-dreams.

142

Tolerance is not peace,
But from tolerance,
In the near or distant future,
Peace may blossom.

143

Your implicit faith
In your heart's peace
Will definitely save you
From the assaults of
    doubt-storms.

144

Fastest is the peace of my soul
At clearing the progress-horizon
Of my mind's doubts
And my heart's fears.

145

When my heart does not have
An iota of peace,
I feel that I am living
In the wrong place
At the wrong time.

146

Peace
Is my mind's Heaven-beauty.
Peace
Is my heart's earth-fragrance.

147

Peace
Illumines our
Division-limitation-darkness.

148

Your division-mind
Is the wrong place
For you to search for peace.

149

Your union-heart
Is the right place
Not only to look for
But also to find your Himalayan
    peace.

150

Doubt chases peace
In vain.

151

Peace
Amazes doubt
At every moment.

152

No matter how powerful the hand
    is,
It cannot hold peace.
But a loving and self-giving heart
Has and is peace.

153

Peace
Is not to be found
In the mind's pronouncement.
Peace
Is found only
In the heart's enlightenment.

154

Peace
Does not command.
Peace
Does not demand.
Peace
Does not reject.
Peace
Does not expect.
Peace
Only injects God-Wisdom.

155

A heart of peace
Can never be marred
By the mind's
Continuous inconsistencies.

156

O world of division,
Once peace is victorious,
It will not only outlive everything
But also eternally live.

157

Peace may not be
In today's crying life,
But peace will definitely be
In tomorrow's smiling heart.

158

Peace
Opens up the first door
To every human hope.

159

The reasoning mind
In vain tries to oust
The aspiring heart
From the peace-temple.

160

Everybody has at least one question
For God,
But peace neither has one
Nor needs one.

161

God
Sleeplessly values peace.
Peace
Breathlessly treasures God.

162

Peace
Silences the nightmares of the
    mind.
Peace
Feeds the dreams of the heart.

163

A man of peace
Is constantly ready
To go to all corners of the globe
For God-manifestation.

164

A man with no peace
Is, indeed,
A self-contradiction-champion.

165

O my peace-empty mind,
What are you doing?
"Can you not see
What I am doing?
I am just rushing headlong
Into the arms
Of my own self-destruction!"

166

The peace-boat of the heart
Never fails.
It only sails and sails
Towards our own divinity's
Immortality-flooded destination.

167

Intellectual competitors
Do not win
Peace-trophies.

168

Neither pull down
Nor pull up.
Peace will claim you.

169

God the Smiler
Gives me peace.
God the Sufferer
Takes away my peace.

170

Do not think of
Past blunders.
Do not imagine
Unlit future roads.
You are bound to have peace.

PEACE: GOD'S HEART-HOME

171

Peace
Is at once
The shortest road
And the longest stride
To arrive at
Our God-destination.

172

I received peace
Infinitely more than I expected
From my God-surrender-studies.

173

God has many intimate assistants,
But peace is by far
His most intimate assistant.

174

My heart becomes
Completely peaceful
When I see my Lord Supreme
Preparing to sail His Boat.

175

God cannot believe
That man has no real hunger
For peace.

176

I am peaceful
When God gives me
What I want.
God is peaceful
When He gives me
What I need.

177

A cave
Has no peace.
Even a grave
Has no peace.
But God-surrender-courage
Has and is peace.

178

The division-mind
Is responsible for
The heart's peace-bankruptcy.

179

I derive no peace
From a mountain-height-dream,
But I do derive peace
From a fountain-spontaneity-
   reality.

180

Peace you want?
Then pray to God
Not for escape
But for shelter.

181

Twice I am most sublimely
　peaceful:
Once when God is
My heart-home-guest,
Once when I find myself
In God's Compassion-Smile-Nest.

182

Peace of mind
Expands
Our heart's God-Dream-horizons.

183

Because of my peace of mind,
Every day I bow to God
With my heart's gratitude-tears.

184

I have peace of mind
Exactly because
I have said a final farewell
To the life I used to live.

185

God-surrender is the soil
Where the bumper crop of peace
Grows.

186

When I have peace of mind,
My Lord shares with me
His secret and sacred
Sorrows and Joys.

187

My peace
Is my rare expedition
To God's Paradise-Smile.

188

My Lord,
How can I have an iota of peace,
Since I am not ready
To accept the world as it is?

189

He who has peace
Pacifies others.

PEACE: GOD'S HEART-HOME

190

Nothing astonishes God
As much as my lack of hunger
For peace.

191

Peace
Has always been
A plant of slowest growth.

192

I belong
To God's Smile,
And God belongs
To my peace.

193

My soul's peace
Can easily transform
My mind's commotion and
  emotion
Into
My heart's devotion and
  perfection.

194

When I was empty of peace,
I thought God was ignoring me.
But now, I do not.

195

Once we capture
And give a life-long sentence to
Our ego-thief,
We enjoy peace in abundance.

196

No matter how high
My mind's imperfection-hurdles,
My heart's peace
Can easily jump over.

197

My heart's peace
And my life's freedom
Are divinely and supremely
Inseparable.

198

When I have peace,
What I enjoy most
Is my heart's
God-devotion-sweetness.

199

From the heart's peace-garden
Supremacy is always excluded.

200

God Himself
Rings His Peace-Bell
Inside my heart's
God-surrender-temple.

PART XXI

MY EVENING DESCENDS

MY EVENING DESCENDS

1. 1 January

My evening descends
To feed me
With the Silence-Bliss
Of God's Footfalls.

2. 2 January

My evening descends
To help me breathe the fragrance
Of a new dream-world.

3. 3. January

My evening descends,
And I affectionately offer my
 evening
My day's success-joys
And failure-sorrows.

4. 4 January

My evening descends
To see
The beauty-heart of my day
And the duty-life of my day.

5. 5 January

My evening descends
To liberate me
From my day's paralysing worries
And anxieties.

6. 6 January

My evening descends
To teach me
How to hear in silence
The heartbeat of the vastness-
 world.

7. 7 January

My evening descends
To request me
To welcome its peace-blossoms
With my heart's receptivity-depth.

8. 8 January

My evening descends
To teach me
How to crush all my day's
Wrong and negative thoughts
Underfoot.

9. 9 January

My evening descends,
And I see and feel
That even the very dust
Of my evening-world
Is full of celestial bliss.

10. 10 January

My evening descends
With a powerful shower
Of bountiful silence.

11. 11 January

My evening descends
And smilingly tells me
That tomorrow I will be
A non-stop enthusiasm-dynamo.

12. 12 January

My evening descends
And proudly transforms
My day's oneness-hunger
Into my night's fulness-feast.

13. 13 January

My evening descends
And unconditionally gives me
A new and direct aspiration-line
To my Absolute Lord Supreme.

14. 14 January

My evening descends
And immediately takes away
My day's sighing tears
And gives me
Its own dancing smiles.

15. 15 January

My evening descends
With its silence-wings.

16. 16 January

My evening descends,
And my heart-tears for God
Fall like beauty's ecstasy-rain.

17. 17 January

My evening descends
With a plentiful supply
Of inner patience
And outer tolerance.

18. 18 January

My evening descends
And carries a special message for me
From God:
"I love you, My child.
And I shall always accept your service,
No matter what you think of yourself."

19. 19 January

My evening descends
And summarily dethrones
My mind-president of the day
And smilingly enthrones
My heart-president for the entire
  night.

20. 20 January

My evening descends
And tells my questioning mind:
"Go you must, immediately!"
And tells my questing heart:
"Come in, my child, come in."

21. 21 January

My evening descends,
And my gratitude-heart
Immediately gives my evening
A magnificent welcome.

22. 22 January

My evening descends
And, in no time, expedites
My God-discovery-aspiration-
  journey.

23. 23 January

My evening descends
To bless me
With the warmest affection-
  blanket
Of God's own Eye.

24. 24 January

My evening descends
To advise me
To live in the heart of mankind
And not in the eyes of mankind.

25. 25 January

My evening descends
And assures me
That my God-fulfilment-
  willingness
Can never be wanting in
  capacity.

26. 26 January

My evening descends
And affectionately asks my mind
To leave its information-house
And live in my heart's
  illumination-home.

27. 27 January

My evening descends
To give me a very special award
For my God-surrender-choice.

28. 28 January

My evening descends
And asks my mind
Why it stays in its traffic jam of
 thoughts,
Instead of accepting the kind
 invitation
Of my beautiful and fruitful
 silence-heart.

29. 29 January

My evening descends
And tells me
That it is ready to accept
Unconditionally from me
My day's resentment-mind
And disappointment-heart.

30. 30. January

My evening descends
And smilingly makes me
A peaceful citizen
Of God's inner Universe.

31. 31 January

My evening descends,
And I tell it:
"My heart is all gratitude to you
For your teeming blessings
In increasing my Eternity's
 silence-thirst."

32. 1 February

My evening descends
And blesses me with
 wisdom-light.
It tells me that my outer
 playful life
Is the perfect manifestation
Of my inner prayerful heart.

33. 2 February

My evening descends,
And I notice something
 significant:
I felt during the day
That I was an aspiration-bloom,
But now I feel
That I am an aspiration-blossom.

34. 3 February

My evening descends,
And I ask it:
"What is the fastest way to
　please God?"
My evening answers:
"Just become a God-devotion-
　magnet."

35. 4 February

My evening descends
And tells me
That I must not allow
　ignorance-night
To take me away
From God's Compassion-Light.

36. 5 February

My evening descends
To tell me
That it has brought
A new love-fragrance-promise
For me to please God.

37. 6 February

My evening descends
And tells me
That my cheerfulness-mind
And my fulness-heart
Are God's two extraordinary
　Victories.

38. 7 February

My evening descends
And gives me
A new devotion-magnet-gift
To pull God towards me.

39. 8 February

My evening descends
And I immediately and gladly
Start breathing out
All my mind's destructive
　anxiety-fumes.

40. 9 February

My evening descends,
And my mind is no longer dizzy
With restless and useless
　thoughts.

41. 10 February

My evening descends
And blesses me
With an invincible faith
To brighten all my
　heart-moments.

42. 11 February

My evening descends
And tells me
That during the day
I was a crowd-pleaser,
And now I must be a God-pleaser.

43. 12 February

My evening descends
To tell me
That the progress-train is waiting
To take me
To God's Satisfaction-Station.

44. 13 February

My evening descends
To increase my life's
Self-transcendence-hunger.

45. 14 February

My evening descends
And implores me
Not to remain a self-styled
Freelance seeker,
But to become
A full-time God-lover.

46. 15 February

My evening descends
To energise my tired heart
With new God-reaching hopes.

47. 16 February

My evening descends
To deliver me
From frustration-city,
Which is covered by darkness-fog.

48. 17 February

My evening descends
With a special message from God:
I have His full Approval
To fight against and conquer
My mind's all-devouring
   ignorance-tiger.

49. 18 February

My evening descends
To revive
My God-pleasing readiness-mind
And God-fulfilling willingness-
   heart.

50. 19 February

My evening descends
To remove the heaviest
Confusion-delusion-weights
From my mind.

51. 20 February

My evening descends
With its silence-peace
To soothe my mind
And save my heart.

52. 21 February

My evening descends
To teach me how to shed
Devotion-flooded tears
To please my Lord Supreme
Always in His own Way.

53. 22 February

My evening descends
And advises my mind
To be purity-depth,
Advises my heart
To be sincerity-depth
And advises my life
To be simplicity-depth.

54. 23 February

My evening descends
And tells me
Not to be afraid of any disadvantage
In my life,
For each disadvantage
Unconsciously helps me
To strengthen my mind,
Widen my heart
And enlighten my life.

55. 24 February

My evening descends
And tells me
That my God-aspiration
Is not sufficient unto itself,
My God-dedication
Is not sufficient unto itself,
But my unconditional God-surrender
Definitely is sufficient unto itself.

56. 25 February

My evening descends
And illumines me by telling me
That my speaking mouth
May one day fail,
But my silence-heart
And my silence-eyes
Will never fail.

57. 26 February

My evening descends
And tells me
That when I fail to fulfil
My God-manifestation-promises,
I do not realise
That I crucify the Heart of God.

58. 27 February

My evening descends
And tells me
To be a constant self-giver
During the day
So that I may live
Not only in the Applause,
But also in the Embrace
Of God.

59. 28 February

My evening descends
And advises me
To open my wisdom-eye
And breathe in the fragrance
Of my heart's God-garden.

60. 29 February

My evening descends
And tells me
To be a man-server
During the entire day.
Then only will God make me
A great God-dreamer
And a good God-lover
During the entire night.

61. 1 March

My evening descends
And asks my heart
To help my soul
Place my giant ego-mind
Under arrest.

62. 2 March

My evening descends
And lovingly teaches me
How to be imperturbable
In my aspiration-heart
And how to be indomitable
In my dedication-life.

63. 3 March

My evening descends
And I see deep down
In the privacy of my heart
That my Lord is whispering to me
To sing the song
Of God-satisfaction on earth.

64. 4 March

My evening descends
And tells me that soon
God will hire my peace-flooded heart
To carry Him wherever He wants to go.

65. 5 March

My evening descends,
And from it I learn
How to soar in silence
And also how to silence
My vital-roars.

66. 6 March

My evening descends,
And I ask my Lord Supreme:
"Will humanity ever receive Your Light?"
My Lord Supreme immediately tells me
That humanity's life-train
Is definitely proceeding forwards
And not backwards.

67. 7 March

My evening descends,
And I ask the Goddess of the Evening
What happens when I hurt God
During the day.
She says to me:
"If you hurt Him during the day,
Then God limps throughout the entire night."

68. 8 March

My evening descends
To rescue my heart
From my day's God-oblivion.

69. 9 March

My evening descends
And immediately blesses me
With its powerful silence,
So that I can run fast, very fast,
Along the royal road of spirituality.

70. 10 March

My evening descends
And gives me,
Lovingly and smilingly,
The immortal Breath
Of God's Heart-Dream.

71. 11 March

My evening descends
And smilingly presents me
With its fount of infinite
Inspiration-aspiration-
  dedication-delight.

72. 12 March

My evening descends
And cheerfully teaches me
How to knock gently and
  self-givingly
At God's Heart-Door.

73. 13. March

My evening descends
With its fully-blossomed humility
To teach me
How to touch God's Feet.

74. 14 March

My evening descends
To transform my God-service-day
Into my God-worship-night.

75. 15 March

My evening descends
To transform my intense desire-
  day-prayers
Into my God-Will-surrender-
  night.

76. 16 March

My evening descends
To help me stop repeating
My wrong thought-deeds
Of the day.

77. 17 March

My evening descends
To relieve my mind
From the day's
Heaviest ignorance-weight.

78. 18 March

My evening descends
To tell me
The simple Truth:
God is in all;
The simpler Truth:
God is for all;
The simplest Truth:
God is All.

79. 19 March

My evening descends
To tell me
That life is a very strict school
When I want only to possess God.

MY EVENING DESCENDS

80. 20 March

My evening descends
To tell me
That life is the best
 entertainment-enjoyment
When I surrender myself
Untiringly and unconditionally
 to God.

81. 21 March

My evening descends
To advise me
That what I need is an inner
 lighthouse
And not an outer powerhouse.

82. 22 March

My evening descends
To advise me
That my desire-thirst,
Which has been growing for years,
Can and shall finally disappear.

83. 23 March

My evening descends
To advise me
That my aspiration-hunger
Will sleeplessly grow
And breathlessly glow
Eternally.

84. 24 March

My evening descends
And tells me
That my aspiration for fame in life
Can never be God's inner Will
Nor even His outer Intention.

85. 25 March

My evening descends
And most affectionately advises
 me
Not to allow my God-fulfilment-
 eagerness
To hesitate
Even for a fleeting second.

86. 26 March

My evening descends
And tells me
That my hurtful doubt
Has created a bottomless
 confusion-sea
Inside my mind.

87. 27 March

My evening descends
And tells me
That my faith
Is God's fathomless Nectar-
 Ocean-Bliss.

88. 28 March

My evening descends
And tells me
That if I really want to be happy,
Then I must tell God sincerely
That I do believe in Him,
I do feel His Love
And I do want to transform
My earth-bound desire-life into
My Heaven-free aspiration-breath.

89. 29 March

My evening descends
And tells me
To pray to God for only one thing:
For Him to chase away
My aspiration-heart-slumber.

90. 30 March

My evening descends
And tells me
That if I make my surrender to
   God's Will
Complete and perfect,
Then God will not withhold
   from me
Any of His endless Secrets.

91. 31 March

My evening descends
And lovingly advises me
To give equal importance
To the call
Of the crying earth
And to the call
Of the smiling Heaven.

92. 1 April

My evening descends
And tells me
To abandon the desire
To make a noise in the world,
If I really want to be happy.

93. 2 April

My evening descends
To help me transform my
   sorrowful day
Into silence-happiness-night.

94. 3 April

My evening descends,
And I sadly tell it:
"Alas, my noisy and busy day
Hurried me towards nowhere."
My evening consoles me:
"I am bringing silence back
Into your heart and life.
In silence you will see your goal
Everywhere."

MY EVENING DESCENDS

95. 4 April

My evening descends
And tells me
To continue studying the
  oldest philosophy:
"Let Thy Will be done."
This philosophy is not only
  immortal,
But also by far the best.

96. 5 April

My evening descends
And tells me:
"God always cries
For your perfection.
Will you ever cry
For God's Satisfaction
In His own Way?"

97. 6 April

My evening descends
And tells me
That a heart devoid of devotion
For God
Signifies a futile life.

98. 7 April

My evening descends
And tells me:
"Do not hanker after any other
  power
Than mastery over your own
  mind,
If happiness is what you really
  want."

99. 8 April

My evening descends
And tells me
To keep under arrest
My doubt-cherishing mind.

100. 9 April

My evening descends
And tells me I must feel and
  realise
That all the good, inspiring and
Illumining thoughts
That I had during the day
Are unparalleled achievements.

101. 10 April

My evening descends
And advises me
To allow only Eternity's Boatman
To steer my life-boat.

102. 11 April

My evening descends
And tells me
To become the strongest
　God-believer
So that I can also become
The happiest God-lover.

103. 12 April

My evening descends
And tells me
That I do not have to
　torture myself
To become good.
I shall automatically
　become good
If I long for God's
　Compassion-Light
And Forgiveness-Delight.

104. 13 April

My evening descends
And instructs me to become
An unconditional
　surrender-specialist
If I want to be
A most favourite child of God.

105. 14 April

My evening descends
And lovingly tells me
That I shall never be able to
　become
A candidate for God-realisation
Unless and until I make friends
With silence.

106. 15 April

My evening descends,
And I wander no more
In the desert of dissatisfaction.

107. 16 April

My evening descends,
And soulfully I ask it
To show me the gateway to
　goodness.
Gladly it accedes to my request.

108. 17 April

My evening descends
And asks me to be careful
Not to offend my soul
During the day,
For to offend my soul
Is to move farther away
From God the Smiler.

MY EVENING DESCENDS

109. 18 April

My evening descends
And tells me
The secret of secrets:
My sleepless willingness
Is the only thing
That can please God in God's own Way.

110. 19 April

My evening descends,
And to my great surprise
I have now become
Consciously and happily
A member of the Pro-God Party.

111. 20 April

My evening descends,
And to my great joy and satisfaction
I become a full-time God-seeker,
And no longer
A part-time God-seeker,
As I was during the day.

112. 21 April

My evening descends
And immediately inspires and energises me
To seek the way
To my heart's sacred hope-temple.

113. 22 April

My evening descends,
And now I fully understand
The language of the heart,
Whereas during the day
I spoke only the language of the mind.

114. 23 April

My evening descends
And lovingly tells me
To be a God-lover
Who never wants to be off duty.

115. 24 April

My evening descends,
And I discover that
I have escaped from my desire-mind-jungle.
Where am I now?
Lo, I am now inside my aspiration-heart-garden.

116. 25 April

My evening descends,
And it unconditionally employs me
To work at God's Victory-Factory.

117. 26 April

My evening descends,
And I ask it
How I can become perfect.
It tells me:
"To become perfect, what you need
Is a willingness-heart
And an eagerness-breath."

118. 27 April

My evening descends,
And suddenly my mind is energised
And my heart is thrilled
To ring God's Heart-Bell.

119. 28 April

My evening descends,
And I ask it
How I can be happy.
My evening tells me just to invoke
God's Compassion-Eye.

120. 29 April

My evening descends
And immediately helps my Lord Supreme
To plant a new world
Inside my heart-garden.

121. 30 April

My evening descends
And tells me
To collect rainbow-blossoms
To be blessed
With God's brightest and proudest Smiles.

122. 1 May

My evening descends
And tells me
That I should be an inner thrill first
And only then will God ring
His Heart's Satisfaction-Bell.

123. 2 May

My evening descends
And tells me
That a spiritual Master is he
Whose inner life
Is made of breathless cries
And whose outer life
Is made of sleepless smiles.

MY EVENING DESCENDS

124. 3 May

My evening descends
And tells me
That when my heartbeat
And the heartbeat of silence
Are in perfect harmony,
God will immediately come
And stand before me.

125. 4 May

My evening descends
And lovingly advises me
To be extremely conscious
  and cautious
All the time
So that my mind's doubt-dust
Cannot obscure the
  faith-blossoms
Of my God-loving heart.

126. 5 May

My evening descends,
And I immediately join it
In singing God's
  ever-transcending Glories.

127. 6 May

My evening descends
And immediately wipes away
My teeming failure-tears
Of the day.

128. 7 May

My evening descends
And tells me
To love God inside my enemies
Exactly the way I love God
Inside my friends
To make my aspiration-progress
Infinitely faster.

129. 8 May

My evening descends,
And I tell it
That I love its silence-divinity
  immensely.
My evening immediately tells me:
"But I want you to love
Only God's infinite
  Compassion."

130. 9 May

My evening descends
And compassionately tells me
That I do not have to remain
  paralysed any longer
By the worries and anxieties of
  the day.
It will present me with a
  new hope,
A new inspiration, a new
  aspiration
And a pure and sure life of
  dynamism.

131. 10 May

My evening descends
And advises me
To take purity
As an invaluable companion
Of my heart,
Sincerity
As an invaluable companion
Of my mind
And simplicity
As an invaluable companion
Of my life.

132. 11 May

My evening descends,
And I ask it
If it can tell me how to have
A guilt-free mind.
My evening replies:
"Just become a true God-lover.
Then your guilt-torturing mind
Will be forced to leave you
For good."

133. 12 May

My evening descends,
And I tell it
That my day blesses me
With worries
And my evening blesses me
With hopes.
My evening adds:
"And God blesses you
With both powerful promises
And fruitful fulfilments."

134. 13 May

My evening descends,
And I ask it
How I can have
Sleepless and breathless
   aspiration.
My evening lovingly says to me,
"What you need
Is a silent, plus speechless, mind."

135. 14 May

My evening descends,
And I ask it
How I can stay in a cheerful
   frame of mind.
My evening tells me that
   what I need
Is a God-devotion-life
And a God-surrender-heart.

MY EVENING DESCENDS

136. 15 May

My evening descends,
And I ask it
What is the sweetest thing I have
According to God.
My evening tells me
That according to God,
My gratitude-heart
Is by far my sweetest possession.

137. 16 May

My evening descends,
And I ask it
How I can spend my night
With fathomless happiness.
My evening says,
"Do not wave your mind's
  ego-flag
The way you did during the
  entire day."

138. 17 May

My evening descends,
And I ask it
What I can expect from salvation
And from realisation.
My evening tells me I can expect
That salvation will give me
  freedom
From my sins
And realisation will give me
Constant and absolute oneness
With God.

139. 18 May

My evening descends
And advises me
To be careful in what I say
And prayerful in what I do.

140. 19 May

My evening descends
And advises me
To be creative and affirmative
In every possible way
To please both God and humanity.

141. 20 May

My evening descends
And asks me
If I would like to be
God's Perfection-partner
Or His Satisfaction-partner.
I immediately say,
"His Satisfaction-partner."

142. 21 May

My evening descends
And blesses me
With a large supply of peace
So that I can have
A oneness-world-heart.

143. 22 May

My evening descends,
And I ask it
Where real happiness is.
My evening tells me that real happiness
Is beyond the reach of my mind
But within easy reach of my heart.

144. 23 May

My evening descends
And immediately fills my heart-vessel
With peace-purity.

145. 24 May

My evening descends,
And a new wave of joy
Feeds my heart.

146. 25 May

My evening descends,
And I powerfully crush
All my despair-thoughts
Long before they take birth
So that I can pass my evening and night
Happily and cheerfully.

147. 26 May

My evening descends
To make my life
As beautiful as my heart-garden.

148. 27 May

My evening descends,
And I immediately feel
That I have become once more
The intensity-breath of my aspiration-life.

149. 28 May

My evening descends,
And my God-satisfaction-eagerness
Starts to roar.

150. 29 May

My evening descends
And immediately prevents
My doubting mind
From entering into
My heart-temple.

151. 30 May

My evening descends
And replaces my fearful mind
With my tearful heart
So that my breath can be pure
For God-worship.

152. 31 May

My evening descends
And unconditionally helps me
To enjoy my soul's God-
   oneness-beauty.

153. 1 June

My evening descends
And unreservedly teaches my
   heart
To smile and fly
In the silence-flooded sky.

154. 2 June

My evening descends,
Sweetening not only my mind
But also all its thoughts.

155. 3 June

My evening descends
And makes my eyes soulfully
   tearful
For my perfect God-adoration.

156. 4 June

My evening descends,
And I ask it
What I sleeplessly and
   breathlessly need.
My evening smilingly tells me:
"God-obedience, nothing more
And nothing less."

157. 5 June

My evening descends
And blesses me unreservedly
With the silence-peace-beauty
Of the setting sun.

158. 6 June

My evening descends,
And from deep within my heart,
The capacity emerges
For me to fly into the Beyond.

159. 7 June

My evening descends,
And I become a conscious
   God-dreamer,
Whereas during the day
I was an unconscious
   God-thinker.

160. 8 June

My evening descends
To increase the beauty
Of my aspiration-heart-home.

161. 9 June

My evening descends
And commands me
Not to swerve
From the path of God-obedience.

162. 10 June

My evening descends
And advises me
To take regular
   detachment-lessons
From my illumination-soul.

163. 11 June

My evening descends
And in no time gives me
A genuinely God-thirsty mind
And a genuinely God-hungry
   heart.

164. 12 June

My evening descends
And gives me calmness
To increase my eagerness
For my God-oneness.

165. 13 June

My evening descends,
And I no longer see
The iron chains of my desire-day.
What I have now
Is a mind of poise.
What I am now
Is a heart of peace.

166. 14 June

My evening descends,
And I see my mind surrendering
All its restless and useless
   thought-waves
To the infinite peace-ocean of my
   soul.

167. 15 June

My evening descends
And inspires me to become
My heart's sincerity-tears
For God's Compassion-Eye.

168. 16 June

My evening descends
And lovingly teaches me
How to pray to God,
How to meditate on God
And how to love God
Unconditionally.

MY EVENING DESCENDS

169. 17 June

My evening descends
And tells me
That there is only one
　ultimate solution
To all my earthly problems:
My earth-love-life-transformation
For my Heaven-love-life-
　manifestation.

170. 18 June

My evening descends
And tells me
That I must not see spirituality
As a world-frightening force,
But as a world-illumining power.

171. 19 June

My evening descends
And tells me
That my life's loudest voice
Must have a silence-heart-cry
As its only source.

172. 20 June

My evening descends
And tells me
That what I need
Is not a monk-like life,
But a soul-like breath.

173. 21 June

My evening descends
And tells me
To pray self-givingly
To God the Silence
To remove from my mind
All my age-old thought-
　impurities.
God will definitely listen to my
　prayer.

174. 22 June

My evening descends,
And I no longer live inside
My God-reasoning mind.
I now live inside
My God-listening heart.

175. 23 June

My evening descends,
And now I am enjoying
Thought-turbulence-extinction-
　thrill.

176. 24 June

My evening descends,
And now I am more sincerely
And more devotedly trying
To free myself
From my day's desire-bondage-
　shackles.

177. 25 June

My evening descends,
And I replace my day's
　storyteller-mind
With my God-singer-heart.

178. 26 June

My evening descends
And encourages me
To plant my aspiration-plant
Inside my heart
For my tomorrow's
　fulfilment-life-promise.

179. 27 June

My evening descends
And is followed by
God's Forgiveness-Nectar-
　Footsteps.

180. 28 June

My evening descends
And advises me
To combine my heart-patience
And my mind-courage
To establish God-Victory
In my life.

181. 29 June

My evening descends,
And I tell my
　God-peace-lover-friends
That evening is by far the
　best time
To make the mind
Peaceful, beautiful and fruitful.

182. 30 June

My evening descends
And immediately blesses me
With a new supply of
　aspiration-flames
And a new supply of
　dedication-blossoms.

183. 1 July

My evening descends,
And my day's frustration-life
Meets with God's
　Compassion-Heart-Smile.

184. 2 July

My evening descends
And tells me
That during the day
My mind has amassed
A mine of information,
And now I must inspire my heart
To sit on the top
Of silence-mountain.

MY EVENING DESCENDS

185. 3 July

My evening descends
And tells me
That the easiest and safest way
Of winning God's infinite Love
Is to ply my life-boat
Between my heart's
  eagerness-shore
And my life's enthusiasm-shore.

186. 4 July

My evening descends
And tells me
That I can approach God
Only after I have forcefully
  placed ignorance
At my Lord's Feet.

187. 5 July

My evening descends
And tells me
To revive my willingness-mind
And my eagerness-heart
So that God can breathe in
His Satisfaction-Delight.

188. 6 July

My evening descends
And tells me
Not to abide in
Expectation-frustration-
  volcanoes,
But to participate in
The soul's aspiration-expedition.

189. 7 July

My evening descends
And tells me
That if I am really sincere,
God will show me
  His hidden Paths
To arrive at my destination.

190. 8 July

My evening descends,
And I tell myself that I must not
Keep my Lord Supreme waiting.

191. 9 July

My evening descends
And commands my mind
To enjoy my love-fragrance-heart
For God.

192. 10 July

My evening descends
And shows me the way
To walk along the road
Of God-Fulfilment-Satisfaction.

193. 11 July

My evening descends,
And my God-hunger-torn heart
Helplessly sheds tears
For God's Compassion-Eye-
   Arrival.

194. 12 July

My evening descends
And blesses me
With a heart-hope-blossom.

195. 13 July

My evening descends
And tells me
That I must not
Even for a fleeting second
Be found inside my mind's
Ruthless confusion-net.

196. 14 July

My evening descends
And tells me
To pull down God's
   Satisfaction-Heart
With my devotion-heart-magnet.

197. 15 July

My evening descends
And tells me
That God will read my
   heart-letters
Only if they are sent
By my life's gratitude-post.

198. 16 July

My evening descends
And tells me:
"Collect God-Satisfaction-Smiles."

199. 17 July

My evening descends
And tells me what I need:
Not my mind-crucifixion,
But my mind-perfection.

MY EVENING DESCENDS

200. 18 July

My evening descends
And immediately takes me
Into the temple
Of God-surrender-bliss.

201. 19 July

My evening descends
And tells me to be satisfied
Only when I can enjoy
God-Satisfaction-Heart-dreams.

202. 20 July

My evening descends
And tells me
That if I want my
 heart-garden to thrive,
I must immediately welcome
 Silence
From all corners of the globe.

203. 21 July

My evening descends
And tells me
That unconditional surrender
Is the only essence
Of a true God-lover.

204. 22 July

My evening descends
And tells me
That because pride found me,
I lost my way.

My evening descends
And tells me
To allow humility to find me
So that I can find my way.

205. 23 July

My evening descends
And advises me
To surrender unconditionally
To God's Will,
So that my heart's
 aspiration-flames
Can reach the summit-heights.

206. 24 July

My evening descends
And lovingly whispers:
"Each self-offering heart
Is a God in the making."

207. 25 July

My evening descends
And tells me
That God keeps His Heart's
   Peace-Door
Wide open
Only to my heart's
   surrender-smiles.

208. 26 July

My evening descends
And tells me
That God wants from human
   beings
Only one thing:
Constant progress.

209. 27 July

My evening descends
And tells me
That if I love God
Not only unreservedly,
But also unconditionally,
God Himself will help me
To manifest Him
At His own choice Hour.

210. 28 July

My evening descends
And tells me
That if I do not claim God
As my own, very own,
Then my heart is bound to
   remain heavy
With fear, anxiety and insecurity.

211. 29 July

My evening descends
To tell me
That God will accompany me
Only if I invite peace
To accompany us.

212. 30 July

My evening descends
And advises me
To live between
My self-effacement
And my God-enlightenment.

213. 31 July

My evening descends
And tells me
That my happiness is a God-gift,
And not my aspiration-result.

MY EVENING DESCENDS

214. 1 August

My evening descends
And tells me
That I can go far beyond
The Heavenly stars
If I can offer
My gratitude-heart-blossoms
Sleeplessly and breathlessly.

215. 2 August

My evening descends
And tells me
That what I need is not
A mind to understand,
But a heart to surrender.

216. 3 August

My evening descends
And tells me
That to make my heart-sky
Vaster than the vastest,
I must welcome the
    Compassion-Eye
Of my Lord Beloved Supreme.

217. 4 August

My evening descends
And tells me
That silence has to interview me
    first,
Long before God grants me an
    interview.

218. 5 August

My evening descends
And tells me
That I do not have to offer God
A flood of tears
To conquer His Heart.
What I need to offer is only
A most sincere tear
From my heart-eye.

219. 6 August

My evening descends
And tells me
That a true aspiration-heart
And a true dedication-life
Are founded upon
God the Smiler's Fulness-Heart.

220. 7 August

My evening descends
And advises me
To pray to God for a
    gratitude-fountain
In order to claim
God's Infinitude-Mountain.

221. 8 August

My evening descends
And tells me
To adorn my mind
With purity-thoughts
To see God's Compassion-Eye
And Satisfaction-Heart
Face to face.

222. 9 August

My evening descends,
And my inspiration-mind
Feels God's magic Touch,
While my aspiration-heart
Breathes God's Fragrance-Heart.

223. 10 August

My evening descends,
And my mind's sincerity-waves
Surprise all,
While my heart's purity-sea
Conquers all.

224. 11 August

My evening descends
And tells me
That I need only one thing:
A constantly soaring
  oneness-heart.

225. 12 August

My evening descends,
And I have unreservedly,
  self-givingly
And unconditionally
Become one with all human
  sufferings.

226. 13 August

My evening descends
And tells me
That only with a purity-heart-
  foundation
Shall I be able to fly
In the skies of freedom and peace.

227. 14 August

My evening descends
And tells me
That each and every human being
Needs self-control in abundance
To enjoy the delight of Heaven
Here on earth.

MY EVENING DESCENDS

228. 15 August

My evening descends
And kindly informs me
That no matter what I did
 or said during the day,
God still keeps me as a
 solid member
Of His Light-Manifestation-
 Team on earth.

229. 16 August

My evening descends
And advises me to develop
Sleepless and breathless
 willingness and eagerness
To please God in His own Way.

230. 17 August

My evening descends
And tells me
That if my fear of God was
 powerful
During the day,
Then I must develop my love of
 God
Here and now
Infinitely more powerfully.

231. 18 August

My evening descends,
And my soul's light
Is brightening and expediting
My heart-journey towards God.

232. 19 August

My evening descends
And most compassionately
 tells me
That if I want to win the
 inner race,
Every day without fail,
I must push beyond my
 limitations.

233. 20 August

My evening descends
And tells me
That real happiness blossoms
Only in the soil of God-surrender.

234. 21 August

My evening descends
And advises me
To use my heart's faith-elevator
To ascend faster than the fastest.

235. 22 August

My evening descends,
And whereas during the day
I thought God was logical,
Now I clearly see
That my Lord of Compassion
Is nothing but magical.

236. 23 August

My evening descends,
And whereas during the day
I told God my life-stories
   happily,
Now my Lord is singing
His Heart-Songs for me happily
Plus proudly.

237. 24 August

My evening descends,
And now I am united
With the evening's climbing
   aspiration,
Instead of
With the day's frustration.

238. 25 August

My evening descends,
And now I am a
   God-determination
And God-satisfaction-heart
Instead of a vacillation-
   indecision-mind.

239. 26 August

My evening descends,
And I realise
That I need not travel around
To discover God's Eye,
For now I see not only God's Eye
But also God's Heart
Here, there and everywhere.

240. 27 August

My evening descends,
And I love God
Not for His Eternity,
Not for His Infinity,
Not for His Immortality,
But for His Compassion-Eyes,
For His Compassion-Smiles
And for His Compassion-Tears.

241. 28 August

My evening descends,
And I clearly see and feel
That there is nothing to worry
   about,
Whereas during the day
Each and every thing worried me.

MY EVENING DESCENDS

242. 29 August

My evening descends
And affectionately reminds me
Of my cheerful and unconditional
Love, devotion and surrender
To God's Will.

243. 30 August

My evening descends,
And I ask it:
"Is there any other way
To make the fastest progress?"
My evening replies:
"Just keep your heart young
And your mind innocent."

244. 31 August

My evening descends
And blesses me
With a God-Peace-necessity-heart,
Whereas my morning blessed me
With a God-Power-curiosity-mind.

245. 1 September

My evening descends,
And my mind carefully,
My heart devotedly
And my life self-givingly
Follow the footsteps of peace.

246. 2 September

My evening descends,
And God's Compassion
And my heart's surrender
Sing, play and dance
With carefree abandon.

247. 3 September

My evening descends,
And what do I do?
I just send my day's
God-disobedience-mind
To its extinction.

248. 4 September

My evening descends
And immediately removes from me
My God-acceptance-hesitation-intruders,
My God-doubt-stubbornness-intruders
And my God-unwillingness-indulgence-intruders.

249. 5 September

My evening descends,
And my heart, which during the day
Was a God-hope-fountain,
Is now a God-promise-mountain.

250. 6 September

My evening descends,
And now I am
A world-enlightenment-seeker,
Whereas during the day I was
A world-excitement-enjoyer.

251. 7 September

My evening descends,
And I see that my heart's
Morning God-aspiration-plant
Has now grown into
A God-manifestation-tree.

252. 8 September

My evening descends
And smilingly, lovingly
And self-givingly assures me
That I shall have a fruitful
Aspiration-night.

253. 9 September

My evening descends,
And I join the pilgrim-heart-
   seekers
In their God-pilgrimage-
   destination.

254. 10 September

My evening descends
And gladly helps me
To journey through the kingdom
Of blossoming silence.

255. 11 September

My evening descends
With a peace-flooded dream
From Heaven
For my heart to treasure.

256. 12 September

My evening descends,
And my fleeting
   God-gratitude-mind
Has now become
An abiding
   God-gratitude-heart.

257. 13 September

My evening descends,
And my God-expecting
   seeker-heart
Has now become
A God-surrendering
   lover-life.

MY EVENING DESCENDS

258. 14 September

My evening descends,
And God is no longer knocking
At my mind's hesitation-
　confusion-door.
God is now entering
My heart's wide-open
　aspiration-surrender-door.

259. 15 September

My evening descends,
And now I am
A fulness-heart-hunger
Whereas during the day I was
A newness-mind-thirst.

260. 16 September

My evening descends
And inspires me
To spread my aspiration-wings
And fly and fly
Ceaselessly and self-givingly.

261. 17 September

My evening descends,
And I see that
God's Compassion-Eye
And the beauty of nature
Are feeding my aspiration-heart.

262. 18 September

My evening descends,
And my heart's God-
　Satisfaction-hope-size
Increases enormously.

263. 19 September

My evening descends,
And my world-tolerance-
　forbearance-capacity
Increases astonishingly.

264. 20 September

My evening descends,
And my highest aspiration
And God's surest Compassion
Enjoy playing hide-and-seek.

265. 21 September

My evening descends,
And I greet God,
My Lord Beloved Supreme,
Unconditionally,
Unlike the way I greet Him
During the day.

266. 22 September

My evening descends,
And my Lord Supreme enjoys
Talking to my heart's
   gratitude-smiles.

267. 23 September

My evening descends,
And God now utters a new
   prophecy:
"My child, you are bound
   to succeed
In your self-giving and
   God-depending life."

268. 24 September

My evening descends,
And I unmistakably and
   unreservedly feel
That God and God's Peace
Are taking care of me.

269. 25 September

My evening descends,
And I see and feel everywhere
God's Sweetness-Presence.

270. 26 September

My evening descends,
And now my heart reminds God
To forgive me,
Whereas during the day
God reminds my mind
To remember Him.

271. 27 September

My evening descends,
And God's Eye invites my heart
To ascend,
While God's Feet give my heart
The capacity to ascend.

272. 28 September

My evening descends,
And God's blessingful Eye is asking
For my undivided attention.

273. 29 September

My evening descends
And gives me its silence-peace
To increase my speed
On the path of love, devotion and
   surrender.

MY EVENING DESCENDS

274. 30 September

My evening descends
And immediately invites me
To be in the most gracious
And most precious company
Of peace.

275. 1 October

My evening descends
And reminds me again and again
That my heart was born
For the fastest upward flight
Every day.

276. 2 October

My evening descends,
And I prayerfully see my Lord Supreme
Entering my heart
With His own Heart-Songs.

277. 3 October

My evening descends,
And I feel that now is the right time
For me to spread
My God-devotion-ecstasy-wings.

278. 4 October

My evening descends
And fortifies my mind's
Doubt-shattering confidence
Enormously.

279. 5 October

My evening descends,
And now I am
My heart's surrender-victory
Instead of
My mind's determination-success.

280. 6 October

My evening descends,
And surprisingly enough,
I am climbing my heart-ladder
Most easily, most speedily
And most perfectly.

281. 7 October

My evening descends,
And whereas during the day
My Lord was so demanding,
Now my Lord is so amusing
And entertaining.

282. 8 October

My evening descends,
And quite unsought,
I am having secret and sacred
   glimpses
Of Heaven's Peace-Gardens.

283. 9 October

My evening descends,
And unlike during the day,
My faith in God has become
A power-flooded citadel.

284. 10 October

My evening descends,
And I am now enjoying
The final triumph of my heart's
   faith
Over my mind's doubt
In the realm of my
   God-manifestation.

285. 11 October

My evening descends,
And I am praying and hoping
That I shall soon become the
   possessor
Of a totally transformed mind.

286. 12 October

My evening descends,
And finally the moment has come
To place myself peacefully
At the Feet of God
And to follow the glorious
   example
Of the evening's silence-life.

287. 13 October

My evening descends,
And its very presence
Has increased immensely
My life's God-thirst
And my heart's God-hunger.

288. 14 October

My evening descends,
And I feel Infinity's Peace
And Immortality's Bliss
Unconditionally beckoning me.

289. 15 October

My evening descends
And gives me
Its very own silence-breath
To pray to God and please God
In His own Way.

MY EVENING DESCENDS

290. 16 October

My evening descends,
And while I love the purity
Of my morning prayers,
I love the divinity
Of my evening meditations.

291. 17 October

My evening descends,
And whereas during the day
I was a mind-library member,
Now I am a heart-university student.

292. 18 October

My evening descends,
And my heart begins
A desperate search
For silence-peace-blossoms.

293. 19 October

My evening descends
And helps my heart
  unconditionally
To reach out and touch
Silence-delight-blossoms.

294. 20 October

My evening descends,
And I am prayerfully enjoying
The inexhaustible beauty
Of Nature's self-giving life.

295. 21 October

My evening descends,
And I am choosing silence
Not as my mind's entertainment,
But as my heart's enlightenment.

296. 22 October

My evening descends,
And my heart's oneness-door
Is now wide open.

297. 23 October

My evening descends
And destroys the daily inventory
Of my mind's horrors.

298. 24 October

My evening descends,
And God Himself applauds
My silence-loving heart.

299. 25 October

My evening descends,
And slowly, steadily and
  unerringly
The purity and fragrance of
  silence
Are coming my way.

300. 26 October

My evening descends,
And the path of my
  God-surrender-life
Opens before me all by itself.

301. 27 October

My evening descends,
And I am praying to God
To accept the very best
Of my heart's devotion-flooded
  love.

302. 28 October

My evening descends,
And my God-fulfilment-
  hope-eyes
Are turning prayerfully and
  soulfully
To Heaven.

303. 29 October

My evening descends,
And even my mind is longing
For my heart's peace-home.

304. 30 October

My evening descends,
And I clearly see
The word 'gratitude'
In the heart of my
  God-aspiration-life.

305. 31 October

My evening descends
And immediately prepares me
To climb up to the silence-flooded
  stars.

306. 1 November

My evening descends,
And I simply do not know
How I am arriving so easily
At silence-pinnacle.

307. 2 November

My evening descends,
And God's Silence-Eye tells me
That my God-commitment-life
Is bound to meet with
My God-enlightenment-eye.

MY EVENING DESCENDS

308. 3 November

My evening descends,
And whereas during the day
My mind wanted me to climb
To the Heights of Heaven,
Now my heart wants me
To spread my heart-breath
Throughout the length and
  breadth
Of the earth.

309. 4 November

My evening descends
And tells me
Only one thing:
My heart's cheerfulness
Is God's Victory-Celebration.

310. 5 November

My evening descends,
And whereas during the entire
  day
I did not realise
That God-disobedience
Was nothing but a losing game,
Now my God-obedience
Is the fastest winning game.

311. 6 November

My evening descends
And makes me see
A beautiful purity-glow
Over my aspiration-heart.

312. 7 November

My evening descends,
And I am overwhelmed with joy
To see that my Lord's
  Compassion-Eye
And my gratitude-heart
Have perfect faith in each other.

313. 8 November

My evening descends,
And I clearly see
That my outer world
Is an ongoing ignorance-
  advertisement,
Whereas my inner world
Is an ongoing God-hunger-beauty.

314. 9 November

My evening descends,
And whereas during the day
I was an attachment-life,
Now I am a detachment
Plus enlightenment-soul.

315. 10 November

My evening descends,
And whereas during the day
I thought and felt that I knew
  everything
About God,
Now wisdom has dawned upon
  me.
How I wish to know more of
  everything
About God!

316. 11 November

My evening descends,
And my life-boat,
With the silence-peace of evening,
Is arriving at God-Satisfaction-
  Shore.

317. 12 November

My evening descends,
And whereas during the day
I was self-employed,
Now I am employed
By God's Compassion-Silence-Eye.

318. 13 November

My evening descends,
And whereas during the day
God was fully satisfied
With my self-improvement-
  efforts,
Now God is extremely delighted
With my God-manifestation-
  commitments.

319. 14 November

My evening descends,
And whereas during the day
God asked me for interesting
  news,
Now God is asking me
For inspiring and illumining
  messages.

320. 15 November

My evening descends,
And I smilingly suffer from
  homesickness
For God's Compassion-Eye
And Perfection-Feet in Heaven.

MY EVENING DESCENDS

321. 16 November

My evening descends,
And I am no longer a prisoner
In my mind's God-doubt-
   existence-jail.
I am now a free bird
Flying in God's Silence-flooded
   Sky.

322. 17 November

My evening descends,
And whereas during the day
I saw my Lord's Eye
Streaming with tears,
Now I do not want to see even one
   tear
Dropping from God's Eye for me.
I shall make my Lord happy
In His own Way
During the entire evening and
   night
With my sleepless heart's
   breathless aspiration.

323. 18 November

My evening descends,
And my Lord is full of praise
For my burning silence-hunger-
   heart.

324. 19 November

My evening descends
With its ineffable silence-beauty
To feed my God-searching mind
And God-crying heart.

325. 20 November

My evening descends,
And God wants me to explore
His Compassion-Eye
And Forgiveness-Heart.

326. 21 November

My evening descends
And helps me unconditionally
To drink in
God's Silence-Splendour-Lustre.

327. 22 November

My evening descends,
And I am now entering into
The God-Silence-fed
Dream-world.

328. 23 November

My evening descends,
And my God-loving heart
Is replacing
My God-searching mind.

329. 24 November

My evening descends
With my soul's silence-delight-songs
To feed my God-hungry heart.

330. 25 November

My evening descends,
And I find myself feeding and enjoying
The beauty of
My heart's aspiration-flames.

331. 26 November

My evening descends,
And God hopes to see in me
A climbing heart,
While I hope to see in God
Two descending Feet.

332. 27 November

My evening descends,
And I clearly see
That my God-longing heart
Once more will rise up and fly
In God's Compassion-flooded Sky.

333. 28 November

My evening descends,
And my contemplation-heart is breathless
With God-Arrival-anticipation.

334. 29 November

My evening descends,
And I feel my aspiration-heart
Thrillingly and throbbingly
Close to God.

335. 30 November

My evening descends,
And God, out of His infinite Bounty,
Exchanges His Promise-Blossoms
For my hope-blooms.

336. 1 December

My evening descends,
And my mind-disharmony-day
Grows into
My heart-harmony-evening.

MY EVENING DESCENDS

337. 2 December

My evening descends
And inspires me
To choose God's Compassion-Eye
And Forgiveness-Feet,
Whereas the day inspired me
To choose God's Power-Hands.

338. 3 December

My evening descends,
And whereas during the day
I gave God a thank-you note,
Now I am giving God
My gratitude-devotion-magnet.

339. 4 December

My evening descends,
And God does not want
My mind, vital and body to roar,
But He wants my heart to soar.

340. 5 December

My evening descends,
And God wants me to illumine
My heart-home
With my soul's sweetness-
   fragrance.

341. 6 December

My evening descends,
And what God hungers
To see in me
At last I have:
Poise.

342. 7 December

My evening descends
And immediately helps me
To speed up
My God-realisation-race.

343. 8 December

My evening descends,
And I must realise
That my Lord Supreme
   proudly treasures
My heart's every devotion-
   moment.

344. 9 December

My evening descends
To completely shut down
My mind's loudest volume-noise.

345. 10 December

My evening descends,
And I am amazed to see
That my God-obedience-heart
And my God-willingness-mind
Are together singing and playing.

346. 11 December

My evening descends,
And my God-love, God-devotion
And God-surrender
Are accompanying me
On my way to my Lord's
Heart-Garden.

347. 12 December

My evening descends,
And I am now finally able
To untie the desire-rope
From my life.

348. 13 December

My evening descends,
And whereas during the day
I saw the path,
Now I am taking the path.

349. 14 December

My evening descends,
And whereas during the day
My mind and I were in the world
   of anarchy,
Now my heart and I are in the
   world
Of order and harmony.

350. 15 December

My evening descends
And teaches me
How to give joy
To God's Silence-Eye.

351. 16 December

My evening descends
And tells me
That there is no greater
   stupidity-mistake
Than to think and feel
That God-realisation is not
   meant for me.

MY EVENING DESCENDS

352. 17 December

My evening descends
And tells me
That I have already made a
   Himalayan blunder
By saying that I do not love God,
And now it does not want me
To make it infinitely worse
By saying that I do not need God.

353. 18 December

My evening descends
With a new hope-promise-angel
To touch my eyes,
My heart
And my life.

354. 19 December

My evening descends,
And my Lord Supreme is sighing
With great relief
That I am determined once more
To love Him and please Him
Tomorrow
In His own Way.

355. 20 December

My evening descends
And tells me:
"Remember what you now have:
God's Forgiveness,
And not what you once lost:
Your faith in God."

356. 21 December

My evening descends,
And whereas during the day
I met with a host
Of danger-enemies,
Now I am meeting with a host
Of prayer-friends.

357. 22 December

My evening descends
And asks me to invoke silence
And nothing else,
So that my heart can roar
And my breath can soar
To please God in His own Way.

358. 23 December

My evening descends,
And ceaseless tears are dropping
From the Eye of my
   Lord Beloved Supreme
To make my heart happy.

359. 24 December

My evening descends,
And my silence-soul
Is beckoning
My heart-climber.

360. 25 December

My evening descends,
And I tell it:
"My sister, your blossoming
    silence
Is my last hope-anchor
For God-service-satisfaction."

361. 26 December

My evening descends,
And whereas during the day
Unsolicited and unwanted
    restlessness
Captured my mind,
Now evening has brought
My heart and my life
An unconditional sea of peace.

362. 27 December

My evening descends,
And finally I grow into
My heart's genuine, open and
    sincere
Self-giving God-cries.

363. 28 December

My evening descends
And tells me
That its beauty, purity and silence
Are going to help me feel
That my God-realisation
Is within my hope's reach.

364. 29 December

My evening descends
And tells me
That evening does not mean
The end of my aspiration-day.
On the contrary,
It means the increase of
My heart's mounting aspiration-
    flames.

365. 30 December

My evening descends,
And whereas during the day
Each step I took
Seemed like a step towards
    tearing misery,
Now I see that each step
Is a step towards beaming joy.

366. 31 December

My evening descends
To tell me
That God has scored
His greatest Triumph
In and through my day's
Unconditional surrender-joy.

PART XXII

MY MORNING BEGINS

MY MORNING BEGINS

1. 1 January

My morning begins
With the Sun-Bloom-Blessing
Of my Lord Beloved Supreme.

2. 2 January

My morning begins
With my soul's self-giving smiles.

3. 3 January

My morning begins
With my heart's Heaven-climbing
cries.

4. 4 January

My morning begins
With my mind's truth-searching
eyes.

5. 5 January

My morning begins
With my vital's lethargy-defying
life.

6. 6 January

My morning begins
With my body's pleasure-silencing
thoughts.

7. 7 January

My morning begins
With a soulful salutation
To world-harmony-lovers.

8. 8 January

My morning begins
With a rainbow-dancing delight.

9. 9 January

My morning begins
Without disturbing,
Without ridiculing
And without criticising
The citizens of the city
Of deplorable sleepers.

10. 10 January

My morning begins
With the vision
Of my rose-heart-garden.

11. 11 January

My morning begins
By claiming
God's Compassion-flooded Eye
As its own, very own.

12. 12 January

My morning begins
With a prayerful and soulful
God-gratitude-silence-moment.

13. 13 January

My morning begins
With the thrill
Of my God-fulfilment-
   determination.

14. 14 January

My morning begins
By energising my body,
Commanding my vital,
Directing my mind,
Feeding my heart
And serving my soul.

15. 15 January

My morning begins
By washing, adorning and
   treasuring
God's Forgiveness-Feet.

16. 16 January

My morning begins
By invoking, obeying and
   satisfying
God the Creator.

17. 17 January

My morning begins
With the hope of enjoying
The exquisite beauty of God
   the creation.

18. 18 January

My morning begins
By challenging and devouring
Temptation-ignorance-sea.

19. 19 January

My morning begins
By uniting Heaven's cheerful soul
And earth's tearful heart.

20. 20 January

My morning begins,
And God tells me that He wants
To play with my willingness-
   mind,
Eagerness-heart and oneness-
   breath.

21. 21 January

My morning begins
With a blessingful invitation
From my Lord Supreme to visit
His Existence-Consciousness-
   Bliss-Land.

22. 22 January

My morning begins
With my heart's aspiration-child,
Who drinks nothing
But Nectar-Delight.

23. 23 January

My morning begins
With my sleepless support
For those who fulfil
God's each and every Wish.

24. 24 January

My morning begins
With a God-intoxicated
   willingness-heart.

25. 25 January

My morning begins
With my blank check-surrender-
   offering
To my Lord Supreme.

26. 26 January

My morning begins
By looking far beyond
Tomorrow's golden dawn.

27. 27 January

My morning begins
With my God-obedience-
   readiness-
Willingness-eagerness-reality
For the entire day.

28. 28 January

My morning begins
Not with my mind's
Success-pleasure,
But with my heart's
Progress-measure.

29. 29 January

My morning begins
With singing,
At the Request of God's
   Compassion-Eye.

30. 30 January

My morning begins
With dancing,
At the Command of God's
   Forgiveness-Heart.

31. 31 January

My morning begins
With a solemn warning
From God:
"Ignorance-indulgence no
   more!"

32. 1 February

My morning begins
By echoing and re-echoing
God's constant Concern
For my transformation-life.

33. 2 February

My morning begins
With God's Compassion-flooded
   Message
That my aspiration will never
Be out of date
And never
Be out of truth.

34. 3 February

My morning begins
With the exquisite fragrance
Of my soul's delight.

35. 4 February

My morning begins
With the Heaven-rising voice
Of my God-Satisfaction-prayers.

36. 5 February

My morning begins
With the only real difficulty:
To convince my mind
That its unwillingness to accept
   God's Light
Will end in its utter failure.

37. 6 February

My morning begins
With my heart's tremendous
God-realisation-attempt,
And not
With my relaxation-enjoyment.

38. 7 February

My morning begins
By watching the fastest decline
Of my mind-glory
And the fastest Heaven-climbing
   joy
Of my heart-victory.

39. 8 February

My morning begins
With my heart's
Secret and sacred thirst
For God's Compassion-Eye.

40. 9 February

My morning begins
By avoiding my mind's
Success-strength
And treasuring my heart's
Progress-length.

41. 10 February

My morning begins
With my life-transformation-
   promise.

42. 11 February

My morning begins
With a special Message from God:
"Each second is a golden
   opportunity
To fly to the Beyond."

43. 12 February

My morning begins
By sailing my gratitude-heart's
   life-boat
To God's Golden Shore.

44. 13 February

My morning begins,
And I immediately start flying
With God's universal
   Oneness-Kite.

45. 14 February

My morning begins
By challenging, defying and
   defeating
My mind's doubt-invasion.

46. 15 February

My morning begins
With the sound-speed
Of my silence-soul
To please God in His own Way.

47. 16 February

My morning begins
With a blessingful Whisper from
   God.
He tells me what to immediately
   choose
And what to constantly refuse.

48. 17 February

My morning begins
With my heart's prayerful promise
  to God
That I shall never, never
  disappoint Him.

49. 18 February

My morning begins,
And with my human eyes I see
  the sunlight
Covering a limited distance.
And what do I see with my
  inner eye?
With my inner eye I see the
  God-Light
Covering the length and breadth
Of the entire world.

50. 19 February

My morning begins
With my mind's
  sincerity-determination,
My heart's purity-expansion
And my life's confidence-
  multiplication.

51. 20 February

My morning begins
With a pilgrim-heart-journey
Towards the Unknowable.

52. 21 February

My morning begins,
And something within me tells
  me
Not to detain my Lord Supreme
  any longer,
But to invite Him
To come into my heart
  immediately.

53. 22 February

My morning begins,
And my soul compassionately
  tells me
That I must not accuse Nature
Of uneven beauty,
For Nature, unlike human beings,
Obeys God implicitly.

54. 23 February

My morning begins,
And my human ears
Not only hear,
But also listen to
God's express Commands.

55. 24 February

My morning begins,
Only that I may receive
Unconditional Help from God
To enter into the Heart
Of His Rainbow-Soul-Vision.

56. 25 February

My morning begins,
And God tells me
That the breath of bliss
Is not far beyond.
It is within easy reach
Of my heart's breathless cries.

57. 26 February

My morning begins,
And lo and behold,
I receive a most precious Gift
From my Lord Supreme:
Silence-Delight.

58. 27 February

My morning begins,
And God openly expresses His
Fondness
For each fragrance-breath
Of my heart.

59. 28 February

My morning begins,
And I tell myself in unmistakable
  terms
That whoever loves God
Is my only ideal hero-friend.

60. 29 February

My morning begins,
And my Lord invariably teaches
  me
How to bridle my high
  horsepower-mind.

61. 1 March

My morning begins,
And my Lord Supreme most
  powerfully claims
Each aspiration-dedication-
Surrender-breath of mine
As His own, very own.

62. 2 March

My morning begins
By watching
God's Compassion-Feet
  descending
Affectionately,
Charmingly
And self-givingly.

63. 3 March

My morning begins,
And I am immediately embraced
By world-peace-dreamers
And world-happiness-lovers.

64. 4 March

My morning begins
With a most beautiful Present
From my Lord Beloved Supreme.
What is the Present?
A huge love-tree
To shelter many, many
   God-crying hearts.

65. 5 March

My morning begins,
And my Lord Supreme
Blessingfully and unconditionally
Asks me to drink in
His Ecstasy's Perfection-Ocean.

66. 6 March

My morning begins
With my heart's only prayer to
   God:
My Beloved Lord Supreme,
May Your cosmic Dream-Tree
One day completely blossom.

67. 7 March

My morning begins
Without my self-doubt-tragedy.

68. 8 March

My morning begins
With a most powerful smile
From God's oldest and dearest
   child:
Peace.

69. 9 March

My morning begins
With my soul's
God-satisfaction-determination.

70. 10 March

My morning begins
By sailing with the beauty,
   purity and bliss
Of my heart-boat.

71. 11 March

My morning begins
With the surrender-life
Of my obedience-heart.

72. 12 March

My morning begins
With the newness-fulness-
   rainbow
Of my self-giving heart.

73. 13 March

My morning begins
With my doubt-bulletproof mind.

74. 14 March

My morning begins
With my life's unconditional
God-service-smile.

75. 15 March

My morning begins
With my most God-charming
God-surrender-dance.

76. 16 March

My morning begins
By shaking hands with
My life's readiness,
My mind's willingness
And my heart's eagerness.

77. 17 March

My morning begins
With my soul's deepest
   meditation
To enrich my aspiration-heart.

78. 18 March

My morning begins
With my heart's
   world-oneness-smile
And my life's
   world-fulness-song.

79. 19 March

My morning begins
With my devotion-
   perfection-heart.

80. 20 March

My morning begins,
And I am all eagerness
For my life-transformation-
   lesson
From my Lord Supreme.

81. 21 March

My morning begins,
And I dauntlessly refuse
To surrender to
   ignorance-pleasure-life.

82. 22 March

My morning begins
With my God-satisfaction-
 earnestness
And eagerness,
And not with a picnic-life-
 enjoyment.

83. 23 March

My morning begins,
And my fearful mind
Immediately disappears,
While my cheerful heart
Immediately appears.

84. 24 March

My morning begins,
And my painful past
Unconditionally surrenders
To my joyful and fruitful present.

85. 25 March

My morning begins,
And I unmistakably realise
 the gravity
Of my God-disobedience-
 stupidity.

86. 26 March

My morning begins
Just by envisioning the
 Sweetness-Smile
Of my Beloved Lord Supreme.

87. 27 March

My morning begins
With the mighty supremacy
Of my faith-warrior
Over the forces of doubt.

88. 28 March

My morning begins,
And I immediately reject
My haughtiness-mind
And select my sweetness-heart.

89. 29 March

My morning begins
With my soul's blessingful
And complete God-trust.

90. 30 March

My morning begins
With my soul's adamantine
 will-power
To challenge each and every
Limitation-barrier of my life.

91. 31 March

My morning begins,
And I say to myself
That I shall no longer remain a
  slave
To my success-mind.
I shall become and remain
  a perfect child
Of my progress-heart.

92. 1 April

My morning begins,
And my Beloved Lord Supreme
  tells me:
"My child, no more lip service to
  Me!
What I need from you
Is your constant heart-service."

93. 2 April

My morning begins,
And the real God tells me
That He does not live inside
The supremacy-declaration-
  religions.

94. 3 April

My morning begins,
And I soulfully invite my
  dynamo-heart
And vehemently shun my
  dynamite-mind
And dynamite-vital.

95. 4 April

My morning begins,
And I clearly see
That my mind's inspiration,
My heart's aspiration
And my life's dedication
Will definitely succeed.

96. 5 April

My morning begins,
And I happily and proudly see
My mind's sincerity
And my life's simplicity
Being blessed by my
  Lord Supreme.

97. 6 April

My morning begins,
And I see my soul
Feeding my heart with hope
And my eye with promise.

98. 7 April

My morning begins,
And I ask my Lord Supreme
What He wants from me.
He smilingly says,
"Unconditional surrender."

99. 8 April

My morning begins,
And my Lord Supreme asks me
What I want from Him.
I cheerfully say,
"My Lord, an iota of peace."

100. 9 April

My morning begins,
And I immediately see my
   Lord Supreme
In His supremely
   Transcendental Trance.

101. 10 April

My morning begins,
And my Lord Supreme
   proudly sees me
Performing readily, willingly and
   eagerly
My terrestrial tasks.

102. 11 April

My morning begins,
And I see the flowering
Of my soul's sacred dreams.

103. 12 April

My morning begins,
And I see God
As the Compassion-flooded
   Keeper
Of my silence-aspiration-pulse.

104. 13 April

My morning begins,
And I play music
For the sleeping world,
And I sing
For the awakening world.

105. 14 April

My morning begins
With a surprisingly newborn
Heart-song.

106. 15 April

My morning begins,
And God vehemently shuts
My mind-door
And proudly opens
My heart-door.

107. 16 April

My morning begins,
And I see myself no more
   entangled
In the desire-jungle of yesterday.

108. 17 April

My morning begins,
And I tell my Lord Supreme
That I am prayerfully chained
To His Heart.

109. 18 April

My morning begins,
And God tells me
That He is proudly chained
To my breath.

110. 19 April

My morning begins,
And I solemnly tell myself:
No more exploitation
Of my Lord's Compassion-Ocean.

111. 20 April

My morning begins,
And I tell my God:
"My Lord, I want You to be
My heart-Ruler
And not my life-Observer."

112. 21 April

My morning begins,
And I see my life's ancient
   ignorance-fetters
Being transformed into
My heart's freedom-wisdom.

113. 22 April

My morning begins,
And I enjoy both
The majesty of my soul-mountain
And the beauty of my
   heart-fountain.

114. 23 April

My morning begins,
And the first thing God does for
   me
Is bless me with a cheerful
   frame of mind.

115. 24 April

My morning begins,
And my heart and I in no time
Grow into two
   God-remembrance-smiles.

116. 25 April

My morning begins,
And I pray to God to bless me
With His Heart-Assurance,
And not His Life-Exuberance.

117. 26 April

My morning begins,
And I pray to God to accept
My life's real servitude,
And not my mind's
   imaginary plenitude.

118. 27 April

My morning begins,
And I invariably see my soul
Feeding my heart
With God-Fulfilment-whispers.

119. 28 April

My morning begins,
And God wants me to be
A choice instrument of His.
Therefore, He asks me not to
   wallow
In my self-destructive pride.

120. 29 April

My morning begins,
And I pray to God
To make my mind
A God-determination-warrior
And my heart
A God-aspiration-lover.

121. 30 April

My morning begins,
And I pray to God
To make me
A goodness-believer
And a greatness-disbeliever.

122. 1 May

My morning begins
With a totally God-absorbed heart
And a God-transformed mind.

123. 2 May

My morning begins,
And I ache with longing
For my oneness-heart-home.

124. 3 May

My morning begins
By treasuring my Lord's smiling
   Eye
And becoming my Lord's
   fulfilling Heart.

125. 4 May

My morning begins
By sowing soulfully
The seeds of self-perfection.

126. 5 May

My morning begins
By serving God's Feet
And feeding God's Heart.

127. 6 May

My morning begins
Not by fearing God the Knower,
But by loving God the Forgiver.

128. 7 May

My morning begins
By crying for
God's Compassion-Feet-
   Protection.

129. 8 May

My morning begins
By watering prayerfully
My heart's God-gratitude-plants.

130. 9 May

My morning begins
By prayerfully asking God
Where I should go to please Him.
God says:
"Nowhere!
Just stay inside your heart-garden
And smell the fragrance of your
   soul-rose
To please Me."

131. 10 May

My morning begins
By commanding thorny doubts
Not to invade my mind.

132. 11 May

My morning begins
By applauding
   world-peace-dreamers.

133. 12 May

My morning begins
By graduating from
   self-interest-stupidity
To God-interest-multiplicity.

134. 13 May

My morning begins,
And God arrives
To uproot from my mind-jungle
God-fulfilment-uncertainty-tree.

135. 14 May

My morning begins,
And I ask myself
Whether I want to remain
A helpless slave to my mind,
Or whether I want to become
A guileless and deathless child
Of my heart.

136. 15 May

My morning begins
By bidding a final farewell
To my desire-life.

137. 16 May

My morning begins
With my heart's endless
Gratitude-expansion
To please my Lord Supreme
In His own Way.

138. 17 May

My morning begins
With a new and thrilling
   discovery:
Everybody's aspiration-life
Is my heart-home.

139. 18 May

My morning begins
With an unprecedented
   discovery:
God feeds on my
   purity-heart-blossoms.

140. 19 May

My morning begins,
And my Lord Supreme blesses me
With the Silence
That explains the inexplicable
And plumbs the unfathomable.

141. 20 May

My morning begins,
And God asks me
To concentrate on the plenitude
Of my soul's will,
And not on the poverty
Of my mind's thoughts.

142. 21 May

My morning begins,
And God tells me
That if I really want to love Him,
Then I must love Him
  unconditionally
All the time,
Without a trace of fear.

143. 22 May

My morning begins,
And God tells me
That I am permitted to speak
  about peace
Only after I have invoked peace.

144. 23 May

My morning begins,
And God compassionately asks me
How I am,
And I devotedly ask God
If He has a special Message for me.

145. 24 May

My morning begins,
And I tell my hope
That it must not retire;
It must continue to aspire.

146. 25 May

My morning begins,
And my mind's readiness
Wants to do all that it must do
For God;
But my heart's willingness and
  eagerness
Are ready to do everything
In God's own Way.

147. 26 May

My morning begins,
And I am not at all interested
In my mind's abstract philosophy;
But I am deeply inspired
By my heart's concrete spirituality.

148. 27 May

My morning begins,
And my Lord smilingly and
  blessingfully
Says to me,
"I am ready to give you anything
For the asking,
But, My child, be wise."

149. 28 May

My morning begins,
And I prayerfully ask my
 Lord Supreme
To tell me something nice.
My Lord Supreme says,
"I am giving you My
 Heart's unlimited
Compassion-Credit Card."

150. 29 May

My morning begins,
And I ask my Lord Supreme:
"What is the most beautiful
 thing on earth?"
My Lord Supreme
 immediately tells me:
"The most beautiful thing on
 earth
Is your gratitude-heart-flower."

151. 30 May

My morning begins,
And I tell my Lord Supreme
That the whole world touches
 His Feet.
Can I do something else?
My Lord Supreme tells me
That certainly I can do
 something else.
He asks me to feel the pulse
Of my own gratitude-heart.

152. 31 May

My morning begins,
And I ask my Lord Supreme
To tell me which bird
Has the largest wings.
My Lord Supreme tells me
That His universal Peace-
 Dream-Bird
Has the largest wings.

153. 1 June

My morning begins,
And I cleverly escape
From my mind-prison,
And immediately enter into
And stay inside my heart-garden.

154. 2 June

My morning begins,
And God asks me
What I want from Him:
His impenetrable Mind
Or His accessible Heart.
I tell Him:
"My Lord, definitely Your
 accessible Heart."

MY MORNING BEGINS

155. 3 June

My morning begins,
And I ask God what He prefers:
A powerful world-mind
Or a peaceful world-heart.
God says to me:
"You fool!
You have nothing better to ask Me?
Of course, a peaceful world-heart."

156. 4 June

My morning begins,
And I give God what I have:
My precious ego,
While God gives me what He is:
His spacious Heart.

157. 5 June

My morning begins,
And I see myself meditating
Inside my meditation-heart-room.
And what does God do?
He attentively guards my meditation-heart-door.

158. 6 June

My morning begins,
And my Lord advises me
Not to do anything
For my future satisfaction,
But to do everything
For my present perfection.
Inside my present perfection
My future satisfaction
Is bound to loom large.

159. 7 June

My morning begins,
And my most special Guest
Is arriving.
Who is my special Guest?
God the Compassion-Sky
And the Forgiveness-Ocean.

160. 8 June

My morning begins,
And I see a tug-of-war
Between my mind's dire unwillingness
And my heart's fire-willingness
To please God in His own Way.

161. 9 June

My morning begins,
And God gives me prayer-capacity
And meditation-capacity.
But He tells me that I must
  acquire myself
Gratitude-capacity.

162. 10 June

My morning begins,
And I ask God if there is anything
  in me
That pleases Him most.
He says:
"Your sleepless eagerness-heart."

163. 11 June

My morning begins,
And God finds my mind's
  attempts
At unconditional surrender
  to His Will
At once amusing and touching.

164. 12 June

My morning begins,
And I ask my mind to tell me
If it knows where peace is.
My mind tells me
It does not know where peace is,
And it does not want to know.

I ask my heart the same question.
My heart says
It does not know where peace is,
But it does want to know.

I ask my soul where peace is,
And my soul says:
"Where else can peace be,
If not inside your own
Silence-meditation-breath?"

165. 13 June

My morning begins,
And my mind asks me
What I want it to do.
I tell my mind
That there is only one thing
It must do:
It has to immediately team up
With my heart.

166. 14 June

My morning begins,
And my heart asks me
What is the thing that I like most
About my heart.
I tell my heart that what I like most
Is its legendary longing
For a God-surrender-life.

167. 15 June

My morning begins,
And I ask my Lord Supreme
What I can do about my doubtful mind.
My Lord says:
"Just shake it off the way you shake off
A persistent fly!"

168. 16 June

My morning begins,
And I immediately try to see
What God is doing.
What do I see?
I see Him weaving and weaving
And enlarging and enlarging
His Heart's Compassion-Net.

169. 17 June

My morning begins,
And I immediately want to hear
What God is saying.
I hear Him repeating
Again and again:
"I need only one thing –
A satisfaction-world!"

170. 18 June

My morning begins,
And I see that my poor God
Is amazed at the endless confusion
Of my mind,
And my proud God
Is amazed at the endless supplication
Of my heart.

171. 19 June

My morning begins,
And I hear my Lord telling my heart
That He wants to entrust my heart
With His birthless and deathless
Cosmic Duties.

172. 20 June

My morning begins,
And I give God
My smiling heart of newness,
While God gives me
His dancing Breath of Fulness.

173. 21 June

My morning begins
With my heart's
God-surrender-breath.

174. 22 June

My morning begins
With a new Message-Light from
 Above:
Man's hope-dream is God.
God's Promise-Reality is man.

175. 23 June

My morning begins
With a powerful Message from
 God:
My mind is made
Of glaring absurdity;
My heart is made
Of glowing reality.

176. 24 June

My morning begins,
And lo, I have become
The singing smile of my life.

177. 25 June

My morning begins
With a Compassion-Blessing-
 Assurance
From God:
My life-boat is sailing extremely
 fast
Towards the Golden Shore.

178. 26 June

My morning begins,
And I smile and smile,
For I see no more
My desire's tenacious grip
On my life.

179. 27 June

My morning begins,
And I closely listen
To the singing heartbeat
Of my life.

180. 28 June

My morning begins,
And I take my
Self-transcendence-perfection-
   attempts
As my only real friends.

181. 29 June

My morning begins
With a most powerful
Perfection-oneness-hunger.

182. 30 June

My morning begins
By watching the sacred flames
Of my enthusiasm-heart.

183. 1 July

My morning begins,
And God comes and tells me
That He wants me to be
His universal peace-partner.

184. 2 July

My morning begins,
And God assures me
That I shall be able to enjoy
The imminent demise
Of my doubting mind.

185. 3 July

My morning begins,
And my soul secretly teaches me
How to remain untouched
By worldly problems.

186. 4 July

My morning begins,
And my Lord tells me
That if I want real happiness,
Then my inner life can brook no
   compromise.

187. 5 July

My morning begins
With my heart's
Aspiration-extension-dream.

188. 6 July

My morning begins,
And I see a pendulum swinging
Between my prayer-cries
And my meditation-smiles.

189. 7 July

My morning begins,
And I sing with my
   heart-hope-friend
And run with my
   soul-promise-friend.

190. 8 July

My morning begins,
And God wants my heart
To be His bravest and
　staunchest friend.

191. 9 July

My morning begins,
And my heart, my life and I
Say to God:
"Our Lord, only to please You
In Your own Way
We came into the world."

192. 10 July

My morning begins,
And God greets my life's
Surrender-smile
With thunderous applause.

193. 11 July

My morning begins
By watching my soul and my Lord
Exchanging victory-garlands.

194. 12 July

My morning begins
By receiving a promotion-smile
From God Himself
For my aspiration-life.

195. 13 July

My morning begins
With my emptiness-mind-
　perfection.

196. 14 July

My morning begins
With my fulness-heart-
　satisfaction.

197. 15 July

My morning begins,
And my life and I are immediately
　drawn
Towards the brilliant horizon of
　faith
By God Himself.

198. 16 July

My morning begins
By watching God and
　His dearest child, Peace,
Walking straight towards
My surrender-life and
　gratitude-heart.

199. 17 July

My morning begins
By enjoying the beauty of my
　soul's
Perfection-manifested bliss.

200. 18 July

My morning begins,
And God tells me to play
Sincerely, devotedly and
　self-givingly
The role of three aspirants:
A truth-believer,
A truth-teller
And a truth-dweller.

201. 19 July

My morning begins,
And God tells me that,
If I really love Him,
Then I must claim His
　Eternity's infinite Breath
As my own, very own.

202. 20 July

My morning begins,
And I beg God to tell me
When He will accept the full
　ownership
Of my aspiration-breath
And dedication-life.

203. 21 July

My morning begins,
And to my greatest joy, I see
That God's Compassion-Peace-Eye
Has become invaluable
To mankind.

204. 22 July

My morning begins,
And I try to become
God's Satisfaction-Delight
By destroying my
　desire-bondage-chain.

205. 23 July

My morning begins,
And I promise God that at
　every moment
I shall claim Him as my own,
　very own,
Happily and self-givingly.

206. 24 July

My morning begins,
And God compassionately and
    blessingfully
Promises me
That He will never disown me,
No matter what I do,
No matter what I become.

207. 25 July

My morning begins,
And I prayerfully ask God
If He ever thinks of me.
He compassionately replies:
"What else do I do?"

208. 26 July

My morning begins,
And I see that two things never
    cease:
God's Hope for me
And my promise to God.

209. 27 July

My morning begins,
And I see God and His faithful
    companions,
Peace, Light and Bliss,
Coming towards me.

210. 28 July

My morning begins,
And my Lord asks me
With His Compassion-
    Affection-Eye
To offer Him my heart's
    satisfaction-delight.

211. 29 July

My morning begins,
And I become my mind's
    inspiration-tree,
My heart's aspiration-flower
And my life's dedication-fruit.

212. 30 July

My morning begins,
And I am delighted to see
My gratitude-heart-flower
Fully blossomed.

213. 31 July

My morning begins,
And my soul immediately
    sends an invitation
To all world-peace-dreamers,
My heart immediately
    sends an invitation
To all world-peace-lovers,
And my life immediately
    sends an invitation
To all world-peace-servers.

214. 1 August

My morning begins,
And I think of only one thing:
My God-manifestation-promise
Here on earth.

215. 2 August

My morning begins,
And I watch God performing
His countless activities
With my prayerful eyes.

216. 3 August

My morning begins,
And my stupid mind tells me
That God is unapproachable,
But my wise heart tells me
That God is really attainable.

217. 4 August

My morning begins,
And my Lord Supreme assures me
That if I can keep my mind
Sincere and receptive,
Then there will be no shortage
Of His Peace-Supplies.

218. 5 August

My morning begins,
And I clearly see
That my Lord Supreme prizes
My willingness and eagerness
To please Him
Far beyond my imagination's
  flight.

219. 6 August

My morning begins,
And I surprise my
  Beloved Supreme
By offering Him two of my
  possessions:
My confusion-mind-jungle
And my aspiration-heart-garden.

220. 7 August

My morning begins,
And God tells me
That my unconditional
  surrender-road
Is infinitely shorter, safer and
  better
Than any other road
To reach my Destination.

221. 8 August

My morning begins,
And my Compassion-flooded
   Lord Supreme
Immediately stops my mind
From its wilderness-expedition.

222. 9 August

My morning begins,
And my Lord Supreme,
Faster than the fastest,
Silences my active vital-volcano.

223. 10 August

My morning begins,
And my Lord Supreme,
In the twinkling of an eye,
Blesses me with a ceaseless
Heart-dynamo.

224. 11 August

My morning begins,
And I see that God
And His dearest child, Peace,
Are travelling everywhere
With the hope of receiving
   invitations
From true peace-lovers.

225. 12 August

My morning begins,
And I prayerfully ask my
   Lord Supreme
What He means by 'peace'.
He says to me:
"My child, peace is
The confusion-illumination
   of your mind."

226. 13 August

My morning begins,
And I ask my Lord Supreme
What peace can, after all, do.
My Lord Supreme says to me:
"My child, peace can do
   everything for you.
Peace can do even the
   impossible for you,
Such as totally transform
Your desire-mind."

227. 14 August

My morning begins,
And I beg my Beloved Supreme
   to tell me clearly
What self-transcendence means.
He tells me my self-transcendence
   means
His most powerful
   Satisfaction-Assurance
In my life.

228. 15 August

My morning begins,
And God tells me that He wants
   Only one thing from me to feed
      Him,
And that is my unconditional
   service-light.

229. 16 August

My morning begins,
And I ask my Lord Supreme
To tell me what I can expect
From my good meditation.
He tells me that I can expect
The complete silencing of my
   mind-storm.

230. 17 August

My morning begins,
And I regain once more
My long-lost God-gratitude-heart.

231. 18 August

My morning begins
With God the Singer
Before me
And God the Listener
Within me.

232. 19 August

My morning begins,
And my Lord Beloved Supreme
   tells me
To be His worldwide
   peace-distributor,
And not to remain anymore
A self-promoter.

233. 20 August

My morning begins,
And I pave my road towards
   the Destination
With the purity of my heart's
   tears.

234. 21 August

My morning begins,
And I ask my Lord Supreme
   how I can know
That I am pleasing Him.
My compassionate Lord Supreme
Immediately tells me to ask
My purity-mind and
   sincerity-heart
The same question,
And He also tells me that they will
   give me
The absolutely correct answer.

235. 22 August

My morning begins,
And my mind immediately greets me
With its happy inspiration-light.

236. 23 August

My morning begins,
And my heart immediately embraces me
With its nectar-delight.

237. 24 August

My morning begins,
And I see my mind, my heart and my soul
Right in front of me.
What else do I see?
I see my soul
Looking at my mind miserably,
And I see my soul
Seeing through my heart proudly.

238. 25 August

My morning begins,
And my Lord most compassionately tells me
That what I need is not an aggressive
Vital-determination
But a progressive heart-realisation.

239. 26 August

My morning begins,
And my soul smilingly tells me
That the spiritual path
That enjoys supremacy over others
Has a fallible God.

240. 27 August

My morning begins
With a special Message from God:
"My child, your willingness-heart
Will always have room
To accommodate the entire creation."

241. 28 August

My morning begins,
And I ask my soul to tell me
Which spirituality is by far the best.
My soul most affectionately tells me
That the spirituality that embodies
Simplicity's mind,
Sincerity's heart
And purity's life
Is by far the best.

242. 29 August

My morning begins,
And I see the beauty of
 my crying heart
And the divinity of
 my smiling soul
Playing together in
 God's Heart-Garden.

243. 30 August

My morning begins,
And I realise something totally
 new:
What I need is the self-giving life
Of blossoming years,
And not the wisdom-declaring life
Of advancing years.

244. 31 August

My morning begins,
And I see my God-searching mind,
My God-loving heart
And my God-serving life,
Each one succeeding
 unmistakably.

245. 1 September

My morning begins,
And I ask my Lord Supreme:
"How can I stop my mind's
 teeming doubts
From torturing me?"
God answers:
"My child, do not worry.
Soon they will helplessly fall
 down
From their own heavy weight."

246. 2 September

My morning begins,
And my Lord tells me that
Since His Hope for me
And His Promise to me
Are not going to retire,
I must not lose courage.

247. 3 September

My morning begins,
And my mind proudly shows me
What it has for me:
A proud wave of happy
 inspiration.

248. 4 September

My morning begins,
And my heart affectionately
  shows me
What it has for me:
A vast sea of self-giving
  expansion.

249. 5 September

My morning begins,
And I prayerfully ask my Lord
What I can give Him
To make Him happy.
He tells me:
"My child,
I shall be happy
Not only immediately, but also
  permanently
If you just offer Me
Your fully blossomed
  gratitude-heart."

250. 6 September

My morning begins,
And I soulfully ask my
  Lord Supreme
To hear my burdens.
He blessingfully tells me:
"My child, I shall
Not only hear your burdens,
But also unburden your burdens,
If you can offer Me
Your sleepless and breathless
  smile."

251. 7 September

My morning begins,
And my Lord Beloved Supreme
  tells me
That He has no interest
In my life's success-story,
But He has sincere and
  immediate interest
In my heart's progress-song.

252. 8 September

My morning begins,
And I ask my Lord Supreme
How I can be truly happy
When I am with others.
He most compassionately
  tells me:
"My child, if you want to be
  truly happy,
Then appreciate everybody's
  beliefs
And never interfere with
  anyone's beliefs."

253. 9 September

My morning begins,
And I become my heart's
  indomitable courage
To challenge and conquer
The devouring doubt of my mind.

254. 10 September

My morning begins,
And I see my soul
Making round-the-clock
　observations
To liberate me from my
　desire-bound life.

255. 11 September

My morning begins,
And I soulfully ask my
　Lord Supreme
To tell me how I can really make
The fastest progress.
He most compassionately tells
　me:
"My child, just march forward
With your heart's
　cheerfulness-steps.
You are bound to make
The fastest progress."

256. 12 September

My morning begins,
And my desire-freed life
Shows me
What divine satisfaction is.

257. 13 September

My morning begins,
And to my extreme joy,
I see my long-lost gratitude-heart
Coming to the fore.

258. 14 September

My morning begins,
And I see clearly
The most glorious
　God-Victory-days
Fast approaching my
　God-dreaming life.

259. 15 September

My morning begins,
And to my wide surprise and
　great delight,
I see God enjoying the
　beauty and fragrance
Of my mind's willingness
And my heart's eagerness.

260. 16 September

My morning begins,
And I see the infinite vault
Of Heaven's peace and bliss
Entering the life-breath
Of my gratitude-heart-fountain.

261. 17 September

My morning begins,
And I see such a difference of
   opinion
Between my mind and my heart.
My mind tells me
God's Justice-Light is everywhere.
My heart tells me
The mind is wrong,
And it is God's Compassion-Heart
That is everywhere.

262. 18 September

My morning begins,
And I see peace-abundance
Enveloping my
   God-gratitude-heart
Completely.

263. 19 September

My morning begins,
And I am convinced
That God's Forgiveness-Heart
Is accessible everywhere.

264. 20 September

My morning begins,
And my soul shows me once more
The God-Destination-Road
Which I carelessly lost.

265. 21 September

My morning begins,
And my compassion-flooded soul
Inspires my aspiration-flames
To climb faster than the fastest.

266. 22 September

My morning begins,
And I prayerfully and
   enthusiastically
Ask my Lord
What is the best thing that
   I possess.
He lovingly and compassionately
   tells me
That my heart's
   devotion-fragrance
Is by far my best possession.

267. 23 September

My morning begins
With a blessingful Message
   from God
That He and His Heart will
   always take me
Under Their blue-gold Wings.

268. 24 September

My morning begins,
And I tell my mind:
"I admire you because
You long to explore
The realities of the unseen world."

269. 25 September

My morning begins,
And I tell my heart:
"I love you because
You sleeplessly implore
God's Compassion-Eye."

270. 26 September

My morning begins,
And I see God writing my
　heart-speeches
To feed the world,
While I am writing my
　mind-speeches
To astonish the world.

271. 27 September

My morning begins,
And I ask my Lord Supreme:
"Is there anything that can
　cure self-doubt
Faster than the fastest?"
He says: "My child, a
　fountain-heart-faith
In My Compassion-Eye
Is the quickest and by far
　the best
Self-doubt-removing
　medicine."

272. 28 September

My morning begins,
And I make my Lord Supreme
Swim in the sea of Delight
Just by striking an
　enthusiasm-match
Inside my aspiration-heart.

273. 29 September

My morning begins,
And I meditate and meditate
　and meditate.
Then what do I see?
I see my meditation fanning
　my aspiration-flames
Most affectionately and
　most powerfully.

274. 30 September

My morning begins,
And I ask my soul
If I can give a special name
To my meditation.
My soul tells me:
"Definitely you can.
Call your meditation
An atomic oneness-power."

275. 1 October

My morning begins,
And I tell my soul:
"I am so helpless that my
    heart's insecurity
Has become my life's ruler.
What shall I do?"
My soul tells me to smile
Brighter than the brightest,
    ceaselessly,
Within and without.
This will definitely topple
My insecurity-heart-ruler.

276. 2 October

My morning begins,
And I pray to God for happiness.
He tells me that He can make me
    happy
Only if I give Him my unaspiring
    past-mind
And my aspiring present-heart
With equal cheerfulness.

277. 3 October

My morning begins,
And I ask my Lord what
    He will give me
If I adore Him unconditionally.
He tells me that
If I adore Him unconditionally,
Then He will always keep a
    special seat for me
Inside His Sweetness-
    Fulness-Heart-Home.

278. 4 October

My morning begins,
And my Lord Beloved Supreme
    asks me
If I want to have special joy
    from Him.
I tell Him: "Definitely, my Lord!"
And He carries me to my soul's
Silence-flooded summit.

279. 5 October

My morning begins,
And I receive two special presents
From my soul and my heart:
My soul blesses me
With confidence-builder-smiles;
My heart blesses me
With aspiration-distributor-tears.

280. 6 October

My morning begins,
And I am still treasuring my walk
Of the previous night
Along a very long peace-road.

281. 7 October

My morning begins,
And I see my Lord
Happily and proudly watching me
Sprinting with my
   lightning-speed-feet.

282. 8 October

My morning begins,
And my Lord tells me
That He is blessing me with
   His Heart's
Rose-Vision-Fragrance-Delight.

283. 9 October

My morning begins,
And I see my Lord so proud of me.
When I ask Him why,
My Lord immediately tells me
It is because I am spreading
My love-devotion-surrender-
   petals
All around His Compassion-Feet.

284. 10 October

My morning begins,
And I prayerfully ask my Lord
Why He is so extraordinarily
   happy.
He tells me that His Happiness
Knows no bounds
Because my life's
Unconditional surrender to Him
Is genuine.

285. 11 October

My morning begins,
And I ask my Supreme Lord
How I can stop thinking.
He says to me:
"My child, you can stop thinking
Only by loving Me more."

286. 12 October

My morning begins
With a fulness-soul,
An openness-heart
And a newness-life.

287. 13 October

My morning begins,
And I immediately start counting
The Tears of my Lord's
  Compassion-Eye.

288. 14 October

My morning begins,
And I immediately start counting
The Smiles of my Lord's
  Forgiveness-Heart.

289. 15 October

My morning begins,
And I start to please God
In many, many ways.
He most affectionately tells me:
"My child, there is only one way
To please Me, and that way
Is your life's unconditional
  surrender-way."

290. 16 October

My morning begins,
And my Lord wants to play
  with me
A very special game
By exchanging my purity-
  heart-bloom
With His Divinity-Heart-
  Blossoms.

291. 17 October

My morning begins,
And I replace my questioning
  mind
With my God-hungry and
God-questing heart.

292. 18 October

My morning begins,
And my unconditional
  surrender is taking me
To the towering
  realisation-summit.

293. 19 October

My morning begins,
And I see that I am no more
A world-pleasure-seeker,
But a peace-treasure-lover.

MY MORNING BEGINS

294. 20 October

My morning begins,
And I do not allow myself
To be driven by burning
   curiosity,
But by flaming necessity.

295. 21 October

My morning begins,
And my mind tells me that
   it is very happy
Because it is unparalleled
In every way.

296. 22 October

My morning begins,
And my heart tells me that
   it is extremely happy
Because it has no inferiors.
Equality's fragrance-breath
It deeply enjoys.

297. 23 October

My morning begins,
And my Lord blesses me
With a special peace-
   diploma for studying,
Lovingly and self-givingly,
In His universal
   Oneness-Heart-School.

298. 24 October

My morning begins,
And God applauds,
No matter how feeble are
   my attempts
To serve Him in the heart
   of aspiring humanity.

299. 25 October

My morning begins,
And I unmistakably see
   and feel
That my heart is made of
God's Compassion-Smiles.

300. 26 October

My morning begins,
And I throbbingly feel
That my life is made of
God's Forgiveness-Bliss.

301. 27 October

My morning begins,
And my Beloved Lord
   Supreme tells me
That since I am a
   prayer-meditation-lover,
I am indeed His
   Delight-Investment.

302. 28 October

My morning begins
By defending the Truth:
God's Heart is in all,
And God's Love is for all.

303. 29 October

My morning begins,
And God tells me that
My aspiration is a credit card,
My dedication is a check,
But my God-manifestation-
  eagerness
Is cash.

304. 30 October

My morning begins,
And God tells me
That unless I invite happiness
To bless my mind,
He cannot give my heart His
Fulness.

305. October 31

My morning begins,
And I am so happy
That my heart is powerfully
  driven
By divine passion for perfection.

306. 1 November

My morning begins,
And I see God feeding my heart
With His own Heart's
  Rainbow-Smile.

307. 2 November

My morning begins,
And I see God blessing me
Because my life is stationed
Far beyond my mind's
  interference.

308. 3 November

My morning begins,
And my Lord Supreme tells me
That nobody has to understand
The language of the heart.
Nobody has to even study
The language of the heart.
Everybody just has to speak
The language of the heart
To please God in His own Way.

309. 4 November

My morning begins,
And I receive the supreme power
  of silence
Because my heart is all willingness
To please God sleeplessly and
  breathlessly.

310. 5 November

My morning begins,
And I give God my unconditional
  willingness
To please Him in His own Way.
He gives me His
  Heart-Beauty's Peace-Bird
In return.

311. 6 November

My morning begins,
And I claim God's Heart
  prayerfully.
God claims my life proudly.

312. 7 November

My morning begins,
And God tells me that each time
I offend my soul,
God becomes sadness itself.

313. 8 November

My morning begins,
And I tell my heart
Not to mix with part-time seekers.
No, never!
For their aspiration is not serious.

314. 9 November

My morning begins,
And God tells me that mine
  must not be
A possession-barrier-life.
He wants me to have
A possession-service-life.

315. 10 November

My morning begins,
And to my extreme joy,
God is showing me how to listen
To the endless waves of peace
Deep within my aspiration-heart.

316. 11 November

My morning begins,
And God asks me whether I
  believe in Him.
I reply, "I do, my Lord, I do."
God says, "Then, My child, to you
  I belong,
To you I belong."

317. 12 November

My morning begins,
And my Lord tells me
That if I show Him unswerving love
For each and every human being,
Then He will give me
His most valuable possession:
Peace.

318. 13 November

My morning begins,
And I want to make it very clear
To my earth-bound mind
That I am only for
My Heaven-free soul.

319. 14 November

My morning begins,
And my soul wants to know from me
How God is treating me these days.
I tell my soul that God is treating me
Extremely well.
I am now a very special member
Of God's all-fulfilling Association.

320. 15 November

My morning begins,
And God tells me that I must always aim
For the ultimate Existence-Consciousness-Bliss
So that I can proudly receive
Much acclaim from Him.

321. 16 November

My morning begins,
And I am so happy that I am walking
On my heart's meditation-road.

322. 17 November

My morning begins,
And my Lord tells me that if I want to be
A perfect God-lover and God-server,
Then I can never go off-duty.

323. 18 November

My morning begins,
And my soulful meditation
Adds to God's Love for me
In bountiful measure.

MY MORNING BEGINS

324. 19 November

My morning begins,
And I become one with my heart's
Sweet hope-dedication-breath
For my Lord Beloved Supreme.

325. 20 November

My morning begins,
And the divinity of
　oneness-light-road
Beckons the duty of my
　aspiration-heart.

326. 21 November

My morning begins,
And I listen only to my soul's
Wisdom-light-broadcast.

327. 22 November

My morning begins,
And my fruitful meditation
Expands and expands
My heart's world-oneness-waves.

328. 23 November

My morning begins,
And my Lord Supreme blesses me
With a cloud-free mind-sky
To meditate on His entire
　creation.

329. 24 November

My morning begins,
And the aspiration-climber in me
Receives a direct invitation
From God's Palace.

330. 25 November

My morning begins,
And God at once most
　affectionately
And most proudly
Accepts my heart's
Gratitude-fragrance-blossoms.

331. 26 November

My morning begins,
And my Inner Pilot Supreme
　blesses me
With His blazing Heart-Torch
For the total transformation
　of my mind.

332. 27 November

My morning begins,
And the Heart of my
　Lord Supreme
Powerfully and proudly admires
My heart's enthusiasm-
　dynamism.

333. 28 November

My morning begins,
And lovingly, faithfully, I take courses
At my Lord's Oneness-World-University.

334. 29 November

My morning begins,
And my Inner Pilot tells me
That my mind's desirelessness
Is my life's complete freedom.

335. 30 November

My morning begins,
And my Inner Pilot tells me
That my heart's mounting aspiration-flames
Are quite successful
In sending ignorance-night
A final farewell letter.

336. 1 December

My morning begins,
And my heart-boat steers speedily
And self-givingly
To God's Oneness-Fulness-Shore.

337. 2 December

My morning begins,
And my concentration-spear
Frightens and silences
My mind's swirling confusion.

338. 3 December

My morning begins,
And God Himself blesses me
With purity's ever-rising aspiration-flames.

339. 4 December

My morning begins,
And I enjoy deeply the complete oneness
Of my life's shining newness
And my heart's illumining fulness.

340. 5 December

My morning begins,
And I enjoy and enjoy
Watching the radiance of my heart's
God-devotion-sweetness.

341. 6 December

My morning begins,
And to my great joy and relief,
Doubts do not dare to bark at my mind
And insecurities do not dare
To torture my heart.
I now have become high, higher, highest-flying
Aspiration-delight.

342. 7 December

My morning begins,
And my Inner Pilot tells me
That the beauty of my
   gratitude-heart-tears
Is undoubtedly unparalleled.

343. 8 December

My morning begins,
And my Inner Pilot tells me
That to conquer His Heart
I do not have to weep a river of tears,
But to become a sea
Of prayerful and soulful smiles.

344. 9 December

My morning begins,
And my Lord Supreme advises me
To be satisfied
Only with the Grace of God
In my inner life,
And not with the face of prosperity
In my outer life.

345. 10 December

My morning begins,
And my Lord Supreme tells me
That He wants me to be
The permanent conqueror
Of my ego
And the sleepless server
Of my soul.

346. 11 December

My morning begins,
And I see no more the quick descent
Of dark ignorance-night,
But an abundance of
   all-illumining light
Within and without.

347. 12 December

My morning begins,
And my Inner Pilot makes my
  aspiration-heart
Sweeter than the sweetest
And purer than the purest
So that He can bless me
With His Plenitude-Harvest.

348. 13 December

My morning begins,
And to my extreme surprise,
My mind is begging my heart
For an abundant supply
Of inner cries.

349. 14 December

My morning begins,
And God supplies my mind
With the message-light of
  vastness,
God supplies my heart
With the message-light of
  oneness,
And God supplies my soul
With the message-light of fulness.

350. 15 December

My morning begins,
And I cannot believe that I have,
All of a sudden,
Become the sweetest
  nectar-delight
Of my self-giving.

351. 16 December

My morning begins,
And I see my life's absolute
  obedience
And my Lord's infinite Delight
Smiling at each other
And singing and dancing
  together.

352. 17 December

My morning begins,
And my Lord Supreme tells me
That my life-rejection will take
  me away
Farther than the farthest
From Him,
And my acceptance of life will
  bring Him
Closer than the closest
To me.

353. 18 December

My morning begins,
And I pray to my Inner Pilot
   most sincerely
For one thing:
May my heart's gratitude-smile
Remain beautiful, more beautiful,
   most beautiful
And never grow old.

354. 19 December

My morning begins,
And I come to realise
That my heart's abundance-love
Will result in oneness-radiance.

355. 20 December

My morning begins,
And my Lord Supreme tells me
That my heart's prayerful songs
Have a special source:
The Voice of His own Divinity.

356. 21 December

My morning begins,
And I see that my heart's
   forgiveness-light
And God's Fulness-Delight
Are unimaginably fond of each
   other.

357. 22 December

My morning begins,
And my soul immediately
   shows me
God the Beautiful
And gives me
God the Bountiful.

358. 23 December

My morning begins,
And my Lord Supreme forbids me
To sit on the chair of outer noise,
But inspires me
To sit on the throne of inner poise.

359. 24 December

My morning begins,
And I want to become
The beauty of inspiration-joy,
But my Lord makes me
The fragrance of
   aspiration-intensity.

360. 25 December

My morning begins,
And I tell my Inner Pilot,
"My Lord, no more
   playthings from You.
My mind now wants only You,
My heart now needs only You,
And my life now claims only You."

361. 26 December

My morning begins,
And I am fully convinced
That my teeming God-
  manifestation-projects
Are saving the human in me
And helping the divine in me
For the full God-manifestation
  here on earth.

362. 27 December

My morning begins,
And my Beloved Lord Supreme
Starts teaching me most
  compassionately
How to take the longest
  progress-strides.

363. 28 December

My morning begins,
And my Inner Pilot takes me
To a special Kingdom of Divinity
Where I can be in the
  sunshine-company
Of liberated souls.

364. 29 December

My morning begins,
And I give my Absolute Lord
My heart's willingness-smile,
And He immediately gives me in
  return
His Fulness-All.

365. 30 December

My morning begins,
And I ask my dearest and sweetest
Beloved Lord Supreme:
"My Lord, please tell me once and
  for all
Who I am."
He answers:
"My child, I am telling you once
  and for all
That you are My Infinity's
Dream-Preparation
And My Immortality's
  Reality-Perfection."

366. 31 December

My morning begins,
And my Lord asks me smilingly
To walk towards my Goal.
Instead of walking, I start
  sprinting.
Seeing me sprinting, my Lord tells
  me
With boundless pride,
"My child, that is what I actually
  meant."

PART XXIII

POWER AND LOVE

POWER AND LOVE

1

Power conquers.
Love wins.

2

Power devours.
Love feeds.

3

Power says to me,
"Come here!"

Love says to me,
"Let us be together,
Always together."

4

Power says to me,
"Go away!"

Love says to me,
"We are our Eternity's oneness."

5

Power does not know
What it is doing
And
Why it is doing.

Love knows
What it is doing
And
Why it is doing.

6

Power is superiority's head.
Love is equality's heart.

7

Power and truth
Are often strangers
To each other.

Love and truth
Are two mutual
Admirers and supporters.

8

The hands of
Power
Are often destructive.

The hands of
Love
Are always creative.

9

Power's blindness
Power is rarely aware of.

Love's oneness
Love is always conscious of.

10

Power, name and fame
Together march.
Destination: nowhere.

Love, oneness and fulness
Together fly.
Destination: Heaven's
  smile-blossoms.

11

Power is
Heaviness-haughtiness-mind.

Love is
Sweetness-fondness-heart.

12

Power is
Duty-emptiness.

Love is
Duty-willingness.

13

Power is narrow.
Power is shallow.
Power is callous.

Love is auspicious.
Love is gracious.
Love is precious.

14

Power does not think;
Therefore, it sinks.

Love sings God's Songs;
Therefore, it is a God-bliss-singer.

15

Power is
Self-aggrandisement.

Love is
God-enlightenment.

16

Ultimately,
Power and frustration
Are compelled to walk along
The destruction-road.

Eternally,
Love and fulfilment
Are favoured by God
  Himself
To walk along
The satisfaction-road.

17

Power tries to
Conceal its weakness.

Love spontaneously not only
Reveals its strength,
But also God's Power.

18

Power used;
Gone, completely gone.

Love used;
Expands, multiplies.

19

Power keeps God's Grace
At a distance.

Love not only values
But also treasures
Sleeplessly and breathlessly
God's Grace.

20

Power
Does not want to carry anybody
But wants to be carried
By the whole world.

Love
Carries each and every human
  being
From the cradle to the grave.

21

When the world suffers,
Power does not shed
Even a single tear.

When the world suffers,
Love becomes
A sea of tears.

22

Power is
Complicated-mind's wild
  adventure.

Love is
Simple-heart's cheerful journey.

23

There is not a single day
That power does not give trouble
To poor God.

There is not a single day
That love does not give joy
To its Beloved Supreme.

24

When power wants to speak to
  God,
God tells power,
"I do not have much time,
Tell Me everything in a nutshell."

When love wants to speak to God,
God tells love,
"Since Eternity is at My disposal,
I am eager to hear from you
  in detail."

25

Power's promises
Can never be taken seriously.

Love's promises
Are doubtless fulfilments.

26

Power takes a tremendous start,
But never wins the inner race.

Love, no matter how it starts,
Always wins the race.

27

The stupidity of power
Wants to interview God.

The wisdom of love
Is always eager to pursue God.

28

Unfortunately,
The very nature of outer power
Works unwisely, hurtfully
And maliciously.

Fortunately,
The very nature of inner love
Works lovingly, graciously
And self-givingly.

POWER AND LOVE

29

When power conducts me,
I see God's Feet nowhere.

When love leads me,
I see God's Feet everywhere.

30

Power quenches the thirst
Of my mind's eye.

Love feeds the hunger
Of my life's heart.

31

Because of power's supremacy,
Our world is heavy
With evening sighs.

Because of love's intimacy,
Our world is light
With morning songs.

32

Power misused is as useless
As a handful of ashes.

Love properly used is as beautiful
And useful
As the starlit sky.

33

Power is
Man's sweet dream-slayer.

Love is
Man's sweet dream-fulfiller.

34

Every day
Power brings embarrassments to God.

Every day
Love brings refreshments to God.

35

Power does not know
What self-offering is.

Love's very existence
Is founded upon self-offering.

36

Power has no power to change
The darkness of the world.

Love hurls not only defiance
At the darkness of the world,
But is absolutely certain
In transforming
World-darkness into world-light.

37

Power flies to meet
With power's allies: super-powers.

Love travels to meet
With love's only Friend: God.

38

Power's Bible
Is for God's Justice-unbelievers.

Love's Gospel
Is for God's Justice-believers,
God's Compassion-dreamers
And for
God's Forgiveness-treasurers.

39

Power is
A mind-sophisticated frown.

Love is
A God-intoxicated smile.

40

Power lives inside
Its own volcano-laughter.

Love lives inside
God's sunshine-Smile.

41

Each new beginning of power
Is world-punishment.

Each new beginning of love
Is world-enlightenment.

42

Power's palace
Has no God-entry.

Love's cottage
Has only a God-entrance all
   around.

43

Power dies
In power's own hands.

Love lives
At God's own Feet.

44

Power:
Who are you?

Love:
You I am.

45

God's Justice
Demands power's
Immediate presence.

God's Delight
Blessingfully offers love
Its immediate embrace.

PART XXIV

SCIENCE AND NATURE

SCIENCE AND NATURE

1

Science assails.
Nature prevails.

2

Science says:
"I can."
Nature says:
"I eternally am."

3

Science goes
Forward and backward.
Nature goes
Inward and upward.

4

Science says to nature:
"I do not need you."
Nature says to science:
"But I love you."

5

Science is
Science's power-hands.
Nature is
Nature's purity-heart.

6

The human mind
Takes help from science
To succeed.
The divine heart
Takes help from nature
To proceed.

7

Science is
Prone to theory.
Nature is
Prone to practice.

8

Science is
Man's mind-experience.
Nature is
God's Life-Proclamation.

9

Science likes to duplicate.
Nature loves to emancipate.

10

When Science speaks,
God cries.
When Nature smiles,
God dances.

11

Science is
Power-supremacy.
Nature is
Love-intimacy.

12

Man relies on science.
God relies on nature.

13

Science says:
"God, I can live
Without You."
Nature says:
"Lord, I cannot breathe
Without You."

14

Science is at times known
And at times unknown.
Nature is always
Unknowable.

15

Science is revolution.
Nature is evolution.

16

Science longs
For matter's prosperity.
Nature longs
For beauty's universality.

17

Science says to the heart:
"Choose me if you dare to."
Nature says to the heart:
"Let us live forever together."

18

Science is
Mind-sound-communication.
Nature is
Soul-silence-union.

19

Science is
What man's mind has.
Nature is
What God's Heart is.

SCIENCE AND NATURE

20

Science does not know
And does not want to know
Where God is.
Nature knows where God is.
Furthermore,
Nature wants to live in God,
With God and for God.

21

Science uproots
Resistance-weeds.
Nature embraces
Resistance-weeds
For her total transformation.

22

Science believes in
Tomorrow's
Most powerful noon.
Nature believes in
Tomorrow's
Most beautiful dawn.

23

Science is
Complexity's seriousness.
Nature is
Simplicity's sweetness.

24

Science admires division.
Therefore,
It has division-adversaries.
Nature loves oneness.
Therefore,
She has oneness-fulness.

25

Science does not
Accept God's Invitation.
Nature is always all eagerness
To accept God's Invitation.

26

Science is spirituality's
Negativity-volcano.
Nature is spirituality's
Protection-umbrella.

27

The love-life of science
Is science.
The love-breath of nature
Is spirituality.

28

Science says to nature:
"Do you want to be recorded
By my camera?"
Nature says:
"Unfortunately not."

Nature says to science:
"Do you want to be captured
By God's Camera?"
Science says:
"No, definitely not!"

29

Science says to nature:
"To me, you are utterly useless!"
Nature says to science:
"To me, you are deplorably
  harmful!"

30

Science is always in a hurry.
Nature has Eternity
At her disposal.

31

Science is God-oblivion.
Nature is the living God.

32

Science, at its very best,
Amuses God.
Nature, at every moment,
Satisfies and fulfils God.

33

In the absence of science,
The proud mind can take its place.
In the absence of nature,
Nothing truly can take her place.

34

The human in us
Takes science very seriously.
The Divine in us
Takes nature lovingly,
Affectionately and proudly.

35

Science is energy-supplier
Of the mind.
Nature is love-multiplication
Of the heart.

SCIENCE AND NATURE

36

Science thinks
That it knows everything.
Nature feels
That God has given her
  everything.

37

Science is
The mind's warship.
Nature is
The heart's worship.

38

Science does not believe in
God's Will.
Nature loves to be within
The orbit of God's Will.

39

Science is the mind's
Glorification and gratification.
Nature is the heart's
Affection and satisfaction.

40

Science can shorten and frighten
The sound-pride of distance.
Nature can brighten and gladden
The silence-light of distance.

41

Science likes
Faultless exactitude.
Nature likes
Breathless sanctitude.

42

Science is
Science's capacity.
Nature is
Nature's Divinity.

43

Science is
The mind's ego-parade.
Nature is
The heart's God-revelation.

44

The unreal part of my life
Likes science.
The real part of my life
Loves nature.

45

Science is desperately searching
For the cosmic key.
Nature already has it.

46

Science is constantly demanding
Victory's success-trumpet.
Nature is beautifully dreaming of
Victory's progress-flute.

47

Science is
Earth-fame-gain.
Nature is
Heaven-flame-game.

48

Science is
A roaring lion-courage.
Nature is
A blossoming God-poise.

49

Sciences dances
With its stupendous discoveries.
Nature dances
To her God-gratitude-heartbeat.

50

Science, I salute you
With my humility-head.
Nature, I love you
With my affection-heart.

PART XXV

A TRUE DISCIPLE

A TRUE DISCIPLE

1

A TRUE disciple
Never argues
With his Master.

2

A TRUE disciple
Is the divine pride
Of his Master's heart.

3

A TRUE disciple
Smiles
When his Master's eye smiles.

4

A TRUE disciple
Cries
When his Master's heart cries.

5

A TRUE disciple
Lessens his Master's
World-transformation-
   responsibilities.

6

A TRUE disciple equally loves
His Master's frightening eye
And enlightening heart,
For he knows both are for
His fastest progress-delight.

7

The Master knows
That his TRUE disciple
Is not only available,
But also serviceable
Around the clock.

8

A TRUE disciple
Wants his life to be made of
His Master's nectar-touches
And thunder-kicks.

9

A TRUE disciple
Is
Insecurity-heart-proof.

10

A TRUE disciple
Is
Jealousy-mind-proof.

11

A TRUE disciple
Is
Negativity-thought-proof.

12

A TRUE disciple
Is
Impurity-vital-proof.

13

A TRUE disciple
Is
Lethargy-body-proof.

14

A TRUE disciple
Is
Unwillingness-life-proof.

15

A TRUE disciple
Adores his Master's
Tiptoe-footstep-whispers.

16

A TRUE disciple's
Genuine surrender to his Master
Is his indomitable courage.

17

A TRUE disciple
Knows that his Master's eye
Is the only Way
And
His Master's heart
Is the only Goal.

18

A TRUE disciple
Does not want to know
What his Master does not know.

19

A TRUE disciple
Does not want to know
What his Master
Does not want him to know.

20

A TRUE disciple
Is the amplifier
Of his Master's silence-life.

21

A TRUE disciple
Has the painful task
Of informing his Master
Of his brother-sister-disciples'
Aspiration-famine-life.

22

A TRUE disciple
Knows that his Master
Does everything
In God's own Way.

23

A TRUE disciple
Knows that his Master
Has no will of his own.
God's Will
Is his Master's will.

24

A TRUE disciple
Loves his Master,
The Love.

25

A TRUE disciple
Serves his Master,
The Service.

26

A TRUE disciple
Never dares
To limit his Master,
The Limitless.

27

The Master's blessingful smile
Is a TRUE disciple's
Nectar-delight.

28

A TRUE disciple
Knows that his perfection-dream-life
Is founded upon
His Master's satisfaction-heart.

29

A compassion-flooded glance
From his Master's eye
Is a TRUE disciple's whole world.

30

A TRUE disciple
Feels that every moment
Is a golden opportunity
To mould and shape his life
To satisfy his Master-Lord.

31

A TRUE disciple
Breathes in and breathes out,
Uttering one solitary mantra:
"My Master for my Master's sake."

32

A TRUE disciple
Feasts on
His Master's choice Hour.

33

A TRUE disciple
Is the beauty and fragrance
Of his Master's
God-manifestation-promise.

34

A TRUE disciple
Replaces his self-indulgence
With God-radiance.

35

A TRUE disciple
Knows that his Master's heart
Is his only home.

36

A TRUE disciple
Knows that the unhappy mind
Is the happiness-heart-killer.

37

A TRUE disciple
Knows no self-deception
And no God-dissatisfaction.

38

A TRUE disciple
Knows that if ever
He disappoints his Master,
He becomes a havoc
To his own self.

39

When a TRUE disciple
Asks his Master for protection,
The Master says,
"Behold, immediate rescue!"

40

A TRUE disciple
Says to his Master,
"Master, as your boosting is
    powerful,
Even so your scolding is merciful."

41

A TRUE disciple says to his
  Master,
"Master, in your compassion-eye
I am complete."
The Master says to his TRUE
  disciple,
"My child, in your
  satisfaction-heart
I am complete."

42

A TRUE disciple begs his Master
To bind him and blind him,
So that he can prayerfully and
  proudly
Walk with his Master along the
  way,
All the way.

43

Every day a TRUE disciple
Tearfully begs his Master,
"Master, do bless me with a new
  life
With the dust of your
  forgiveness-feet."

44

A TRUE disciple says to his
  Master,
"Master, it breaks my heart
That you have to wait
Such a long time
For my God-realisation."
The Master says to his
  TRUE disciple,
"My child, do not be a fool!
The Goal has already come to you
In the form of your Master."

45

A TRUE disciple
Knows that his past
Was in his Master's eye,
His present
Is at his Master's feet,
And his future
Will be in his Master's heart.

46

A TRUE disciple does not hesitate
Even for a fleeting second
To claim his Master as his own,
Very own.
Indeed, the Master is extremely
  proud
Of his disciple's self-taught lesson.

47

A TRUE disciple
Every day enjoys voraciously
Two meals:
His Master's compassion-eye-meal
And
His Master's forgiveness-heart-meal.

48

The Master
Every day enjoys voraciously
Two meals:
His TRUE disciple's
Devotion-beauty-meal
And
His TRUE disciple's
Surrender-fragrance-meal.

49

A TRUE disciple
Begs his Master to juggle his life
At the Master's sweet will.

50

A TRUE disciple
Prayerfully devours
The Master-obedience-nectar-drink.

51

A TRUE disciple
Vehemently shuns
The Master-disobedience-poison-drink.

52

A TRUE disciple
Begs his Master to make of him
A volleyball, basketball,
    ping-pong ball
And "love-and-serve" tennis ball.

53

A TRUE disciple
Begs his Master
Not to allow him to remain
A divided man,
But to make him a united man.

54

A TRUE disciple
Embarks on the spiritual journey
Thinking that his Master's way
Is by far the best way.
But while walking, marching,
    running
And sprinting
On his Master's way,
He realises that his Master's way
Is the only Way.

A TRUE DISCIPLE

55

A TRUE disciple
Has learnt from his Master
That the way of expectation
Has nothing in it.
But the way of surrender
Not only has everything,
But also is everything.

56

A TRUE disciple knows
That his Master's footfalls
Will compassionately, ceaselessly
And unfailingly
Call him to follow.

57

Each time a TRUE disciple
Comes to see his Master,
He comes with a burst of song-delight.

58

A TRUE disciple
Knows that he came into the world
To proudly hoist
His Master's greatness-life-banner.

59

A TRUE disciple
Knows that he came into the world
To sleeplessly fly
In his Master's goodness-heart-sky.

60

A TRUE disciple
Knows that his Master's heart-palace
Has thousands of entrances,
But no exit.

61

A lifelong prison sentence
The doubting mind receives
From a TRUE disciple.

62

A TRUE disciple
Eagerly collects
The harvest of his Master's will.

63

A TRUE disciple
Leaves his self-assertion-will
Scattered in the dust.

64

A TRUE disciple's heart-cries
And his Master's soul-smiles
Deeply enjoy
The hide-and-seek game.

65

The Grandfather-God tells
His TRUE disciple-grandchild,
"You are so cute!
You are so adorable!
My Love is all for you.
My Pride is all in you.
I am all for you,
My grandchild!"

66

The Grandfather-God
Says to His TRUE
  disciple-grandchild,
"My grandchild, you are so
  fortunate.
I placed before your father
An infinitely longer way,
But he has unimaginably
  shortened it
For you."

PART XXVI

I CLIMB UP, I FALL DOWN

I CLIMB UP, I FALL DOWN

1

I climb up
Immediately
When I love God only.

2

I fall down
Justifiably
When I want God
To love me only.

3

I climb up
When I have dedication-smiles
Inside my aspiration-tears.

4

I fall down
When my aspiration is empty of tears
And my dedication is empty of smiles.

5

I climb up
When my mind's equanimity
And my heart's divinity
Enjoy their transcendental
And universal partnership.

6

I fall down
When my mind and my heart
Are at daggers drawn.

7

I climb up
When my heart becomes
A God-obedience-feast.

8

I fall down
When I attend my mind's
God-unwillingness-banquet.

9

I climb up
When my heart's sincerity-tears
And purity-smiles
Grow, glow and flow together.

10

I fall down
When I jump into
The hostile turmoil
Of my mind's confusion-life.

11

I climb up
When I pine for
My Lord's Forgiveness-Smiles.

12

I fall down
When I indulge in
My God-unawareness
And God-unwillingness-life.

13

I climb up
When I readily, gladly
And eagerly accept
My heart's God-wisdom-light.

14

I fall down
When I greedily, stubbornly
And willfully cherish
My mind's ignorance-futility-
    night.

15

I climb up
And fly and fly in Infinity's Sky
On God-Compassion-Plane.

16

I fall down
And fracture all my limbs
When I board my
Ego-gratification-plane.

17

I climb up
When my heart becomes
The quintessence
Of angelic sweetness.

18

I fall down
When my mind becomes
The epitome
Of satanic bitterness.

19

I climb up
When my aspiration-heart
Is supercharged
With God-manifestation-
    eagerness.

20

I fall down
When I consciously
And deliberately enjoy
My God-indifference-mind.

I CLIMB UP, I FALL DOWN

21

I climb up
When I prayerfully long for
God-Satisfaction-Breath.

22

I fall down
When I arrogantly enjoy my
　mind's
Self-aggrandisement-game.

23

I climb up
When I stoically and callously
Disregard my mind's
Doubt-summons.

24

I fall down
When my heart deliberately
　embraces
God-faith-famine.

25

I climb up
When I have an allergic reaction
To name and fame.

26

I fall down
When I richly indulge
In name and fame.

27

I climb up
The moment I become
My desire-cremator.

28

I fall down
The moment I become
My frustration-follower.

29

I climb up
When I burn down
My doubt-bridge.

30

I fall down
When I sleeplessly and
　breathlessly
Build my doubt-bridge.

31

I climb up
The day my mind
Willingly goes with my heart
To visit God.

32

I fall down
The day my mind
Vehemently rejects the idea
Of visiting God.

33

I climb up
When I have complete faith
In my soul-compass.

34

I fall down
When I take my suspicion-mind
As my polestar.

35

I climb up
When I am in perfect harmony
With the world.

36

I fall down
When I cherish my mind's
Disharmony-discovery.

37

When I forcefully tear down
My mind's towering doubts,
I climb up
High, higher, highest.

38

When I sumptuously feed
My mind's brooding doubts,
I fall down
Far, farther, farthest.

39

I climb up
When I become
My oneness-purity-heart.

40

I fall down
When I become
My division-impurity-mind.

I CLIMB UP, I FALL DOWN

41

When I cry for the
God-necessity-experience,
I climb up.

42

When I take pride
In my self-analysis-experiment,
I fall down.

43

I climb up
Extremely high
The moment I relinquish
My ego-crown
And my ego-throne
Forever.

44

I fall down
To the very depths
The moment I proudly
And sovereignly enjoy
My ego-crown
And my ego-throne.

45

I climb up
When I just ring
My aspiration-heart-bell.

46

I fall down
Even when I gently strike
My ostentation-mind-gong.

47

I climb up
When I use
My aspiration-eye
And my faith-heart.

48

I fall down
When I employ
My overconfidence-mind
And my arrogance-vital.

49

When I take God
As my only escort,
I climb up
Immediately.

50

When I take either my mind
Or my vital as my escort,
I fall down
Unavoidably.

51

When I awake
From my spirituality-coma,
I climb up.

52

When I enjoy even unconsciously
My ego-drama,
I fall down.

53

When I use my God-devotion
To raise the world's standard,
I climb up.

54

When I use my pride-mind
To raise the world's standard,
I fall down.

55

When I pray to God:
"My Lord, do not lose
Your Grip on me,"
God smiles
And I climb up.

56

When I think I can steer
My life-boat
Easily and perfectly all by myself,
I fall down.

57

When I receive enormous joy
From every little thing I do,
I climb up.

58

When I get no joy
No matter what I do
Or how I do,
I fall down.

59

When I enjoy
My God-obedience-bliss,
I climb up.

60

When I enjoy
My God-disobedience-volcano,
I fall down.

I CLIMB UP, I FALL DOWN

61

When I become
My God-devotion-heart,
I climb up.

62

When I become
My confusion-addiction-mind,
I fall down.

63

When God's Compassion
Steers my heart-boat,
I climb up
Into the skies.

64

When I allow my mind
To steer my life-boat,
I fall down
Into the abysmal abyss.

PART XXVII

THE DIFFERENCE BETWEEN GOD AND ME

THE DIFFERENCE BETWEEN GOD AND ME

1

The difference between
God and me:

I ask God
To keep His Eye closed.

God asks me
To keep my heart open.

2

The difference between
God and me:

Independence
I want.

Interdependence
God wants.

3

The difference between
God and me:

I tell God
That my mind is now ready
  to do
Everything for Him.

God tells me
That His Heart has already done
Everything for me.

4

The difference between
God and me:

I love God
To fulfil my desire-life.

God loves me
Because He does not know
Anything else.

5

The difference between
God and me:

When I think of God,
I become my dissatisfaction-vital.

When God thinks of me,
He becomes His
  expectation-Heart.

6

The difference between
God and me:

I blame God
For every little thing
That goes wrong in my life.

God blames Himself
For my imperfection-life.

7

The difference between
God and me:

I pretend
To be the doer.

God pretends
To be the Actor.

8

The difference between
God and me:

God says to me,
"My child, are you ready?"

I say to God,
"My Lord, why are You so late?"

9

The difference between
God and me:

I tell God,
"My Lord, do You want to see
   My mind-forest?
It is so powerful.
You are bound to admire it."

God says to me,
"My child, do you want to see
My Heart-Garden?
It is so beautiful.
You will just love it."

10

The difference between
God and me:

When I see anything wrong
In God's creation,
I bark at Him.

When He sees anything wrong
In my creation,
He simply smiles.

THE DIFFERENCE BETWEEN GOD AND ME

11

The difference between
God and me:

My mind says to God,
"My Lord, why are You inspiring me
To arrive at my destination?
Can You not see that it will take me
Ninety-nine trillion steps?"

My God's Heart says,
"My child, only one more step."

12

The difference between
God and me:

God does not know
How to sleep.

I do not know
How to wake up.

13

The difference between
God and me:

I want
God's prompt attention.

God wants
My total satisfaction.

14

The difference between
God and me:

My dictionary has only one word:
Exasperation.

God's dictionary has only one word:
Compassion.

15

The difference between
God and me:

When there is a severe dispute
Between God and me,
God openly admits His defeat.

I do not accept my defeat
Even secretly.

16

The difference between
God and me:

I tell God,
"My Lord, You are too old
To understand my philosophy."

God says to me,
"My child, you are too young
To appreciate My Song."

17

The difference between
God and me:

When I am angry with God,
God pleads with me
To give Him another chance.

When God is angry with me,
I say to myself, "Who cares!"

18

The difference between
God and me:

I go up to examine
God's Mind.

God comes down
To sweeten my life.

19

The difference between
God and me:

God tells me to go forward.

I ask God, "What is wrong
With my going backward?"

20

The difference between
God and me:

God is ready
To give me everything for the
  asking.

I am not yet prepared
To give God anything.

21

The difference between
God and me:

I tell God,
"You can come to my house.
If I like You, You can stay with
  me."

God tells me,
"You can come to My House
And live with Me permanently.
Here is the key."

22

The difference between
God and me:

God says to me:
"Work is Love."

I say to God:
"Work is torture."

THE DIFFERENCE BETWEEN GOD AND ME

23

The difference between
God and me:

God whispers dreams.

I plunder realities.

24

The difference between
God and me:

Forgiveness
Is God's Meal.

Revenge
Is my banquet.

25

The difference between
God and me:

I proudly tell God
That ignorance is my boss.

God tearfully tells me
To give Him only one chance
And see if He is better.

26

The difference between
God and me:

I tell God
That I doubt Him quite often.

God tells me
That He trusts me all the time.

27

The difference between
God and me:

I angrily ask God,
"My Lord, where are You?"

God eagerly asks me,
"My child, how are you?"

28

The difference between
God and me:

I tell God,
"My Lord, how can I believe You
When You tell me
That You think of me all the
    time?"

God tells me,
"My child, how can I believe you
When you tell Me
That you love Me only?"

29

The difference between
God and me:

I am afraid of God's
Perfection-Dream for me.

God is not afraid of transforming
My imperfection-life
Into His Satisfaction-Heart.

30

The difference between
God and me:

I do not believe God at all
When He tells me that I am
His Heart's All.

God does not believe me at all
When I tell Him that my mind
Is my all
And I want my mind to remain
  my all
All my life.

31

The difference between
God and me:

I say to God,
"My Lord, it pains me so deeply
That I often speak ill of You."

My Lord says to me,
"My child, not true, not true,
Not true."

32

The difference between
God and me:

I say to God,
"My Lord, Your infinite Greatness
I desire."

My Lord says to me,
"My child, your inseparable
  oneness
I need."

THE DIFFERENCE BETWEEN GOD AND ME

33

The difference between
God and me:

I say to God,
"My Lord, I need perfection from
 You
For my life."

My Lord says to me,
"My child, I need aspiration from
 you
For My Heart."

34

The difference between
God and me:

I ask God,
"My Lord, when will You give me
Eternal freedom?"

My Lord says to me,
"My child, when will you
Cheerfully become
A citizen of My Heart-Kingdom?"

35

The difference between
God and me:

My very nature
Is to rectify God.

God's very nature
Is to justify me.

36

The difference between
God and me:

"My Lord, is there anything
That You would like to have
From me?"
"Yes, My child.
I would like to have
Your haughty head."

"My child, is there anything
That you would like to have
From Me?"
"Yes, my Lord.
I would like to have
Your pretty Feet."

37

The difference between
God and me:

Before entering into
A very serious argument, I tell
    God,
"My Lord, this time
I shall defeat You badly."

God says to me,
"My child, this time
I shall illumine you permanently."
Alas,
Neither of us wins.

38

The difference between
God and me:

God does not know
What frustration is.

I do not know
What satisfaction is.

39

The difference between
God and me:

God wants to feed
The world.

I want to transform
The world.

40

The difference between
God and me:

God consciously
Reveals Himself
To Himself.

I unconsciously
Conceal myself
From myself.

41

The difference between
God and me:

I cannot
Take care of myself.

God takes cares of Himself,
Plus He takes care of me
Lovingly, compassionately
And self-givingly.

42

The difference between
God and me:

God is satisfied
In governing Himself.

I am satisfied
Only when I govern others.

43

The difference between
God and me:

I enjoy living
In my mind-prison.

God enjoys living
In His Heart-Country.

44

The difference between
God and me:

I have no courage
To face myself.

God has the courage
Not only to face Himself,
But also to face me
And transform me.

45

The difference between
God and me:

My Lord's
Unimaginable Greatness
Surprises me.

My self-limitation
Surprises my Lord.

46

The difference between
God and me:

My Lord's
Unfathomable Goodness
Astonishes me.

My self-oblivion
Astonishes my Lord.

47

The difference between
God and me:

I want to impress God
By frequenting libraries
And reading and studying
Thousands of books.

God wants to impress me
By not reading
One single book.

48

The difference between
God and me:

I want to save the world.

God tells me,
"My child, I am pleading
With you
Not to take away My job."

49

The difference between
God and me:

When I go to God for help,
He tells me,
"My child, My help
Is immediately available."

When God comes to me for help,
I say to God,
"My Lord, my help
Is approachable, no doubt,
But not guaranteed."

50

The difference between
God and me:

I am
A stupid thought-carrier.

God is
A wise thought-observer.

51

The difference between
God and me:

I want my popularity
And nothing else.

God wants His Creativity
And nothing else.

52

The difference between
God and me:

I want to perfect
God's creation.

God wants to protect
My creation.

53

The difference between
God and me:

My teachings
Are locking me
Most deplorably.

God's Teachings
Are unlocking the whole world
Most compassionately.

54

The difference between
God and me:

When God teaches me
His Philosophy,
He tells me that His Philosophy
Has only three words:
Here and now."

When I teach my philosophy
To God,
I tell Him that my philosophy
Has only one word:
"Eternity."

55

The difference between
God and me:

I hesitate indefinitely
Before I speak about God.

God meditates most seriously
Before He speaks about me.

56

The difference between
God and me:

My motto is:
"Give up, give up
If you do not succeed."

God's Motto is:
"Wake up, wake up —
You will never fail!"

57

The difference between
God and me:

God enjoys
Humour-lightness.

I enjoy
Rumour-ugliness.

58

The difference between
God and me:

When I give God my good news
That I am
Unconditionally surrendering
To His Will,
God tells me,
"My child, I am extremely,
Extremely proud of you."

When God gives me His good
　news
That I am a perfect devotee,
I say to God,
"My Lord,
You could have told me that
A long time ago."

59

The difference between
God and me:

God is horrified
To see me greedily devouring
Ignorance-meal.

I am stupefied
To see that God has no interest
In my Nectar-meal.

60

The difference between
God and me:

God never thinks that He is
Extremely great.

I never think that I am
Shamelessly useless.

61

The difference between
God and me:

I talk and talk
About the roaring lions
Of my mind-forest.

God talks and talks
About the beauty and fragrance
Of His Infinity's Heart-Garden.

62

The difference between
God and me:

God asks me to be hungry
For His infinite Love.

I ask God not to be angry
With my finite anger.

63

The difference between
God and me:

When I offer a gratitude-flower
From my heart-garden to God,
God says to me,
"My child, you have given Me
Everything that I need."

When God offers a
    Satisfaction-Smile
From His Heart-Garden to me,
I say to God,
"Is that all?"

64

The difference between
God and me:

God asks me
To be perfect in my inner life
And my outer life.

I ask God,
"My Lord, I beg of You
Only one thing:
Just fall asleep until I wake You
    up."

PART XXVIII

GOD'S GREATNESS AND GOD'S GOODNESS

GOD'S GREATNESS AND GOD'S GOODNESS

1

God, Your GREATNESS
Has confused me.
God, Your Goodness
Has illumined me.

2

God, Your GREATNESS
Has entangled me.
God, Your Goodness
Has freed me.

3

God, I admire
Your GREATNESS.
God, I love
Your Goodness.

4

God, Your GREATNESS
Is one of the things
That I want.
God, Your Goodness
Is the only thing
That I need.

5

God, Your GREATNESS
Is my inspiration-greed.
God, Your Goodness
Is my aspiration-hunger.

6

God, I am praying to You
To hide from me
Your GREATNESS.
God, I am praying to You
To reveal to me
Your Goodness.

7

God, I salute
Your GREATNESS.
God, I embrace
Your Goodness.

8

God, do use Your GREATNESS
To control my mind-factory.
God, do use Your Goodness
To pilot my heart-boat.

9

God, Your GREATNESS
Frightens me.
God, Your Goodness
Enlightens me.

10

God, I pray to Your GREATNESS
Out of helpless fear.
God, I meditate on Your Goodness
Out of sheer love.

11

God, I tremble
At Your GREATNESS.
God, I marvel
At Your Goodness.

12

God, Your GREATNESS-House
Is unimaginably powerful.
God, Your Goodness-Home
Is unimaginably peaceful.

13

God, Your GREATNESS
Silences my pride.
God, Your Goodness
Feeds my humility.

14

God, Your GREATNESS
Shakes my entire being.
God, Your Goodness
Cradles my life.

15

God, I obey
Your GREATNESS.
God, I follow
Your Goodness.

16

God, Your GREATNESS
Feeds my curiosity-eyes.
God, Your Goodness
Feeds my sincerity-heart.

17

God, when I think of
Your GREATNESS,
I become the sun-driver.
God, when I think of
Your Goodness,
I become the moon-dancer.

GOD'S GREATNESS AND GOD'S GOODNESS

18

God, Your GREATNESS
Is Your transcendental
Vision-Eye.
God, Your Goodness
Is Your universal
Compassion-Heart.

19

God, Your GREATNESS
Changes my mind
With great difficulty.
God, Your Goodness
Changes my mind
Easily.

20

God, Your GREATNESS
Thunders.
God, Your Goodness
Whispers.

21

God, to me Your GREATNESS
Is nothing but a life-destroying
  Machine-gun.
God, to me Your Goodness
Is nothing but a
  life-immortalising Flute.

22

God, Your GREATNESS
Strengthens my mind-fort.
God, Your Goodness
Blesses my heart-shrine.

23

God, to Your GREATNESS
I submit my desire-list.
God, to Your Goodness
I offer my aspiration-list.

24

God, Your GREATNESS
Is Your stupendous Detachment.
God, Your Goodness
Is Your gracious Tolerance.

25

God, Your GREATNESS
Is our darkness-destroyer.
God, Your Goodness
Is our darkness-transformer.

26

God, Your GREATNESS
Is Your Mind-Orator.
God, Your Goodness
Is Your Heart-Listener.

27

God, my determination-mind
Looks at Your GREATNESS-Eye
With folded hands
And prays to You
For Your Blessings.
God, my devotion-heart
Sits at Your Goodness-Feet
And prays to You
For Your Forgiveness.

28

God, Your GREATNESS
Shuts my open eyes.
God, Your Goodness
Opens my closed heart.

29

God, Your GREATNESS
Waits for my receptivity.
God, Your Goodness
Creates receptivity in me.

30

God, Your GREATNESS
Is conditional:
"Give and take, My son."
God, Your Goodness
Is unconditional:
"Take, My child, take."

31

God's GREATNESS,
You are my mind-astonishment.
God's Goodness,
You are my heart-fulfilment.

32

God's GREATNESS,
My soul is extremely and
 extremely
Proud of You.
God's Goodness,
You are extremely and extremely
Proud of my heart.

33

God's GREATNESS,
I have an irresistible urge
To become like You.
God's Goodness,
I have a sleepless thirst
And a breathless hunger
To please You.

34

God's GREATNESS,
I shall proudly give You
As much as possible.
God's Goodness,
I shall give You my very existence
As soon as possible.

35

God's GREATNESS,
You are the Power,
Not mixed with limitations.
God's Goodness,
You are the Bliss,
Not mixed with frustrations.

36

God's GREATNESS,
When I am with You,
I become a readiness-mind
And a willingness-life.
God's Goodness,
When I am with You,
I am an eagerness-heart
And a selflessness-breath.

37

God's GREATNESS,
I fly into You
To enjoy myself.
God's Goodness,
I dive into You
To enjoy You.

38

God's GREATNESS,
You are Your Power-Sun.
God's Goodness,
I am Your Peace-Sky.

39

God's GREATNESS,
Your infinite Power tempts me.
God's Goodness,
Your infinite Love tames me.

40

God's GREATNESS,
The moment I touch You,
My life is blessed
With the greatest privilege.
God's Goodness,
The moment I touch You,
My heart is blessed
With the fastest opportunity.

41

God's GREATNESS,
You chide my slowness.
God's Goodness,
You encourage my readiness.

42

God's GREATNESS,
With my head I fly
Into Your high, higher, highest
Realities.
God's Goodness,
With my heart I dive
Into Your deep, deeper, deepest
Dreams.

43

God's GREATNESS,
You tell me:
"My son, just try and see
How great I am."
God's Goodness,
You tell me:
"My child, just cry and become
All that I am."

44

God's GREATNESS,
You are Your Victories.
God's Goodness,
You are Your Mysteries.

45

God's GREATNESS,
You are Your
Miracle-Summits.
God's Goodness,
You are Your
Blessing-Dreams
All-where.

46

God's GREATNESS,
You are my hope-excellence.
God's Goodness,
You are my promise-radiance.

47

God's GREATNESS,
You are my mind's
Mountain-summit
On my life-journey.
God's Goodness,
You are my heart's
Fountain-delight
Inside my heart-garden.

48

God's GREATNESS,
In Your Presence
I enjoy the proudest moment
Of my life.
God's Goodness,
In Your Presence
I enjoy the happiest moment
Of my heart.

49

God's GREATNESS,
The child in me wants to become
As great as You are.
God's Goodness,
The child in me wants to become
Inseparably one with You.

GOD'S GREATNESS AND GOD'S GOODNESS

50

God's GREATNESS,
When I look at You,
I become a pride-ocean.
God's Goodness,
When I look at You,
I become a peace-sea.

51

God's GREATNESS,
I am coming to You
With a return ticket.
God's Goodness,
I am coming to You
With a one-way ticket.

52

God's GREATNESS,
You command my obedience.
God's Goodness,
You inspire my obedience.

53

God's GREATNESS,
I am coming to You
With my heart's
Aspiration-flames.
God's Goodness,
I am coming to You
With my life's
Dedication-blossoms.

54

God's GREATNESS,
You tell me to conquer
The ignorance-world
Immediately.
God's Goodness,
You tell me to love
The weakness-world
Unreservedly.

55

God's GREATNESS,
I see the entire universe
Inside Your ever-widening Eye.
God's Goodness,
I feel the entire universe
Inside Your ever-blossoming
  Heart.

56

God's GREATNESS,
Your direct descendants,
Sri Krishna, the Buddha, the
  Christ
And others,
Have come from You.
God's Goodness,
These supremely chosen children
Of Yours
Live in You.

57

God's GREATNESS,
The Avatars come down
To extol Your Reality.
God's Goodness,
The Avatars come down
To manifest Your Divinity.

58

God's GREATNESS,
At times the divine Avatars
Play their roles in a human way
To lift up humanity and thus
Please You only, in Your own Way.
God's Goodness,
The Avatars cry for You,
Cry with You and cry in You;
Smile for You, smile with You
And smile in You,
Only to please You in Your own
  Way.

59

God's GREATNESS says:
"I have.
Eternity I have.
Infinity I have.
Immortality I have."
God's Goodness says:
"I am.
Eternity's Tears I am.
Infinity's Smiles I am.
Immortality's Song I am."

PART XXIX

I AM FLYING AND FLYING AND FLYING

I AM FLYING AND FLYING AND FLYING

1

I am flying and flying and flying
On my new God-obedience-wings
In Infinity's Sky.

2

Aspiration is singular.
Manifestation is plural.

3

Doubt rightly deserves
To be
A homeless beggar.

4

Love is
Mistake-proof.

5

Bury your impatience
Here, there and
All-where.

6

God asks for volunteers
And not for soldiers.

7

Man-teacher preaches.
God-Teacher teaches.

8

I am looking for
A permanent doubt-remedy.

9

God accompanies
My opportunities.

10

The outer smile is beautiful.
The inner smile is perfect.

11

Cancel your
Hesitation-performance.

12

Aspiration-decline
Does not become you.

13

Negativity's bloom
Is
Negativity's doom.

14

God does not command,
But expects
An eager audience.

15

Effort needed.
Grace indispensable.

16

I am bettering myself
To increase humanity's
Divine pride.

17

Soulfulness-barrenness
Is
Terribly shocking.

18

Nobody can outlive
His usefulness on earth.

19

There is a sempiternal bond
Between
My nothingness
And
God's fulness.

20

What is God doing?
God is looking
For a self-giving,
God-hungry seeker.

21

I must trust
The peace-dreamer,
I must.

22

I must trust
The peace-bringer,
I must.

23

I must trust
The peace-receiver,
I must.

24

I am giving you
The happiest news:
Your long alienation
From your soul
Is just over!

25

The perfection-soul is by far
The best mediator
Between
The two secret rivals:
The mind and the vital.

26

Imitation is an unforeseen
Failure-frustration.

27

I keep only four books
In my heart library:
Simplicity,
Sincerity,
Humility
And
Purity.

28

May each life become
A flower-blossom-beauty.

29

May each heart become
A fountain-God-obedience.

30

Man's outer life
Is
A fading experience.

31

Man's inner life
Is
An ever-heightening
And
Ever-deepening Realisation.

32

One flight can NEVER reach
The God-realisation-height.
Countless stopovers
Are absolutely needed.

33

Miracle-Masters are fated
To deplorable disciple-conditions
And
Blessed with a miracle-audience.

34

Devotion-superfluity
Is an absurdity
Plus impossibility.

35

The perfection-song
Hides
In the imperfection-gong.

36

The King of Light
Lovingly expects
My heart.

37

The king of darkness
Ruthlessly demands
My blood.

38

A delight-heart
Is the tailwind
Of a surrender-life.

39

Our God-aspiration-heart
Does not sleep.

40

Our God-dedication-life
Does not sleep.

41

When I claim God
To be my own, very own,
I do not need sleep.

42

My doubting mind
Wants to be
A self-illumination-questioner.

43

My aspiring heart
Wants to be
Self-illumination-billionaire.

44

My utter disaster
Is only a hair's breadth away
From my God-disobedience.

45

Do not wait
For God to approach you.
He may deliberately
Forget you.

46

There is no
Quick and sudden journey
To perfection.

47

I want my heart-compass
To turn towards
God's Polestar-Eye.

48

Our suffering does not pay
The admission fee to Heaven,
But our God-surrender
Happily does.

49

A surrender life
Is a perfect
God-answer.

50

A great many times
My life has been saved
By a wee iota
Of God-obedience.

51

You fool!
Grace descends
For your immediate acceptance
And not for your total rejection.

52

O my God-searching mind,
Fly and fly
Far beyond the domain
Of world-complaint-criticism-
   torture.

53

My Lord,
Please give me anything else –
But not freedom.
Freedom I misuse;
Destruction I invite.

54

Every day God loves to have
A letter from me.
Even my volcano-anger-letter
Gives Him true joy.

55

God and I disagree
Only on one point:
He emphatically tells me
That I am another God.

56

My Lord Supreme,
I just love
Your high Commands.
They are at once
Extremely challenging
And extremely inspiring.

57

My Lord Supreme,
I quite dislike
Your mild Requests.
They are so weak
And completely empty
Of inspiration.

58

My mind,
I have already chosen
My heart
And not you
To be my destiny-maker.
You can remain silent.

59

The longer I sit
On my knees,
The sooner God comes down
To kiss my eyes.

60

The ignorance-thief
Does not know
How
To stop stealing.

61

My pride is
My self-applause
Thunder.

62

Immortality loves
To live
In the heart
Of fleeting moments.

63

God's Face quenches
My eye-thirst.
God's Feet feed
My heart-hunger.

64

Not out of dire compulsion
But out of sterling affection
I always say YES
To my soul.

65

Change of work
Is rest.
This is my God-lesson.

66

The aspiration-elevator
Is available
Only in the heart-palace
And *not* in
The mind-cottage.

PART XXX

RETIREMENT NOT GRANTED

RETIREMENT NOT GRANTED

1

God does not want me
To have any retirement,
Not to speak of
Early retirement.

2

God with the Form
Awakens me.
God without the Form
Beckons me.

3

Conches blew
And trumpets blared
In Heaven
When my life became
An unconditional surrender
To God's Will.

4

I stand before
My Lord's Eye,
But I sing inside
My Lord's Heart.

5

A self-reliance-man
Unawares
Is hastening
His own doom.

6

A God-reliance-man
Is, indeed,
God's successor.

7

God's Compassion-Eye
Sows;
Man's gratitude-heart
Reaps.

8

Whomever I meet
On my way to God,
I ask only one thing:
Does God really love me?
This question has completely
Occupied my mind.

9

Alas,
Who will meet me
And tell me that
God is waiting for me?

10

Silence-teacher
Is ignored.
Sound-preacher
Is extolled.

11

When I walk towards God,
God happily
Shakes hands with me.

12

When I fly towards God,
God proudly
Embraces me.

13

Self-confidence
Founded upon
Self-importance
Is the most deplorable
Stupidity.

14

O insecurity-cherishing
Seekers,
Can you not hear
God's warning Bell
Ringing?

15

God loves us equally,
Even on the days we enjoy
Our ignorance-desire-life.

16

God safely breathes
Inside our minds
Only when our minds
Sincerely smile
At Him.

17

My oneness-heart
Never participates
In my mind's
Comparison-game.

18

Do you not believe
In God's Promise
That He will NEVER
Fail you?

19

My blossoming soul-flower
Is singing and dancing
Inside
My morning heart-garden.

RETIREMENT NOT GRANTED

20

Arise in the morning,
Proclaiming
The Victory of God
Inside the body
Of humanity.

21

Smile in the evening,
Proclaiming
The Victory of God
Inside the breath
Of humanity.

22

I prayerfully give God
The green leaves
Of my
Surrender-life-tree.

23

My soul's peace
Is
My heart's feast.

24

My Lord,
Do You know
That Your worst punishment
Is Your Indifference-Eye?

25

May each forward step of mine
Be blessed
By God's ever-new Face.

26

May my heart
Be precious
In quality-fragrance.

27

May my life
Be gracious
In quantity-beauty.

28

In the inner life,
Self-doubt is
The worst possible
Nightmare.

29

My self-giving life
Attracts God's Attention
Sooner than at once.

30

Power rises and falls.
This is the very nature
Of power.

31

Love rises and rises
And rises –
High, higher, highest.
This is the very nature
Of love.

32

What has fettered
My heart and my life,
If not my mind's misuse
Of my freedom?

33

Every day
God wants my heart
To be
An ultra-distance lover.

34

May my mind
Become
An inspiration-mountain.

35

May my heart
Become
An aspiration-fountain.

36

May my life
Become
A dedication-train.

37

My heart is always ready
To embrace my mind
With infinite affection.

38

Alas,
My mind is never ready
Even to say hello
To my heart.

39

God blessingfully tells
The regularity-seekers
To sit at His Feet.

40

God fondly tells
The regularity-punctuality–
Seekers
To come and sing
Inside His Heart-Garden.

41

My mind desires
To have an interview
With God
The Greatness-Height.

42

My heart pines
To have an interview
With God
The Goodness-Light.

43

My life wishes
To have an interview
With God
The Forgiveness-Delight.

44

My Lord,
Do give me the heart
Of a million tears
To embrace the dust
Of Your Feet.

45

My God-acceptance-mind
Is good.

46

My God-dependence-heart
Is very good.

47

My God-surrender-life
Is very, very good.

48

On my way
To God's Palace,
I am my gratitude-heart.

49

On my way back
From God's Palace,
I am my surrender-life.

50

My sweet heart-melodies
Are the sweet results
Of my sweet Lord's
Sweet Flute.

PART XXXI

A HEART OF ONENESS-PEACE

A HEART OF ONENESS-PEACE

1

Peace is God's own
Progress-Perfection-Satisfaction
In man's birthless and deathless
God-hunger-life.

2

Peace smilingly challenges
And immediately silences
My mind's doubt-thunder.

3

Peace and nothing else
Can ever be humanity's
Perfection-dream-fulfilled
Happiness-reality.

4

Peace is at once the safest
And the highest ascent
Of a truth-seeker and a God-lover.

5

Peace is humanity's
Ignorance-liberated
And God-treasured
Eternal life and infinite breath.

6

Peace is my conscious
And constant obedience
To the Will of my Inner Pilot
Lord Beloved Supreme.

7

My peace-heart blossoms
The moment it sees
My ego-mind's eclipse.

8

My heart and I receive
Abundant peace
Only when my mind loses
Its elephant-heavy
Unwillingness-weight.

9

My soulful love for my
   Lord Supreme
And
His bountiful Faith in me
Give me fruitful peace.

10

When my Lord's descending
Compassion-Eye
And my ascending
Aspiration-heart meet,
I feel in the inmost recesses
Of my heart
Peace in infinite measure.

11

The absence of peace
In your heart
Is the presence of my Lord's
Sorrowful sigh.

12

My Lord Supreme,
How can I have peace of mind
Every morning before I enter into
The hustle and bustle of life?
"My child,
Every morning ask your heart
To count My Heavenly Blessings
Long before you allow your mind
To count your earthly bills.
My child,
This is the only way
You can have peace of mind
Early in the morning
And during the entire day."

13

My life desperately needs peace.
Therefore, on the strength
Of my heart's aspiration-cries,
I must immediately silence
My mind's ego-thunder.

14

Farewell, farewell,
My old expectation-friends.
I must have an absolutely new
    friend,
Detachment,
If I sincerely need peace
In the very depths of my heart.

15

Reluctance, leave me alone,
Leave me alone!
Willingness, I am of you
And I am for you.
Let us pray together
To our Inner Pilot,
Let us together meditate
On our Inner Pilot
For peace,
Abundant peace, infinite peace.
He will grant us,
Out of His infinite Bounty,
At His choice Hour,
Peace, peace, peace
In infinite measure.

16

Only a heart of gratitude
And
A life of surrender
Can offer the seeker
Peace, abundant peace.

17

Peace I feel
In the depths of my heart
The moment my dedication-life
Rings the oneness-bell.

18

No resentment within,
No resentment without
If I want peace.
Enlightenment
In my heart of aspiration
And
In my life of dedication
Is what I eternally need.

19

I can have abundant peace
Only when my heart,
My mind, my vital
And my body
Are loving, faithful
And self-giving
To one another.

20

Peace is my soulful heart's
Gratitude-bridge
To God's Homeland.

21

Peace is my
Unconditionally surrendered life
To God's Compassion-Eye.

22

Peace is my sleepless love
For God's Protection-Feet
And His Compassion-Eye.

23

Peace I feel in abundant measure
In the inmost recesses of my heart
When I do not allow my
  mind-elephant
And my vital-tiger
To attack my heart-lamb.

24

Peace I feel in infinite measure
Only when I give the key
To my Lord Supreme
To open my heart-door
At His sweet Will.

25

I get peace of mind
The moment I ask my mind
To stop running
And I ask my heart
To start singing.

26

I receive peace
In abundant measure
When I take my mind
To fly with me
In my simplicity, sincerity,
Humility and purity-plane
In the Sky of God's Compassion,
Protection and Satisfaction.

27

What I need is a life of peace.
And to have a life of peace,
What I need is a heart of bliss.
And to have a heart of bliss,
My entire being has to become
A mounting flame of aspiration.

28

I can have peace
In abundant measure
Only from a non-stop surrender
To the Will
Of my Lord Beloved Supreme.

29

The moment I pray to God
For peace,
He immediately promises me
A better world.

30

Whenever I soulfully meditate
On world peace,
My Lord Supreme gives me
His blessingful surprise Visit.

31

Peace is in my secret
And sacred pathway
To my supreme
   gratitude-destination.

32

Peace I feel
In abundant measure
When my heart becomes
The rainbow-beauty
Of my soul.

33

Peace I feel
In infinite measure
When my life becomes
The fragrance
Of my gratitude-heart.

34

Every day,
Out of His infinite Bounty,
My Lord Supreme comes to visit
My heart-garden
With His Compassion-flooded
　Peace.

35

My heart's gratitude-tears
And
My life's surrender-smiles
Have given me immense peace.

36

I have peace of mind
Precisely because
I do not walk any more
Along the road of self-doubt.

37

Expectation-extinction
Is the very beginning
Of the heart's satisfaction-peace.

38

Purify my heart,
O my Lord Supreme.
I need peace.
Advise my mind,
O my Lord Supreme.
I need peace.
Guide my life,
O my Lord Supreme.
I need peace.

39

Liberate me,
O my Lord Supreme,
From my
Expectation-entanglement.
I need peace.

40

Great men come and go.
Oh, where are the men of peace,
Where?
I need them; I need peace.

41

In my hope-abundance-light,
I am all peace.
In my promise-abundance-
    delight,
I am all peace.

42

Only a heart of constant gratitude
And
A life of unconditional surrender
To God's Will
Are the two true possessors
Of peace infinite.

43

I can have abundant peace
If I can ring
My heart's temple-bell
Every day
Without fail.

44

I can have abundant peace
If I can sit
At my heart's temple-shrine
And pray and meditate
Every day.

45

I need peace
In the inmost recesses of my heart.
Therefore,
I must say good-bye
To my age-old restlessness.

46

I need peace
In the inmost recesses of my heart.
Therefore,
I must say good-bye
To my age-old insecurity.

47

Peace is in
The surrender-smile
Of my gratitude-heart.

48

Peace means
My conscious and constant
Willingness
To fly with God's Compassion-Eye
In His Infinity's Sky.

49

The pure appearance
Of my heart's blossoming peace
Compels the sure disappearance
Of my mind's teeming doubts.

50

I feel abundant peace
In the depths of my heart
When my mind loves
The oneness-songs
Of my wisdom-flooded soul.

51

If we want peace,
Then we must be fluent
In our soul's language.
What is our soul's language?
Oneness-light and fulness-delight.

52

God blesses only
An unconditionally surrendered heart
With His Infinity's Peace.

53

Expectation is everywhere,
In each and every individual.
But where is our aspiration?
Where is our dedication?
How can we have even an iota of peace
Without our heart's aspiration
And our life's dedication?

54

Peace will be yours,
Peace will be his,
Peace will be mine,
Peace will be ours,
Our treasure supreme.
Let us offer our heart's
Love-candle-flame
All over the world.

55

Instead of making ourselves famous,
Let us make
Our Lord Beloved Supreme famous
Here on earth
With our heart's mounting cry
And
With our life's dedication-smile.
Then ours will be peace eternal,
Infinite and immortal.

56

Peace is in
The purity-life
Of my ceaseless prayer.

57

Peace is in
The fragrance-heart
Of my sleepless meditation.

58

Peace is in
The fragrance-delight
Of my soul's birthless
And deathless dream.

59

We can have boundless peace
Only when we are fully awakened
From the slumber of millennia.

60

I feel peace infinite
When I climb up and reach
The highest height
Of my faith-mountain
And when I dive deep and reach
The deepest depth
Of my gratitude-sea.

61

I must be brave
To silence my mind,
If I want to have peace
In the depths of my heart.

62

It is I who have to come out
Of my mind's self-created
Melancholy-night,
If I want to have peace of mind.

63

I can have peace
In abundant measure
If I can sleeplessly maintain
My heart's aspiration
And observe my Lord's Footsteps
Inside the depths
Of my heart's constant cry.

64

Every morning,
At the end of my soulful
  meditation,
I receive peace from my heart's
Soulful rainbow-faith.

65

If my God-longing is sleepless
And sincere, absolutely sincere,
Then my Lord's blessingful Peace
Can never remain a far cry.

66

Not on the strength of austerity,
But by virtue of aspiration,
I can and I shall have peace.

67

Peace is always available
In the fragrance
Of my sleeplessly aspiring heart.

68

If I stop walking
Along the road
Of my dry desert-mind,
Then I am bound to get peace,
Abundant peace.

69

I must convince my mind
That God loves me
   unconditionally
No matter what I do,
No matter what I say,
No matter who I am.
He is moulding me and shaping me
In His own Way.
His unconditional Love,
   Compassion
And Blessings
I must try to feel
At every moment of my life
If I truly want to have peace
In the depths of my heart
Daily and sleeplessly.

70

If I want to succeed
In my outer life,
Then I must nourish hope
At every moment.
It is only with hope
That I can embark on my journey
In my outer life.
Then there shall come a time
When my outer life
Will be flooded with peace.

71

If I want to proceed
In my inner life,
Then I need confidence
At every moment.
It is by virtue of my confidence,
Divine confidence,
That I shall be able to make
　progress
In my inner life,
And this progress is all peace,
Peace.

72

A heart of oneness-peace
Is always beyond the reach
Of a doubting mind.

73

Let me not try to perfect the
　world.
I shall have peace of mind
Immediately.

74

God's Wisdom-Sun-Peace
Will claim me as its own,
Very own,
The moment I disown
My ignorance-mind-sound.

75

To become a servant
Of surrender-light
Is to become a master
Of peace-delight.

Notes to *A heart of oneness-peace*

1-5. Yale University, New Haven, Connecticut, 26 February 1989.
6-10. Brown University, Providence, Rhode Island, 5 March 1989.
11-12. Buchman Hall, New York City, 7 March 1989.
13-15. Buchman Hall, New York City, 13 March 1989.
16-19. Cornell University, Ithaca, New York, 16 March 1989.
20-24. Princeton University, Princeton, New Jersey, 27 March 1989.
25-27. University of Vienna, Vienna, Austria, 1 April 1989.
28-31. Kurhalle Oberlaa, Vienna, Austria, 1 April 1989.
32-34. Friedrich Ebert Halle, Ludwigshafen, Germany, 3 April 1989.
35-37. University of Heidelberg, Heidelberg, Germany, 4 April 1989.
38-42. Johns Hopkins University, Baltimore, Maryland, 13 May 1989.
43-46. Stanford University, Palo Alto, California, 22 May 1989.
47-50. McGill University, Montreal, Canada, 27 May 1989.
51-55. Chiles Auditorium, Portland, Oregon, 12 June 1989.
56-60. Homebush Stadium, Sydney, Australia, 5 July 1989.
61-65. Logan Campbell Centre, Auckland, New Zealand, 7 July 1989.
66-71. University of Auckland, Auckland, New Zealand, 8 July 1989.
72-75. Arie Crown Theatre, Chicago, Illinois, 20 July 1989.

PART XXXII

GOD WAS SIMPLY SHOCKED

GOD WAS SIMPLY SHOCKED

1. Introduction

On the strength of my inseparable oneness with the souls of my students all the world over, I ventured to write this book for their fastest spiritual progress.

If anybody takes these heart-rending and soul-stirring messages seriously and devotedly, and works on them cheerfully, bravely and unreservedly, they definitely will before long become supremely chosen hero-warrior-children of our Lord Absolute Beloved Supreme to fight against the age-old ignorance-night and establish His full manifestation on earth.

– Sri Chinmoy

2

God was simply shocked
To find my abominable
Plus unquestionably
   unpardonable
Carelessness, nay, callousness,
In not feeding Him
Every day
In the small hours of the morning
With my prayers and meditations,
Which He so desperately needs
And rightly deserves.

3

God was simply shocked
When I criticised
His beautiful creation
Ruthlessly.

4

God was simply shocked
When He saw me
Majestically and proudly
   complacent
And not at all concerned
About my spiritual life.

5

God was simply shocked
When He saw
My most precious enthusiasm-life
Had considerably disappeared.

6

God was simply shocked
To see
My devotion-heart-tears
Were totally missing.

7

God was simply shocked
To see me playing happily
With my ceaseless
Self-doubts.

8

God was simply shocked
To see me listening
To my doubting mind
Very faithfully.

9

God was simply shocked
To see
My vital and my mind
Secretly deserting
My aspiration-heart.

10

God was simply shocked
To see me
Extolling to the skies
My stupendous success-life
And giving Him
No credit whatsoever.

11

God was simply shocked
To see my heart totally empty
Of gratitude-flowers.

12

God was simply shocked
To see that I was doubting
His unconditional
Compassion-Eye.

13

God was simply shocked
To see
My unthinkable delay
In delivering
His express Messages.

GOD WAS SIMPLY SHOCKED

14

God was simply shocked
To see my doubting mind,
Restless vital
And lethargic body
Working together
Against my aspiring heart.

15

God was simply shocked
To see me feeding
My doubting mind
So happily and proudly.

16

God was simply shocked
To see
That I was not listening
To His lectures
Most attentively.

17

God was simply shocked
To see
That there was not even
An iota of sincerity
Inside my gratitude-heart.

18

God was simply shocked
That I was not maintaining
The same beauty and fragrance
In my devotion-heart.

19

God was simply shocked
To see
That I had lost
Two most valuable virtues:
Simplicity and patience.

20

God was simply shocked
That I was giving all importance
To my self-assertion
And not to God's Will
At all.

21

God was simply shocked
To see
That there was no genuine
Sincerity-breath
In my dedication-service-life.

22

God was simply shocked
To see me entering into
A self-styled
And self-sufficient life.

23

God was simply shocked
To see me losing so rapidly
My inspirational joy
In my spiritual life.

24

God was simply shocked
To see me incapable
Of knowing
What true surrender is.

25

God was simply shocked
To see me building fast,
Very fast,
My self-indulgence-tower.

26

God was simply shocked
To see
That I so often
Deliberately ignore
My Heaven-climbing
Responsibilities.

27

God was simply shocked
To see me playing
Happily and proudly
With hesitation, doubt
And suspicion.

28

God was simply shocked
To see
My spiritual discipline-life
So drastically dwindling.

29

God was simply shocked
To see me forcing
My aspiration-heart
To starve to death.

30

God was simply shocked
To see
That I was thinking of God
Less and less
As the days were passing by,
And thinking more and more
About my desire-fulfilment-life.

31

God was simply shocked
To see
That my overconfidence-life
Was taking me away from Him
Fast, very fast.

32

God was simply shocked
To see
That I was drinking deep
My success-glories
And not placing them devotedly
At His Feet.

33

God was simply shocked
That I was not at all anxious
To regain
My aspiration-heart's
Devotion-tears.

34

God was simply shocked
To find me
Wallowing in the pleasures
Of extravagant lethargy.

35

God was simply shocked
To find the drastic descent
Of my life's purity-height.

36

God was simply shocked
To find me quite happy
And unconcerned about my
Readiness-willingness-eagerness-
   heart-bankruptcy.

37

God was simply shocked
To see
The most unfortunate decline
Of my aspiration-dedication-
   speed.

38

God was simply shocked
To see
My utterly baseless feeling
Of inferiority
In every aspect of my life.
He also feels sad and miserable
That my inferiority-poison
Is slowly but unerringly killing
My aspiration-life.

39

God was simply shocked
To see
That I have given myself
A totally new name
Without His permission –
Even without His knowledge:
God-attention-expectation-
   frustration.

40

God was simply shocked
To see
My sesquipedalian list,
To be purely and breathlessly
   precise,
Of my catastrophic expectations
In my inner life of aspiration
And my pathetic expectations
In my outer life of dedication.

41

God was simply shocked
To see
My hopelessly weak inability
To establish
My inseparable oneness
With the streaming tears
And bleeding hearts
Of humanity,
Even for a fleeting day.

42

God was simply shocked
To discover
That I was enjoying
My stone-life-consciousness-
   emptiness-heart
For a very long duration.

43

God was simply shocked
To find
That I had already sold
My illumination-soul
And aspiration-heart
In order to pay the exorbitant fee
To become a brave soldier
Of ignorance-night.

44

God was simply shocked
To have
An unprecedented experience
In His Eternity's Existence:
My earth-bound insecurity-life
Devoured His Heaven-free Breath,
Instead of my devouring Him
With my unconditional love,
Devotion and surrender.

45

God was simply shocked
To find
That I was, in secrecy supreme,
Beating my mind-drum
Harder than the hardest,
Consciously and deliberately,
To obliterate my previous
God-readiness
And God-acceptance-life.

46

God was simply shocked
When He entered into
My sleeping, snoring
And utterly God-oblivious
And sanctimoniously
    self-amorous
Body, vital, mind, heart and life.

47

God was simply shocked
And unspeakably perplexed
And confused
When He entered into
My abysmal abyss-stupidity-mind
That had convinced me
Of my indispensability
In God's Life.

48

God was simply shocked
To see me playing
Hide-and-seek
With useless and lifeless
Desert-barrenness
Instead of treasuring and
    enjoying
The breathless beauty and
    fragrance
Of my heart-garden.
God whispered into my
    non-listening
And unwilling ears
That my darkest
Ignorance-enjoyment-life
Beggars description.

PART XXXIII

MY LORD READS MY LETTERS

MY LORD READS MY LETTERS

1

My Lord reads
My gratitude-surrender-letters
Long before
He does anything else.

2

The mind
Satisfies itself
By criticising God.

3

The vital
Satisfies itself
By disobeying God.

4

The body
Satisfies itself
By forgetting God.

5

The heart
Satisfies itself
By worshipping God.

6

The soul
Satisfies itself
By manifesting God.

7

I satisfy myself
By devouring
The dust of God's Feet.

8

My mind
Wants to possess
God's Height.

9

My heart
Wishes to be possessed
By God's Depth.

10

My philosophy
Is
An independent life.

11

God's Philosophy
Is
An interdependent existence.

12

My philosophy
Is
The manifestation of my
Supremacy-mind.

13

God's Philosophy
Is
The manifestation of His
Intimacy-Heart.

14

Alas,
My heart is afraid
Of diving.

15

Alas,
My mind is afraid
Of climbing.

16

Alas,
My vital is afraid
Of surrendering.

17

Alas,
My body is afraid
Of waking.

18

Alas,
I am afraid
Of transcending.

19

When God comes to me
As God,
I do not understand Him.

20

When God comes to me
As man,
I do not believe Him.

21

When God comes to me
As God,
I ignore Him.

22

When God comes to me
As man,
I ridicule Him.

23

When God comes to me
As God,
I hide from Him.

24

When God comes to me
As man,
I run away from Him.

25

When God comes to me
As God,
I instruct Him.

26

When God comes to me
As man,
I betray Him.

27

When God comes to me
As a flower,
I love Him.

28

When God comes to me
As a child,
I treasure Him.

29

When God comes to me
As His Life-Breath-Sacrificer,
I immediately become Him.

30

I forget
To tell God
That I love Him.

31

God forgets
To tell me
That He needs me.

32

I forget
To tell God
That He is extraordinary.

33

God forgets
To tell me
That I am not transitory.

34

I forget
To tell God
That He is always perfect.

35

God forgets
To tell me
That I am always correct.

36

I forget
To tell God
That He is indispensable.

37

God forgets
To tell me
That we are inseparable.

38

I intentionally forget
To touch
God's blessingful Feet.

39

God intentionally forgets
To touch
My boastful mind.

40

I forget
To ask God
Who I am to Him.

41

God forgets
To ask me
What I have for Him.

42

My forgetfulness
Of God,
God does not announce.

43

God's forgetfulness
Of me,
I vehemently and openly
Denounce.

44

My Lord,
Please tell me frankly
What You think
Of my spiritual life.

45

"My child,
Please tell Me frankly first
What you think
Of My unconditional
Forgiveness-Heart."

46

My Lord,
Please tell me
Once and for all
If You really love me.

47

"My child,
Please tell Me
Once and for all,
If you really love Me,
Then why do you always
Remain far away from Me?"

48

My mind
Cannot imagine
How my heart
Can be so self-giving.

49

My heart
Cannot imagine
How my mind
Can be so unwilling.

50

My mind
Cannot imagine
How the Heart of God
Inspires my heart.

51

My heart
Cannot imagine
How the very thought of God
Bewilders my mind.

52

God wants
Our minds to see
That His creation
Is divinely beautiful.

53

God wants
Our hearts to feel
That His creation
Is supremely fruitful.

54

God wants me
To add to
His eternally blissful creation.

55

May my mind
Every day
Play its role nobly.

56

May my heart
Every day
Play its role prayerfully.

57

May my life
Every day
Play its role unreservedly.

58

May I
Every day
Play my role unconditionally.

59

May my heart's aspiration-tree
Every day grow to reach
The highest height.

60

May my life's
Dedication-branches
Every day try to reach
The longest length.

61

May my outer life
Belong
To Eternity's Tears.

62

May my inner life
Belong
To Immortality's Smiles.

63

The desiring mind
Competes
With the world.

64

The aspiring heart
Completes
The world.

65

The desiring mind
Is indeed
A possession-hunger.

66

The aspiring heart
Is indeed
A renunciation-meal.

67

The desiring mind
Is our life's
Backward march.

68

The aspiring heart
Is our life's
Forward run.

69

The desiring mind says:
"I want,
Even if God
Does not want me to have."

70

The aspiring heart says:
"I need
Only what God
Wants me to need."

71

Sorrows and tears
Torture
The desiring mind.

72

Smiles and cheers
Promptly welcome
The aspiring heart.

73

The desiring mind
Does not realise
That its search for satisfaction
Is useless.

74

The aspiring heart
Cannot even imagine
That God has infinite Love, Peace
And Bliss
For the aspiring heart.

75

The desiring mind
Is the inevitable
Kiss of death.

76

The aspiring heart
Is the imperishable
Embrace of life.

77

The desiring mind
Kills the true fragrance
Of our inner life.

78

The aspiring heart
Creates a new beauty
In our outer life.

79

The desiring mind
And Infinity
Are not destined to meet.

80

The aspiring heart
And Immortality
Are destined not only to meet,
But also to become
Inseparably one.

81

When I go to God,
God asks me:
"My child,
When will you
Come back again?"

82

When God comes to me,
I say to God:
"I never thought
That You would
Come back again!"

83

When I go to God,
God asks me:
"My child,
Do you not know
Who you really are?"

84

When God comes to me,
I ask God:
"My Lord,
Do You ever care to know
What I am suffering from?"

85

When I go to God,
I am astonished to see
God's unimaginable Hospitality.

86

When God comes to me,
He is shocked to see
My irresponsible unreceptivity.

87

When I go to God,
God surprisingly asks me:
"My child,
What has brought you
To Me today?"

88

When God comes to me,
I angrily ask Him:
"My Lord,
What has kept You away
For such a long time?"

89

When I go to God,
He reminds me
Of the fact
That I am at once
His partner and collaborator.

90

When God comes to me,
I tell Him that
My mind is His secret admirer,
My heart is His sleepless lover
And my life
Is His breathless worshipper.

91

A peace-dreamer is he
Who sows peace-seeds
Everywhere.

92

A peace-lover is he
Who grows bliss-truth
Everywhere.

93

I am desperately trying
To change
God's Mind.

94

God is desperately trying
To open
My mind's eye.

95

I do not know
Where the salvation-food
Is prepared –
Perhaps in Heaven.

96

I definitely know
That the realisation-meal
Is prepared
Here on earth.

97

I pray to God
To give me
All that He has and is.

98

God prays to me
To give Him
All that I do not actually need.

99

I pray to God
To give me
His Beauty and Divinity.

100

God prays to me
To give Him
My duty and responsibility.

101

The doubting mind
Cannot preface
The aspiring heart,
But the aspiring heart
Easily can.

102

The doubting mind
Cannot efface
The aspiring heart,
But the aspiring heart
Easily can.

103

The doubting mind
Cannot chase
The aspiring heart,
But the aspiring heart
Easily can.

104

The doubting mind
Cannot race with
The aspiring heart,
But the aspiring heart
Easily can.

105

The doubting mind
Cannot face
The aspiring heart,
But the aspiring heart
Easily can.

106

The doubting mind
Cannot trace
The aspiring heart,
But the aspiring heart
Easily can.

107

The doubting mind
Cannot embrace
The aspiring heart,
But the aspiring heart
Easily, definitely
And lovingly can.

108

The doubting mind
Can obviously ignore
The aspiring heart,
But the aspiring heart
Cannot.

109

The doubting mind
Can obviously belittle
The aspiring heart,
But the aspiring heart
Cannot.

110

The doubting mind
Can obviously ridicule
The aspiring heart,
But the aspiring heart
Cannot.

111

The doubting mind
Can obviously falsify
The aspiring heart,
But the aspiring heart
Cannot.

112

The doubting mind
Can obviously berate
The aspiring heart,
But the aspiring heart
Cannot.

113

The doubting mind
Can obviously torture
The aspiring heart,
But the aspiring heart
Cannot.

114

The doubting mind
Can obviously bisect
The aspiring heart,
But the aspiring heart
Cannot.

115

God does not understand
The most complicated prayers
Of the mind.
Therefore
He fails to answer.

MY LORD READS MY LETTERS

116

God easily understands
The most simple prayers
Of the heart.
Therefore
He immediately answers.

117

The real friends
Are those
Who unburden your life.

118

The real friends
Are those
Who minimise your sorrows.

119

The real friends
Are those
Who maximise your joys.

120

The real friends
Are those
Who cannot brook
Insults and humiliation
Thrust upon you.

121

The real friends
Are those
Who dine with your success
And progress.

122

The real friends
Are those
Who brave your dire enemies
To save you.

123

The real friends
Are those
Whose lives are made
Of sacrifice-delight.

124

The real friends
Are those
Who unreservedly
And unconditionally
Help you
In secrecy supreme.

125

The real friends
Are those
Who sincerely connive
At your mistakes.

126

The real friends
Are those who take
Your Himalayan-tall blunders
As short as anthill foibles.

127

God the invisible
Becomes visible
In the beautiful eyes
And powerful hands
Of the real friends.

128

God the Heart
Lives most proudly
In the oneness-heart
Of the real friends.

129

Self-glorification
Delays
Our Godward journey.

130

Self-deprecation
Delays
Our Godward journey.

131

Self-affirmation
Delays
Our Godward journey.

132

Self-negation
Delays
Our Godward journey.

133

Self-mortification
Delays
Our Godward journey.

134

Self-acceptance,
Founded upon God-dependence,
Expedites
Our Godward journey.

135

God asks me:
"How are you?"
And not:
"Who are you?"

136

I ask God:
"Who are You?"
And:
"Why are You?"

137

God asks me
To do Him
A big favour:
"Smile."

138

My mind,
On my behalf,
Answers and shares with God
Its philosophy,
Free of charge:
"Give not and take not."

139

My mind wants to teach
My heart
Everything that it knows.

140

My heart wants to teach
My mind
Whom to love: God.

141

My mind
Is
My morning God-queries.

142

My heart
Is
My evening God-answers.

143

Now is the time
To make ourselves
Perfect.

144

Here is the place
For us to fulfil
Our Lord Supreme.

145

Determination is an award
That my mind gives
To my heart.

146

Satisfaction is an award
That my heart gives
To my mind.

147

God the Eye
Secretly
Scolds me.

148

God the Heart
Openly
Praises me.

149

My joy is in
My heart's
Pulling my life upward.

150

When I become
A man of success,
Worries chase me.

151

When I become
A man of progress,
God Himself comes
And embraces me.

152

My mind saddens me often
With its
Superiority-hunger.

153

My heart always gladdens me
With its
God-Compassion-hunger.

154

I am complete
Not when others
Love me.

MY LORD READS MY LETTERS

155

I am complete
When I love and need
Only God.

156

When I am in my soul,
I am
All illumination.

157

When I am in my heart,
I am
All aspiration.

158

When I am in my mind,
I am
All inspiration.

159

When I am in my vital,
I am
All determination.

160

Alas,
When I am in my body,
I am
All frustration.

161

Try to please your own mind.
You will have a new name:
Failure.

162

Try to please your heart.
You will have a new name:
God's Smile.

163

My mind has to arrive
At God's
Perfection-Shore.

164

My heart has to arrive
At God's
Satisfaction-Shore.

165

I must arrive
At my
Self-transcendence-shore.

166

In the morning
God gives my heart
His special Love.

167

In the evening
God gives my life
His special Peace.

168

My heart
Satisfies God
With its devotion-tears.

169

God
Satisfies my heart
With His Compassion-Smiles.

170

God
The Compassion-Heart
Gives.

171

Man
The confusion-mind
Refuses.

172

When God speaks,
The mind
Does not care to listen.

173

When God speaks,
The heart readily,
Willingly and eagerly
Cares to listen.

174

My heart
Is well-known
For its streaming tears.

175

God's Heart
Is well-known
For its Fountain-Forgiveness.

176

God's Eye
Frightens
The animal in us.

177

God's Heart
Awakens
The human in us.

178

God's Life
Feeds and treasures
The divine in us.

179

The aspiring heart
Throws itself into
Each and every project
Of God.

180

The doubting mind
Interferes in
Each and every project
Of God.

181

May our aspiration
Be the hope
Of the present generation.

182

May our realisation
Be the promise
For the future generation.

183

My mind
Shows my heart
The wrong way.

184

My heart
Shows my mind
The right way.

185

My Lord shows my mind
And my heart
His Way:
"Come My children,
Come to My Heart-Home."

PART XXXIV

THE DIFFERENCE BETWEEN A
FALSE MASTER AND A TRUE MASTER

THE DIFFERENCE BETWEEN A FALSE MASTER AND A TRUE MASTER

1

What is the difference
Between
A false Master
And
A true Master?

UNFATHOMABLE.

2

The false Master
Says,
"Be good.
I shall come and see you
Later."

3

The true Master
Says,
"I am here.
Come to me
Or
Stay where you are.
I am coming."

4

The false Master
Says,
"This world is full of suffering.
Run away!"

5

The true Master
Says,
"Make the world better.
Join me.
You are starting late.
Alas, so did I."

6

The false Master
Says,
"You are nothing.
Come to learn from me."

7

The true Master
Says,
"God tells me
That you are perfect.
But He also tells me
To help you
So that you can become
Infinitely more perfect."

8

The false Master
Says,
"Although God is in all,
Be careful, be careful!"

9

The true Master
Says,
"Since God is All,
Love and become."

10

The false Master
Says,
"I alone have seen
The Face of God."

11

The true Master
Says,
"Like everybody else,
I am also
The Heart of God."

12

The false Master
Says,
"Fear God.
If you do something wrong,
He will punish you."

13

The true Master
Says,
"Love God.
Without your love,
God says He is incomplete."

14

The false Master
Says,
"God is watching you.
Be extremely careful!"

15

The true Master
Says,
"God is loving you.
Be soulful,
Infinitely more soulful."

16

The false Master
Says,
"No hope for you,
No hope,
Absolutely none!"

17

The true Master
Says,
"Here and now, look!
You have done it."

18

The false Master
Says,
"Think of your
Countless imperfections first,
If you want to see
The Face of God."

19

The true Master
Says,
"Multiply and heighten
Your aspiration-flames,
If you want your heart
To be God's fondness-child."

20

The false Master
Says,
"I am God."

21

The true Master
Says,
"I am fortunate to know
That God is both
My Lover and my Beloved."

22

The false Master
Says,
"My perfection-feet
Are for you all."

23

The true Master
Says,
"My satisfaction-heart
Embodies and treasures
You all."

24

The false Master
Says,
"I have reached
The ultimate Height.
No more, no more to climb."

25

The true Master
Says,
"I am
An ever-transcending Dream
Of God."

26

The false Master
Says,
"My spiritual children,
What have you done for me?"

27

The true Master
Says,
"I am all ready.
Tell me, my children,
How can I be of service to you
In every possible way?"

28

The false Master
Says,
"I am
A supreme superstar."

29

The true Master
Says,
"God is
My supreme Joy-Giver."

30

The false Master
Says,
"Always enjoy
Your superiority-roar."

31

The true Master
Says,
"Always keep open
Your equality-heart."

32

The false Master
Is
Dynamically active
And
Dramatically assertive.

33

The true Master
Is
Soulfully and unconditionally
Active
And never assertive.

34

The false Master
Says,
"Give me your soul,
Heart, mind, vital, body
And earthly existence,
Everything that you have
And you are,
To expedite
Your spiritual journey."

35

The true Master
Says,
"I shall show you
How to place your soul,
Heart, mind, vital, body
And earthly existence,
Everything that you have
And you are,
At the Feet of God
To please Him in His own Way."

36

The false Master
Takes all the credit
When the disciples
Do something great for him.

37

The true Master
Gives all the credit
To God
When the disciples
Do something great for him.

38

The false Master
Sincerely believes
That he is God Himself
And, without hesitation,
He tells his disciples as well
That he is God.

39

The true Master
Does not claim to be God,
But he tells his disciples
That it is much easier for them
To pray and meditate
On God inside the Master's heart.

40

The false Master
Separates himself
From the disciple
Whenever anything goes wrong
With the disciple.

41

The true Master
Equally blames himself
When something goes
Seriously wrong
With the disciple.

42

The false Master
Encourages his disciples
To be in the world
Of competition.

43

The true Master
Tells his disciples
To be in the world
Of self-improvement.

44

The false Master
Enjoys playing
The mind-comparison-game.

45

The true Master
Enjoys playing
The oneness-heart-game.

46

The false Master
Does not want to admit,
Even to himself,
That he is false.

47

The true Master
Knows
That nobody can be false
And nothing can be false,
Since we all are
God's express creations.

48

The false Master
Proudly thinks
That God is his monopoly.

49

The true Master
Sincerely feels
That God is everybody's
Unmistakable possession.

50

The false Master
Says to his disciples,
"Empty your purse
To expedite
Your God-realisation."

51

The true Master
Says to his disciples,
"Empty your mind and heart
Completely
To expedite
Your God-realisation."

52

The false Master
Thinks
That Justice-Light
Knows no equal.

53

The true Master
Thinks
That Compassion-Height
Is unreachable.

54

The false Master
Powerfully blames the world
When something goes wrong
In his life.

55

The true Master
Immediately blames himself
When anything goes wrong
In God's creation.

56

The false Master
Is
Mind-power-addition.

57

The true Master
Is
Heart-light-multiplication.

58

The false Master
Is
A martial threat-supremacy.

59

The true Master
Is
Heart-openness-intimacy.

60

The false Master
Feels
His disciple-world
Is his constant headache.

61

The true Master
Feels
His disciple-world
Is his true
God-satisfaction-opportunity.

62

The false Master
Is
A world-life-negativity-announcer.

63

The true Master
Is
A world-life-positivity-affirmer.

64

The false Master
Tells the world
That the world-peace-dream
Is a costly joke.

65

The true Master
Tells the world
That the world-peace-dream-reality-journey
Has already begun.

66

The false Master
Cares for his own success
Infinitely more than
The progress of his disciples.

67

The true Master
Knows that his disciples' progress
Is, indeed,
His real success.

68

The false Master
Always sees his feet
On the top of
His disciple's humility-head.

69

The true Master
Always sees his heart
Inside his disciple's
Confusion-mind.

70

The false Master
Is absolutely sure
That he is
Mistake-proof.

71

The true Master
Sees, knows and feels
That he is
God's ceaseless
Compassion-manifestation.

72

The false Master
Majestically feels that
He is all.

73

The true Master
Happily feels that
He is for all.

74

The false Master
Is
His hallucination-mind-
Product-productivity.

75

The true Master
Is
His God's Heart-creation-
   creativity.

76

The poor false Master
Thinks that
He has been forced
Both by Heaven and earth
To carry
The world-responsibility-burden.

77

The fortunate true Master
Feels and knows that
He has been given
The rare opportunity and
　privilege
By Heaven and earth
To take care of
The world-beauty-garden.

78

The false Master
Says,
"I have, I am,
I can."

79

The true Master
Says,
"God has, God is,
God does."

PART XXXV

TWO DIVINE QUALITIES:
CONFIDENCE AND SINCERITY

TWO DIVINE QUALITIES: CONFIDENCE AND SINCERITY

Part I – Confidence

1

Only a self-giving devotee
Can have ecstatic confidence
In the depths of his heart.

2

If we can earnestly
And soulfully meditate,
Then we can easily have
Cheerful confidence.

3

Perfect confidence is not
In earth-possession
But in self-illumination.

4

To acquire victory's crown,
One must cultivate
Resolute confidence
In one's spiritual life.

5

If a seeker is not
Continuously blessed
With purity-breath,
Then his life
Will unmistakably betray
Arrogant confidence.

6

Success on the outer plane
Does not remain a far cry
After the mind has achieved
Solid confidence.

7

Before God-realisation
It is almost an impossible task
To have supreme confidence
In one's aspiration-life.

8

Devilish confidence
And destruction
Are immediate neighbours.

9

To have complacent confidence
Is the beginning
Of one's fast-approaching perdition
In one's inner life.

10

If you are a good seeker,
Then you will try
To earn confidence
In the depths
Of your aspiring heart
And not enjoy confidence
In your obscure and impure vital.

11

A disciplined life
Can unmistakably
Register confidence
In the searching mind.

12

When the clever mind undermines
Your spiritual confidence
In your life,
Do not be doomed to disappointment,
Even for a fleeting second.

13

Confidence in my mind
Wavers.

14

Confidence in my heart
Soars.

15

Confidence in my soul
Prevails.

16

My aspiring heart
Is
My intimate confidant.

17

My searching mind
Is
My faithful confidant.

18

My striving vital
Is
My usual confidant.

19

My awakened body
Is
My receptive confidant.

TWO DIVINE QUALITIES: CONFIDENCE AND SINCERITY

20

My dedicated life
Is
My serving and fulfilling
Confidant.

Part II – Sincerity

21

Sincerity
Is
God the seed.

22

Sincerity
Is
Soul the garden.

23

Sincerity
Is
Heart the plant.

24

Sincerity
Is
Life the tree.

25

Sincerity
Without intensity
Is futility.

26

Sincerity
Without eagerness
Is barrenness.

27

Sincerity
Without cheerfulness
Is callousness.

28

Sincerity
Without humility
Is absurdity.

29

Sincerity
Is the sweetness
Of our outer existence.

30

Sincerity
Is the fulness
Of our inner existence.

31

God embraces
The heart of
Sincerity.

32

God blesses
The mind of
Sincerity.

33

God treasures
The life of
Sincerity.

34

When a seeker is wanting
In sincerity,
His aspiration-heart
And dedication-life
Are bound to become
Spiritually bankrupt
Sooner than at once.

35

Sincerity
Is by far the best
God-Protection-assurance.

36

A sincerity-mind,
An openness-heart
And
A fulness-soul
Are most intimately
Inseparable.

37

When I become my own
Sincerity-heart,
God becomes
His fastest and strongest
Magnet-Heart.

38

The more I value
My sincerity-breath,
The stronger becomes
God's Manifestation-Promise
In and through me on earth.

TWO DIVINE QUALITIES: CONFIDENCE AND SINCERITY

39

In the battlefield of life,
We become the victors
Over ignorance-night
Only when
The sincerity of the mind,
The spontaneity of the heart,
The rapidity of the vital
And
The purity of the body
Work in perfect oneness.

40

Sincerity,
I do love you and need you.
But I am telling you
In all sincerity
That I love and need
God's Will-Manifestation-Delight
On earth
Infinitely more.
Nay, God's Fulfilment-Smile
Is the only thing
That I sleeplessly need.

41

Sincerity,
You are morality's
Loftiest height.

42

Morality is the excellence
Of the mind, heart and life.
Although spirituality
Is in morality and for morality,
It goes far beyond
Morality's territory-confines.

43

The human in us needs
Sincerity's perfect perfection
And
Morality's complete satisfaction.

44

The divine in us
Also needs the same.
But the divine in us,
Being consciously and constantly
One with God's Will,
At times does not abide
By morality's strict injunctions.

45

Humanity's complete fulfilment
Can and shall dawn
Only when humanity prayerfully,
Bravely and self-givingly
Accepts Divinity
For the sake of Divinity.

46

"Let Thy Will be done,"
Him to fulfil in His own
  Way:
This is sincerity's sleepless
  dream
And breathless reality.

Notes to *Two divine qualities: confidence and sincerity*

1-20. These twenty poems on confidence were written on 14 December 1981.
21-46. These twenty-six poems on sincerity were written on 20 October 1995.

PART XXXVI

EMPEROR-SMILES. ORPHAN-TEARS

EMPEROR-SMILES. ORPHAN-TEARS

1

I give God
A piece of good news.
God gives me
His Emperor-Smiles.

2

I give God
My proud views.
God gives me
His Orphan-Tears.

3

God the creation-lover
Is
A universal citizen.

4

My self-giving drill
Is
God's Heartbeat-Thrill.

5

My heart feeds
On God's Compassion-Will.
God's Heart feeds
On my world-concern.

6

My gratitude-heart
And God's Beatitude-Eye
Deeply love
Their interdependence.

7

I bid adieu
To my self-indulgence.
God gives me back
My self-effulgence.

8

Sleeplessly
My aspiration-heart
Enjoys the Beauty
Of my Lord's starlit Feet.

9

My God-surrender
Is shepherded
By God's constant Concern.

10

The mind-prayer
Is a long-distance call
To God.

11

The heart-meditation
Is a local call
To God.

12

Frustration
Is a useless zero.

13

Enthusiasm
Is a real hero.

14

I must begin my life
Once again
By dreaming the impossible.

15

Things that money-power
Cannot buy:
God's Pride
And
God's Satisfaction.

16

Is there anything on earth
As unreliable
As the human mind?

17

To be God's favourite,
The seeker must cherish
God's firm Grip
On his life.

18

Today's impossible dreams
Tomorrow give birth to
Not only possible
But also inevitable realities.

19

God does not trust you
Unless
You trust yourself first.

20

God needs you
Only when you love Him
The way God wants you to.

21

As God feeds my heart,
Even so,
God's Feet free my heart.

22

A faith-boat
Is always
Smooth sailing.

23

The clever mind proves to be
The worst fool
When it fails to see
Its destination.

24

The Whispers of God's Heart
Awaken my heart,
Inspire my heart,
Energise my heart
And
Immortalise my heart.

25

The ancient sincerity
Is needed
For the modern peace.

26

May my God-gratitude-heart
Be my full
Soul-satisfaction.

27

Superiority is a total loss
And not even an iota
Of gain.

28

May my life be a
Constant,
God-comforting smile.

29

Today I must unearth
My long-buried
Heart-riches.

30

You can never have
An iota of peace
If you are not willing
To wrestle with your doubts.

31

God tells me that
My surrender-life
Is the brightest star
In His Divinity's Firmament.

32

My starlit
Marathon meditations
Are paving the way
To my God-realisation.

33

My readiness,
My willingness
And my eagerness
Are the blossoming buds
Of my life-tree.

34

Self-doubt means
A thick forest of fears.

35

Aspiration's summit-rewards:
My life-mastery
And
My God-discovery.

36

Man dreams
Of drinking ambrosia
While enjoying
The lap of inertia.

37

God increases
His Love-Power for us
Infinitely more
When He sees our heart
Diving inward,
Our mind marching onward
And
Our life flying upward.

38

God's miraculous achievement
Is my unconditional
Surrender-life.

39

A self-giving heart
Grows younger
Every new day.

40

World-shakers
Are world-misguiders.

41

World-lovers
Are instant
God-discoverers.

42

An unseen God-server
Is undoubtedly
The God-Heart-winner.

43

The mind
Is a broken sleep.

44

The heart
Is a golden dream

45

Ambitions
Can be devoured
By a giant doom.

46

Aspiration
Can be embraced
By instant bloom.

47

Every morning
God makes a new selection
Of His crew members.

48

There is only one
True sanctuary:
The fulness of peace.

49

He who puts God-service
On hold
Will never be embraced
By God's Heart
Of gold.

50

God-devotion
Has the power to be
Infinite expansion.

51

Prayer-cries
Strengthen.

52

Meditation-smiles
Enlighten.

53

Prayer-fulfilment
Is a future tense.

54

Meditation-fulfilment
Is a present tense.

55

God cradles me
Between
My morning sunrise-prayers
And
My evening sunset-meditations.

56

God every morning asks me
To keep an eye on my mind,
My vital and my body,
Specially on my mind.

57

As it is true
That my life was
A God-ingratitude-gloom,
Even so,
My life is now
A God-gratitude-bloom.

58

God-aspiration-beauty
I was.

59

God-realisation-fragrance
I now am.

60

My Lord,
If You really love me,
Then every day
You must bless my heart
With the Sahara-thirst.

61

My mind wants
Immediate
World-attention.

62

My heart needs
Fond
God-Affection.

63

My mind,
Run, run!
Hide, hide!
Pride is fast approaching you.

64

Each time I go to visit
My mind-desert,
My Beloved Lord Supreme
Brings me back
And most compassionately
Helps me bathe
In my heart-river.

PART XXXVII

THE MOMENT I PLEASE
GOD IN GOD'S OWN WAY

THE MOMENT I PLEASE GOD IN GOD'S OWN WAY

1

The moment
I please God
In God's own Way,
God gives my eyes
The Beauty of His Eye
And gives my heart
The Fragrance of His Heart.

2

The moment
I please God
In God's own Way,
He makes my life
His Heart's own
Ambrosial Affection.

3

The moment
I please God
In God's own Way,
He takes me as an urgent need
Before He does anything.

4

The moment
I please God
In God's own Way,
My life becomes
An immortal protection-cradle.

5

The moment
I please God
In God's own Way,
My heart becomes
A flaming and climbing
Aspiration-flower-blossom.

6

The moment
I please God
In God's own Way,
The purity-goddess
Starts living permanently
Inside my heart-temple.

7

The moment
I please God
In God's own Way,
Each thought of mine
Grows into
An abiding affinity
With all the human beings
Of the world.

8

The moment
I please God
In God's own Way,
God compels me to forget
All my human foibles
And frailties.

9

The moment
I please God
In God's own Way,
A failure-life becomes
A total impossibility.

10

The moment
I please God
In God's own Way,
He blesses me
With His transcendental
Vision-Light-Award.

11

The moment
I please God
In God's own Way,
The doubt-deluge of the
   entire world
Does not dare approach
My life's progress-harvest.

12

The moment
I please God
In God's own Way,
He becomes my heart
And I become His Heartbeat.

13

The moment
I please God
In God's own Way,
The first thing He does
Is to illumine
Bright, brighter, brightest
The dark alley of my mind.

14

The moment
I please God
In God's own Way,
He and I immediately become
Two mutually enthusiastic
Oneness-offerings.

15

The moment
I please God
In God's own Way,
I feel inspired from deep within
To write God every morning
A gratitude-heart-letter.

THE MOMENT I PLEASE GOD IN GOD'S OWN WAY

16

The moment
I please God
In God's own Way,
He makes me an excellent player
In His Cosmic Game.

17

The moment
I please God
In God's own Way,
He commands me
Not to ever ride
My mind's ego-horse.

18

The moment
I please God
In God's own Way,
I see nowhere
Temptation-snares.

19

The moment
I please God
In God's own Way,
God tells me,
"My child, happily and proudly
I shall become
The slave of your slave."

20

The moment
I please God
In God's own Way,
God says to me,
"My child, I am burying
All your past
Evil deeds
And hurrying your future
Divine deeds."

21

The moment
I please God
In God's own Way,
God says to me,
"My child,
I have conquered your head;
You have conquered My Crown."

22

The moment
I please God
In God's own Way,
God says to me,
"My child, you have given Me
What you presently have.
I am giving you
What I eternally am."

23

The moment
I please God
In God's own Way,
God says to me,
"My child,
Now that you have pleased Me,
Ask Me for a boon.
I shall immediately fulfil you."

My Lord,
Please give me the capacity
To love You infinitely more
Than You love me.
"My child, ask for another boon.
How can I allow you to steal
My own most precious desire?"

24

The moment
I please God
In God's own Way,
God says to me,
"My child,
You have played your first role
As My lover most successfully.
Now I want you to succeed
In exactly the same way
As My Eternity's partner."

25

The moment
I please God
In God's own Way,
God says to me,
"My child, I am placing
The animal in you
Before My Eye,
The human in you
Inside My Heart,
The divine in you
At My Feet."

26

The moment
I please God
In God's own Way,
God says to me,
"My child, as it is true
That I am your shrine,
Even so it is equally true
That you are My temple."

27

The moment
I please God
In God's own Way,
God says to me,
"My child,
From today on I shall be
Your dearer than the dearest
And better than the best
  Messenger."

THE MOMENT I PLEASE GOD IN GOD'S OWN WAY

28

The moment
I please God
In God's own Way,
God says to me,
"My child, you and I
Have cried for each other
For a very, very long time.
Now let us start smiling
At each other
Throughout Eternity."

29

The moment
I please God
In God's own Way,
He whispers
Enlightenment
And I whisper
Astonishment.

30

The moment
I please God
In God's own Way,
I remain far beyond the reach
Of the random arrows
Of hostile fate.

31

The moment
I please God
In God's own Way,
Both my Mother Earth
And my Father Heaven
Become extremely proud of me.

32

The moment
I please God
In God's own Way,
My God-loving, God-serving
And God-manifesting capacities
Become the pride
Of God's Infinity.

33

The moment
I please God
In God's own Way,
My mind does not remain
Any more
An avalanche of impurity.

34

The moment
I please God
In God's own Way,
God welcomes me to study
At His Perfect Perfection-
   Satisfaction-School.

35

The moment
I please God
In God's own Way,
God tells me
That from now on
I shall have to follow only
A one-way road
To my Destination.

36

The moment
I please God
In God's own Way,
God asks me
If I am sincerely interested
In His manifestation on earth.
If so, He will bless me
With a two-way road
To my Destination.

37

The moment
I please God
In God's own Way,
He asks me to drink deep,
Very deep
His Nectar-flooded Will.

38

The moment
I please God
In God's own Way,
I see nowhere
My mind's
God-unwillingness-confines.

39

The moment
I please God
In God's own Way,
He asks me to sprint
For His world-astonishing
And world-fulfilling
Peace award.

40

The moment
I please God
In God's own Way,
God says to me,
"My child, stop watching Me.
Start participating
In My Cosmic *Lila* (Play)."

41

The moment
I please God
In God's own Way,
God says to me,
"My child, now is the time
For you to spread
The transcendental glories
Of My Vision-Light
Upon My creation."

42

The moment
I please God
In God's own Way,
God puts my life's desire-night
To eternal sleep.

43

The moment
I please God
In God's own Way,
God awakens my heart's
Aspiration-days
To play with
His Eternity's Silence
And
His Infinity's Sound.

44

The moment
I please God
In God's own Way,
God says to me,
"My child,
Claim My Immortality's
Ever-transcending Smile.
It is all yours."

45

The moment
I please God
In God's own Way,
I clearly see
My very earth-existence-life
Submerged
In an ocean of bliss.

46

The moment
I please God
In God's own Way,
God asks me to row
And He provides me with the oars
To arrive at the Golden Shore
Of the Beyond.

47

The moment
I please God
In God's own Way,
God puts an end
To my life's endless rounds
Of mistakes.

48

The moment
I please God
In God's own Way,
God asks my heart-quality
And my life-quantity
To smile at each other.

49

The moment
I please God
In God's own Way,
My self-glory-desire
Surrenders
To my self-discovery-aspiration.

50

The moment
I please God
In God's own Way,
I become
My gratitude-heart-presentation
And God becomes
His Infinitude-Heart-
   Compassion.

51

The moment
I please God
In God's own Way,
God tells me,
"My child, I am sure,
Like Me,
You will never take
A leave of absence."

52

The moment
I please God
In God's own Way,
My Lord promises me
That every morning
He will take a pleasure-walk
In my heart-garden.

53

The moment
I please God
In God's own Way,
God teaches me the supreme art
Of tuning my heart
To His universal Heart.

54

The moment
I please God
In God's own Way,
I am shocked to see God
Taking me as another God.

55

The moment
I please God
In God's own Way,
God immediately wants me
To enjoy
His thunderous applause.

56

The moment
I please God
In God's own Way,
God opens the door
Of His Eternity's Silence.

57

The moment
I please God
In God's own Way,
My heart-sky starts ringing
With the music of angels.

58

The moment
I please God
In God's own Way,
God tells me that from now on
I will be able to touch
His Feet
At any moment I want to.

59

The moment
I please God
In God's own Way,
God tells me to draw in
The fragrance
Of His Eternity's Breath.

60

The moment
I please God
In God's own Way,
God blesses me
With the blissful waves
Of His Touch.

61

The moment
I please God
In God's own Way,
God starts defending me
Against both earth and Heaven's
Accusations.

62

The moment
I please God
In God's own Way,
I become the "News of the Day"
Both in Heaven and on earth.

63

The moment
I please God
In God's own Way,
My heart throbs
With devotion-tears
And God's Heart throbs
With Pride-Smiles.

64

The moment
I please God
In God's own Way,
My life becomes
A fully blossomed lotus-heart
For God-worship.

65

The moment
I please God
In God's own Way,
My heart becomes
A sleepless aspiration-boat
And my life becomes
A breathless dedication-train.

66

The moment
I please God
In God's own Way,
He immediately asks me
To decorate
His Heart-Home
In my own way.

67

The moment
I please God
In God's own Way,
I tell Him, "My Lord,
I do not need
Even Your infinite Delight.
I need only
Your constant Command."

68

The moment
I please God
In God's own Way,
I devour the dust
Of God's
Sweetness-Oneness-Fulness-Will.

69

The moment
I please God
In God's own Way,
God gives me the capacity
To fulfil Him
At every moment
On a very colossal scale.

70

The moment
I please God
In God's own Way,
He tells me to become
An everlasting contribution
To His Mission.

71

The moment
I please God
In God's own Way,
I compel the long expedition
Of ignorance-night
To halt.

72

The moment
I please God
In God's own Way,
My heart-gratitude-smiles
Thrill God's Heart
Far more
Than I can ever imagine.

73

The moment
I please God
In God's own Way,
I revel in God's
Peaceful Heart
And
Blissful Embrace.

74

The moment
I please God
In God's own Way,
He tells me that
Each heartbeat of mine
Has to be His own
Manifestation-life's watchword.

75

The moment
I please God
In God's own Way,
I dance in the core
Of God's
Compassion-flooded Fondness.

76

The moment
I please God
In God's own Way,
God tells me,
"My child, from now on
You will be
The doctor of your mind."

77

The moment
I please God
In God's own Way,
God tells me,
"My child,
I am inhaling
Your life-tears.
You inhale
My Heart-Smiles."

78

The moment
I please God
In God's own Way,
God tells me,
"My child,
Start immediately
Energising yourself
With self-mastery
And God-discovery."

79

The moment
I please God
In God's own Way,
I come to realise that
Heaven-Beauty is God's Eye
And
Earth-fragrance is God's Heart.

80

The moment
I please God
In God's own Way,
God tells me,
"My child, from now on
I shall set your pace
According to My need.
You must neither push
Nor pull yourself."

THE MOMENT I PLEASE GOD IN GOD'S OWN WAY

81

The moment
I please God
In God's own Way,
God tells me,
"My child, no more rest!
Rest is a luxury
And not a necessity."

82

The moment
I please God
In God's own Way,
God tells me,
"My child, from now on
Yours will be a life of heart-living
And not a life of
   mind-scheduling."

83

The moment
I please God
In God's own Way,
God tells me,
"My child, from now on
Watch and listen to your heart-sky.
It speaks.
It speaks exactly like Me."

84

The moment
I please God
In God's own Way,
God tells me,
"My child, from now on
My Heart shall direct your choice
And
My Hand shall direct your voice."

85

The moment
I please God
In God's own Way,
God tells me,
"My child,
Although life has dealt you
Many, many, many cruel blows,
Remember,
You are my Eternity's Concern,
Infinity's Joy
And Immortality's Pride."

86

The moment
I please God
In God's own Way,
God immediately quickens
My heart's God-pulse.

87

The moment
I please God
In God's own Way,
He promises me
That He will unmistakably
Count on me
In times of His spiritual
Emergencies.

88

The moment
I please God
In God's own Way,
I come to realise
That my God-obedience
Is such a small price
To pay.

89

The moment
I please God
In God's own Way,
God says to me,
"My child, from now on
My Will only
Will prevail in your life –
This fact is certain."

90

The moment
I please God
In God's own Way,
I come to realise
That from that very moment
My life shall thrive only
On God-hunger.

91

The moment
I please God
In God's own Way,
God says to me,
"My child,
The telephone line
Between your heart
And My Heart
Will never be out of order."

92

The moment
I please God
In God's own Way,
God tells me
That from now on
His Sculptor-Hands
Shall fashion my life.

93

The moment
I please God
In God's own Way,
To my great surprise,
God shows me
That my God-longing-tears
Are at once
Birthless and deathless.

94

The moment
I please God
In God's own Way,
He tells me His Life-Story
And makes me
His Heart-dictionary.

95

The moment
I please God
In God's own Way,
My Lord blesses me –
My heart, my mind, my vital
And my body –
With gigantic soul-strides
To arrive
At my ultimate Goal.

PART XXXVIII

MY SUNRISE-HEART, PART 1

MY SUNRISE-HEART, PART 1

1

God's Eye watches me.
God's Heart waits for me.
God's Life feeds my all.

2

My mind,
Stop making constant excuses.
My heart,
Stop making daily excuses.
Can you not see
That your older brother, soul,
Makes no mistake?

3

From today on, like my soul,
My heart, my mind, my vital,
My body —
Everything that I have and am —
Shall love God only.
A lifelong dream
Has finally come true.

4

My heart-wisdom needs
God-blessed humility.
Humility needs
The feet of universality
For its complete illumination
And total satisfaction.

5

Ignorance-walls can imprison
My God-doubting mind,
But never my God-loving heart.

6

With redoubled enthusiasm,
I am feeding my eyes
With the Beauty
Of my Lord's Eye.

7

With redoubled enthusiasm,
I am kissing each speck of dust
Of my Supreme Lord's Feet.

8

There must be no going back
On my full God-manifestation
And God-satisfaction-promises.

9

When we give God
Our world-complaint list,
God swims in the sea
Of His Heart-Tears.

10

Man begs God to increase
His Infinity's capacity
To forgive him.
God begs man to increase
His divinity's capacity
To receive God.

11

We must never dream
Of enlightenment
Unless and until we have
Prayerfully and soulfully offered
Our absolute loyalty
To our God-satisfaction-
 commitment.

12

The mind and the vital every day
Must go to the iron
 discipline-school
To be ready for the acceptance
Of God-Commands.

13

Do you want to know why
God has singled me out?
He has singled me out
Not because I love Him more
Than anybody else loves Him,
But because He has given me
More God-hunger
Than He has given to anybody
 else.

14

Self-mastery pioneers
To the outer world
Of surprising success-life.
God-discovery pioneers
To the inner world
Of astonishing progress-heart.

15

One powerful doubt of the mind
Can easily derail
The running, blissful train
Of the heart.

16

My desire-achievement-fame
Is
My aspiration-enlightenment-
 shame.

17

To love God
Unconditionally
Is to appoint God
Permanently.

18

When I fear God,
God tells me that
I disappoint Him
Infinitely more
Than I can ever imagine.

19

Enthusiasm at once
Uproots my mind-jungle
And
Illumines my heart-temple.

20

God's Love and Fondness
For me
Become measureless
When my heart-tears
Blind His Eye completely.

21

My soul,
Although my heart, my mind
And my vital
Fail you again and again,
Please do not stop showing them
The way
To the Golden Shore.

22

My heart,
Can you not start loving
Our Lord Beloved Supreme
Every day a little more?

23

Each new prayer that I offer
To my Lord Beloved Supreme
Adds a new candle
To my heart-shrine.

24

When my mind steers,
My heart-tears
Become uncontrollable.

25

My knowledge-light
Is my mind-development.
My wisdom-sun
Is my life-enlightenment.

26

My mind,
When are you going to stop
Your marathon criticism
Of our Lord Beloved Supreme?

27

What I need
Is a gramophone-heart
And not a microphone-mind.

28

My vital,
My Lord Beloved Supreme
Wants you to show Him
Your dynamism.
Alas, you are showing Him
Your aggression instead.

29

My body,
My Lord Beloved Supreme
Wants you to be
His own sacred temple.
Alas, you have turned yourself
    into
A lifeless, worthless and useless
Piece of stone.

30

The life that offers everything
Owns
Eternity-Infinity-Immortality's
Absolute Supreme.

31

A gratitude-heart
Is to discover on earth
A Heaven-delivered rose.

32

My surrender-strength
And my Lord's
Satisfaction-length
Simultaneously increase.

33

When my Absolute Beloved
Lord Supreme
Is a *thought,*
I slowly walk.

34

When my Absolute Beloved
Lord Supreme
Is a *will,*
I bravely march.

35

When my Absolute Beloved
Lord Supreme
Is a *smile,*
I speedily run.

36

When my Absolute Beloved
Lord Supreme
Is an *embrace,*
I unmistakably reach
My Destination.

37

When I reach my Destination,
My Absolute Beloved
Lord Supreme tells me:
"My child, I am tired.
I want you to take care of My
  creation
Until I have regained fully
My Paradise-Dream-
  manifestation
On earth."

38

My aspiration-heart
Echoes and re-echoes
One message:
"No gloom, no gloom!
All bloom, all bloom!"

39

My God-faith doubles
And redoubles
Each time I breathe it.

40

Father Heaven greets me
Smilingly and proudly
Only when I am
Sleeplessly and breathlessly
On Mother Earth's side.

41

God loves me more,
Abundantly more
And infinitely more,
When I entertain Him.

42

I love God more,
Abundantly more
And infinitely more,
When He enlightens me.

43

If I constantly keep my eye
On my God-representative-soul
On earth,
Then I will never fail.
My life-boat will only sail and sail.

44

As long as I safeguard
My God-surrender-promise-
   fulfilment,
I do not have to think of
   anything else
On earth.

45

I pray to God's Heart
For His Forgiveness-Sun.
God prays to my heart
For my receptivity-sky.

46

My mind loves
Constant secrecy.
My heart loves
Soulful intimacy.
My soul loves
God-ecstasy.

47

God teaches me how
To invoke Him and welcome Him
Every morning
With my sleepless heart
And my breathless breath.

48

Only my heart-tears
Have the stupendous capacity
To increase
My God-love, God-devotion
And God-surrender-intensity.

49

We just want to watch
God's Cosmic Play,
But God eagerly wants us
To participate in His Cosmic Play.

50

Alas, when will I be ready
To be a self-giving member
Of God's
Peace-Bliss-Manifestation-Society
On earth?

51

I may not be familiar
With God's Will,
But that must not prevent me
From surrendering my earth-existence
To God's Will.

52

If I love God's Will
A little more,
His Love of me
Will immediately be more,
Ever more and infinitely more.

53

Alas, my mind always tells me
That my mind is the only God
And there has been no other God
Since the beginning of creation.

54

My heart tells me in all sincerity
That my heart is not God,
But it is more than willing
And eager
To help me and take me to God.

55

May each and every prayer
And meditation of mine
Become sweet perfume
In my Lord's Heart-Garden.

56

God the Mother tells me,
"My child, do not be in a hurry.
Still there is plenty of time."
God the Father tells me,
"My son, it is so late!
What is wrong with you?"

57

My Lord Beloved Supreme,
From today on
I shall not give You any more
My ingratitude-life-experience.

58

My Supreme,
To You my solemn promise:
No more desire-indulgence,
But aspiration-effulgence.

59

May my aspiration-heart
Have a sleepless
And breathless breath.

60

Meditation is silence.
Silence is God
In His Infinity's Smile.

61

Not for a fleeting second
Do I belong to myself.
I belong only to my
  Lord Supreme
Eternally.

62

Not only tomorrow,
But even the next moment
Is too late
To please my Lord Supreme.

63

My Lord,
You do not come often,
And even when You come,
You do not stay long.
How I wish You could change
Your Cosmic Plan!

64

The highly developed souls
Live in the silence-breath
Of God's Infinity.

65

When I pray soulfully
And meditate deeply,
I see only two things:
God's Protection-Cradle
And
God's Satisfaction-Smile.

66

My aspiration-heart
And my service-life
Must be utilised unreservedly,
Unconditionally, sleeplessly
And breathlessly.

67

I was born to offer
Each and every heartbeat
Of mine
Only to my Lord Supreme.

68

When I banished
My fault-finding mind,
God immediately gave me
His own all-embracing Heart.

69

My heart loves and enjoys
The Beauty
Of my Absolute Lord
   Supreme's Smiles.

70

My Absolute Lord Supreme's
   Heart
Loves and enjoys the fragrance
Of my heart's tears.

71

My God-invocation-heart
And God's Satisfaction-Joy-Pride
Echo and re-echo simultaneously.

72

Unlike the impersonal God,
The personal God cannot be
Beyond the realm of suffering.
This is what I know
From my God-oneness-heart.

73

There is a yawning gulf
Between God taking human birth
And man taking divine birth.

74

My mind loves
Ego-assertion.
My heart loves
Oneness-perfection.

75

My Lord tells me that
I may lose sight of Him
Even if I fix my eyes
On His outer Feet,
But I shall never lose sight of Him
If I fix my eyes
On His inner Heart.

76

My Lord, I am ready
To be scolded by You mercilessly
At every moment,
Provided You tell me that
You will derive true satisfaction
From Your Scolding.

77

When my life becomes
Voracious God-hunger,
God immediately makes me
A perfect
World-ignorance-hunter.

78

My Lord laughs and laughs
At my self-styled austere mind,
But He is all Love for and all
　Pride in
My self-giving, sincere heart.

79

My mind has to unlearn
Almost everything.
My heart has to yearn for God
Sleeplessly and breathlessly.
My life has to earn
God's Compassion-flooded Eye
And His Forgiveness-Ocean-
　Heart.

80

From my life to my death
I am a God-Destination-arriving
Sailboat.
From my death to my life,
I am a God-serving
World-ocean liner.

81

My heart sings, plays and dances
In ecstasy supreme
When it sees my Master's
Gladness-smiles.

82

My heart dies
The moment it sees my Master's
Sadness-tears.

83

Time salutes and stops
When my Master proudly
   expresses
His love, affection, sweetness
And fondness for me.

84

Every morning
My Master helps my heart
To wake up
With his heart's sunrise-beauty.

85

My Master,
Out of his infinite bounty,
Cautioned and warned me
Of the tragic destruction-descent
Of my disobedience-life.

86

O my insecurity-mind,
Do not whine.
O my insecurity-heart,
Do not cry.
Behold, our Master
With his compassion-flooded eye
Is fast approaching us!

87

When my Master appears,
He immediately says
To my frustration-mind,
Frustration-vital and
   frustration-body,
"Stop!
Enough of your stupidity-pride!"
He then says to my heart,
"Enjoy no more ignorance-sleep.
I want you to accept some of my
World-transformation-
   responsibilities."

88

My Master smilingly yet sternly
Appears and says to me:
"I am sure this time
My iron rod will work
Since, up until now,
My sweetness-flute
Has sadly failed."

89

Master, Master,
Please tell me how you love me
More than I love you.
"My child,
Your heart needs repair.
Leave it with me just for an hour.
I will do the needful."

90

My Master does not come alone.
He carries with him
His heart-home
So that his sweet children
Do not wander any more
Inside their mind-jungles.

91

Master, Master, over the years
I have given you so many things.
It seems to me that you have shown me
No sense of appreciation.
Master, this time I have
Two very special gifts for you.
I am sure you will enjoy them.

"My child, tell me, tell me.
I am all eagerness."

Master, this time I shall give you
My gratitude-heart
And
My surrender-life-beauty-fountains.

92

Master, Master,
What is the difference
Between my faith in you
And your faith in me?
"My child,
Your faith in me depends
On your sweet hope-fulfilment by me.
My faith in you entirely depends
On your heart's love-strength
And your life's surrender-length."

93

God does not want us
To weigh His Love for us.
He only wants us
To play with Him.

94

God loves us
Not because
We are either divinely great
Or supremely good,
But because, unlike us,
He knows only one thing:
How to love us.

95

God is always eager to share
His Heart's Secrets with me,
But I am always
My indifferent mind.

96

God's Compassion-Eye
Never, never, never forgets me
Although I am every day climbing
High, higher, highest
Ignorance-tree.

97

God never wants us to give up.
He always asks us
To wake up and shape up.

98

God tells me that
Unless I have a rainbow-heart,
He is not going to allow me
To enter into His Heart-Garden.

99

Each new sunrise-smile
Declares the birth
Of a new God-manifestation.

100

How can we ever hear
God's Nectar-Voice
When we enjoy our mind's
Loud dissatisfaction-noise?

101

Every day we must fulfil
Our God-manifestation-
   responsibilities
With redoubled enthusiasm.

102

When my heart smiles at God,
God's Victory-Bell rings
And His golden Heart-Chain
Binds me.

103

I find everywhere
God's infinite Patience,
But God's immortal Pride
Nowhere.

104

Alas,
Self-pity and
God-displeasure
Are equally harmful and painful.

Notes to *My Sunrise-Heart, part 1*

1-10. PS 117, 19 February 2000.
11-20. PS 117, 26 February 2000.
21-32. PS 86, 1 March 2000.
33-44. PS 86, 4 March 2000.
45-56. PS 86, 8 March 2000.
57-68. PS 86, 11 March 2000.
69-80. PS 86, 18 March 2000.
81-92. PS 86, 22 March 2000.
93-104. PS 86, 25 March 2000.

PART XXXIX

YES, I CAN! I CERTAINLY CAN!!

YES, I CAN! I CERTAINLY CAN!!

1

Yes, I can!
I certainly can!!
I can enjoy the infinite bliss
Of a God-surrendered life.

2

Yes, I can!
I certainly can!!
I can firmly hold
The Compassion-Feet
Of my Lord Beloved Supreme.

3

Yes, I can!
I certainly can!!
I can have a heart
Full of gratitude-songs
Sleeplessly
To thrill the Heart
Of my Lord Beloved Supreme.

4

Yes, I can!
I certainly can!!
I can have
A multiple-entry visa
To God's Heart-Land,
Provided
I have a breathless
God-love, God-devotion
And God-surrender-heart.

5

Yes, I can!
I certainly can!!
I can have a rainbow
Love-devotion-surrender-heart.

6

Yes, I can!
I certainly can!!
I can clearly see
That God is playing
Charmingly, powerfully
And proudly
In my heart-garden.

7

Yes, I can!
I certainly can!!
I can burn
My possession-attachment-mind
To ashes.

8

Yes, I can!
I certainly can!!
I can stop
My God-disobedience-mind
From having its way.

9

Yes, I can!
I certainly can!!
I can devour
God's Compassion-Feet.

10

Yes, I can!
I certainly can!!
I can have my heart ready
To be devoured by God.

11

Yes, I can!
I certainly can!!
I can have a new life
That will please God
Thousands of times and more
Every day.

12

Yes, I can!
I certainly can!!
I can absorb and assimilate
God's Nectar-Will.

13

Yes, I can!
I certainly can!!
I can take the surrender-road,
The fastest of all roads
That lead to God's Palace.

14

Yes, I can!
I certainly can!!
I can have love, devotion
And surrender
To please God on a colossal scale.

15

Yes, I can!
I certainly can!!
I can have a heart
That will escort me
Across life's ocean.

16

Yes, I can!
I certainly can!!
I can begin
My God-manifestation-task
Again, ad infinitum.

YES, I CAN! I CERTAINLY CAN!!

17

Yes, I can!
I certainly can!!
I can have a mind
That will accept God's Will
Without any compromise.

18

Yes, I can!
I certainly can!!
I can see the dangers
Of displeasing God
If I am not alert and careful
Twenty-four hours a day.

19

Yes, I can!
I certainly can!!
I can easily get off
Frustration-see-saw.

20

Yes, I can!
I certainly can!!
I can from now on
Live only to please God
In His own Way.

21

Yes, I can!
I certainly can!!
I can see
That the time has come
To stop ignorance-march
Right now.

22

Yes, I can!
I certainly can!!
I can clearly see my soul
Waving a red flag
At my wild vital.

23

Yes, I can!
I certainly can!!
I can see
That each individual
Has the potential
To earn a Ph.D.
In God-obedience.

24

Yes, I can!
I certainly can!!
I can put
My Lord Beloved Supreme
On my heart's pedestal.

25

Yes, I can!
I certainly can!!
I can protect
My sincerity-mind,
Purity-heart
And simplicity-life.

26

Yes, I can!
I certainly can!!
I can bury my past
And turn over altogether
A new page.

27

Yes, I can!
I certainly can!!
I can climb
The perfection-mountain.

28

Yes, I can!
I certainly can!!
I can clearly see
That God is not hiding
In my mind-closet.

29

Yes, I can!
I certainly can!!
I can be included every day
In God's Invitation List.

30

Yes, I can!
I certainly can!!
I can wake up
From my age-long
Ignorance-sleep.

31

Yes, I can!
I certainly can!!
I can have
A God-surrender-trophy
If I stop fooling myself.

32

Yes, I can!
I certainly can!!
I can have an express train ride
To the God-manifestation-station.

33

Yes, I can!
I certainly can!!
I can become
An impossibility-challenger
In my inner life
And my outer life.

34

Yes, I can!
I certainly can!!
I can have
Ceaseless heart-tears
To be stepping stones
To my Lord's Palace.

35

Yes, I can!
I certainly can!!
I can have a bliss-flooded
Adoration-heart,
Provided my life depends
Solely on God's Grace.

36

Yes, I can!
I certainly can!!
I can seize each and every
God-fulfilment-opportunity.

37

Yes, I can!
I certainly can!!
I can carry my life
To the land
Where God-fulfilment-dreams
Are born.

38

Yes, I can!
I certainly can!!
I can be nested
Deep in God's Nectar-Heart.

39

Yes, I can!
I certainly can!!
I can be a peace-bird
To nestle in my heart's
Gratitude-tree-branches.

40

Yes, I can!
I certainly can!!
I can jump into
God's fond Embrace.

41

Yes, I can!
I certainly can!!
I can have
A God-aspiration-thrill
That never grows old,
But remains ever-new.

42

Yes, I can!
I certainly can!!
I can find my way
To God's Lotus-Feet.

43

Yes, I can!
I certainly can!!
I can have a heart
That hungers for
New challenges in life.

44

Yes, I can!
I certainly can!!
I can dissociate myself
From the devouring
Ignorance-breath.

45

Yes, I can!
I certainly can!!
I can give
Every aspiration-heart
A little sunshine.

46

Yes, I can!
I certainly can!!
I can stop living
In the crossfire
Of desires.

47

Yes, I can!
I certainly can!!
I can clearly see that
My inspiration-aspiration-athlete
Is out of shape.

48

Yes, I can!
I certainly can!!
I can have a peace-heart
To be a resident
Of God's Homeland.

49

Yes, I can!
I certainly can!!
I can devour God's Will
The way I devour
A cake.

50

Yes, I can!
I certainly can!!
I can have a purity-mind –
A priceless treasure.

51

Yes, I can!
I certainly can!!
I can have
An illumination-mind
That will never set
On God's Aspiration-Empire.

52

Yes, I can!
I certainly can!!
I can avoid any accident
On the aspiration-highway.

53

Yes, I can!
I certainly can!!
I can succeed
Where nobody else
Has dared to try.

54

Yes, I can!
I certainly can!!
I can have a heart-phone
To call my Lord's
Home number
At any time.

55

Yes, I can!
I certainly can!!
I can have a life
Far beyond the range
Of desire-arrows.

56

Yes, I can!
I certainly can!!
I can take
My desire-bound mind
And quickly discard it.

57

Yes, I can!
I certainly can!!
I can no longer accept
The slavery
Of desire-tyrant.

58

Yes, I can!
I certainly can!!
I can please God
Only after
I have served Him.

59

Yes, I can!
I certainly can!!
I can clearly see
That God has invented
Death
So that we can value
Breath.

60

Yes, I can!
I certainly can!!
I can have
A totally new beginning
Which is nothing other than
A new winning.

61

Yes, I can!
I certainly can!!
I can clearly see
My teeming imperfections
Screaming at me.

62

Yes, I can!
I certainly can!!
I can easily do away with
My self-deception-mind-
    specialist.

63

Yes, I can!
I certainly can!!
I can have
A God-specialist-smile.

64

Yes, I can!
I certainly can!!
I can easily remove
My torturing and tortured
Mind-plant
From my heart-garden.

65

Yes, I can!
I certainly can!!
I can stop waiting
And I can immediately
Start preparing.

66

Yes, I can!
I certainly can!!
I can stop living
In the dungeon-mind.

67

Yes, I can!
I certainly can!!
I can always be
A front runner
In the spiritual life.

68

Yes, I can!
I certainly can!!
I can clearly see
That there is nothing greater
Than my God-obedience-heart.

69

Yes, I can!
I certainly can!!
I can sacrifice
My mind-rock in no time
For my heart-diamond.

70

Yes, I can!
I certainly can!!
I can have a life
That grows and glows
With challenges
And towering hopes.

71

Yes, I can!
I certainly can!!
I can escape
The dry aspiration-desert.

72

Yes, I can!
I certainly can!!
I can heap
My heart-gratitude-blossoms
At God's Feet.

73

Yes, I can!
I certainly can!!
I can have a mind
With devotion-sweetness-
   fragrance.

74

Yes, I can!
I certainly can!!
I can always remain
In God's Satisfaction-Circle.

75

Yes, I can!
I certainly can!!
I can have my life-roots
In God's infinite Blessing-Soil.

76

Yes, I can!
I certainly can!!
I can have a heart
That sleeplessly rings
With sweet devotion-melodies.

77

Yes, I can!
I certainly can!!
I can have a genuine
God-lover-heart.

78

Yes, I can!
I certainly can!!
I can proudly watch
My enthusiasm-breath
Flying.

79

Yes, I can!
I certainly can!!
I can stop yesterday
From obscuring my today.

80

Yes, I can!
I certainly can!!
I can plunge into
The self-effacement-river.

YES, I CAN! I CERTAINLY CAN!!

81

Yes, I can!
I certainly can!!
I can see my heart
Crying for God
Through my eyes.

82

Yes, I can!
I certainly can!!
I can stop ignorance-dust
From blinding my heart's
Illumination-sun.

83

Yes, I can!
I certainly can!!
I can clearly see God
Correcting my mind
And not rejecting it.

84

Yes, I can!
I certainly can!!
I can have
The Kingdom of Heaven
On earth
Right in my heart's street.

85

Yes, I can!
I certainly can!!
I can use
The God-reference-book
At any moment I want
To illumine me, my all.

86

Yes, I can!
I certainly can!!
I can have
A gratitude-flower-heart
That shall remain open
At all hours.

87

Yes, I can!
I certainly can!!
I can stop walking
Carelessly
In my disobedience-mind-jungle.

88

Yes, I can!
I certainly can!!
I can release my heart's
God-manifestation-hesitation-brake.

89

Yes, I can!
I certainly can!!
I can clearly see
That life's temptation-ocean
Knows no shores.

90

Yes, I can!
I certainly can!!
I can stop
The mocking frown
Of darkest ignorance-night.

91

Yes, I can!
I certainly can!!
I can firmly inform
Ignorance
That my tolerance-days
Are over.

92

Yes, I can!
I certainly can!!
I can see that what I want
Is God's rapt attention
And not His real help.

93

Yes, I can!
I certainly can!!
I can unmistakably see
That God never loses count
Of our God-serving deeds.

94

Yes, I can!
I certainly can!!
I can stop walking
On the heavily crowded
Desire-street.

95

Yes, I can!
I certainly can!!
I can clearly see
That the blissful dust
Of God's Feet
Is indispensable
For my God-realisation.

96

Yes, I can!
I certainly can!!
I can surrender my life
With the rising sun
Of the golden dawn.

97

Yes, I can!
I certainly can!!
I can hasten
To the sweet, beckoning Call
Of God.

98

Yes, I can!
I certainly can!!
I can embrace
God's blissful Feet
With every breath.

99

Yes, I can!
I certainly can!!
I can be madly in love
With God's Sweetness-Smile.

100

Yes, I can!
I certainly can!!
I can clearly see
That God's Will
Will, before long,
Capture my all.

PART XL

GREAT PEOPLE AND GOOD PEOPLE

GREAT PEOPLE AND GOOD PEOPLE

1

Great people
Are
Promise-jugglers.

2

Good people
Are
Promise-cradlers.

3

Great people
Smuggle.

4

Good people
Struggle.

5

Great people
Talk.

6

Good people
Act.

7

Great people
Have many mouths.

8

Good people
Have only one mouth
And one heart.

9

Great people
Estimate
World-sufferings.

10

Good people
Carry
World-sufferings.

11

Great people
Have great sayings.

12

Good people
Have God's Blessings.

13

Great people
Are
World-leaners.

14

Good people
Are
World-lifters.

15

Great people
Have a strong voice.

16

Good people
Have a true choice.

17

Great people
Think that they have.

18

Good people
Know that they are.

19

Great people
Think that good thoughts
Are experimental.

20

Good people
Know that good thoughts
Are essential.

21

Great people
Are
Heart-bankruptcy.

22

Good people
Are
Heart-ecstasy.

23

Great people
Intimidate.

24

Good people
Intimate.

GREAT PEOPLE AND GOOD PEOPLE

25

Great people say,
"O world,
Walk behind me."

26

Good people say,
"O world,
Walk inside my heart-garden."

27

Great people
Challenge darkness –
That's all.

28

Good people
Fully illumine darkness –
Completely illumine.

29

Great people
Are
Greatness-madness.

30

Good people
Are
Sweetness-oneness.

31

Great people
Think
They are fault-free.

32

Good people
Feel
They are fault-prone.

33

Great people
Do not remember
Their misdeeds.

34

Good people
Do not remember
Their good deeds.

35

Great people
Are at times
Reality-strangers.

36

Good people
Are always
Reality-embracers.

37

Great people
Are
Self-esteemed possessors.

38

Good people
Are
Self-esteemed renouncers.

39

Great people
Do not want to face
The truth.

40

Good people
Want to fence
The truth.

41

Great people
Ignore facts.

42

Good people
Adore facts.

43

Great people
Dread
Excellence-sincerity-road.

44

Good people
Tread
Excellence-sincerity-road.

45

Great people
Are
Truth-devourers.

GREAT PEOPLE AND GOOD PEOPLE

46

Good people
Are
Truth-discoverers.

47

Great people
Try to lengthen
Their fame.

48

Good people
Try to strengthen
God's Name.

49

Great people
Destroy their enemies.

50

Good people
Pray for their enemies.

51

Great people
Like to control
The world.

52

Good people
Love to extol
The world.

53

Great people
Want to be judged
By their words.

54

Good people
Want to be judged
By their deeds.

55

Great people think
Sincerity has
A foreign accent.

56

Good people think
Sincerity's accent
Is perfect.

57

Great people
Export pride.

58

Good people
Import love.

59

Great people
Love to play
Self-defence-game.

60

Good people
Love to play
Truth-defence-game.

61

Great people
Have
Complexity-minds.

62

Good people
Have
Simplicity-hearts.

63

Great people
Love
Success-broadcast.

64

Good people
Love
Progress-mast.

65

Great people
Have no time
To listen.

66

Good people
Have Eternity
To listen.

67

Great people
Are
Self-contradictions.

68

Good people
Are
Self-improvements.

GREAT PEOPLE AND GOOD PEOPLE

69

Great people
Know
How to praise themselves.

70

Good people
Know
How to efface themselves.

71

Great people
Chase happiness.

72

Good people
Trace happiness.

73

Great people
Are
Equality-strangers.

74

Good people
Are
Equality-adorers.

75

Who can please
Great people?
Nobody!

76

Who can please
Good people?
Everybody.

77

Great people
Take promise
As a dictionary word.

78

Good people
Take promise
As a fully blossoming
   heart-tree.

79

Great people,
When they say they cannot,
Mean they will not.

80

Good people,
When they say they can,
Mean they have already
Started doing it.

81

Great people accept,
Suspect and inspect
Their friends.

82

Good people accept,
Welcome and treasure
Their friends.

83

Great people
Do everything
Powerfully.

84

Good people
Do everything
Gracefully.

85

Great people
Speak well
Only of the dead.

86

Good people
Speak well
Of the living and the dead alike.

87

Great people
Scare the audience.

88

Good people
Treasure the audience.

89

Great people
Are self-impressions.

90

Good people
Are love-expressions.

GREAT PEOPLE AND GOOD PEOPLE

91

Great people
Do not change
Their opinions.

92

Good people
Value
The world-opinion.

93

Great people
Keep questioning
The world.

94

Good people
Keep giving
To the world.

95

Great people
Are apt
To misuse their power.

96

Good people
Are apt
To spread their love.

97

Great people think
The exercise of power
Is beautiful.

98

Good people think
The exercise of love
Is not only beautiful
But also fruitful.

99

Great people
Want to be nominated.

100

Good people
Wish to be communicated.

101

Great people
Are self-edifiers.

102

Good people
Are self-sacrificers.

103

Great people
Are loud drums.

104

Good people
Are sweet flutes.

105

Great people
Are
Victory-hungry minds.

106

Good people
Are
World-harmony-hungry lives.

107

Sound-pride attracts
Great people.

108

Silence-delight attracts
Good people.

109

Great people
Command
Immediate enemy-surrender.

110

Good people
Leave their heart-door
Wide open
To welcome their enemies.

111

Great people
Take years
To build world-trust.

112

Good people
Live
In world-trust.

GREAT PEOPLE AND GOOD PEOPLE

113

To great people,
Life is, indeed,
A battlefield.

114

To good people,
Life is, indeed,
A garden.

115

Great people
Are God's Life.

116

Good people
Are God's Heart.

117

Great people
Know everything.

118

Good people
Know only one thing:
Goodness of the heart.

119

Great people
Have a suspicion-torturing
And tortured mind.

120

Good people
Have a belief-treasuring
And belief-treasured heart.

121

Fleeting
Is the gratitude-breath
Of the great people.

122

Everlasting
Is the gratitude-breath
Of the good people.

123

I say to great people,
"Wake up!"
And to good people,
"Spread out!"

124

A great person
Can easily and unmistakably
 become
A good person
When his mind's
 fulness-supremacy
Surrenders
To his heart's oneness-ecstasy.

PART XLI

HERE AND NOW

HERE AND NOW

1

Here and now
I must realise
That God's Cosmic Plans
Are neither inexplicable
Nor mysterious.

2

Here and now
I must realise
That God is very simple
And very easy to love –
Like a flower or a child.

3

Here and now
I must realise
That this world
Is not God's Jugglery
And not God's Luxury,
But His Treasury.

4

Here and now
I must prepare my life
To be submerged
In the ocean of bliss,
Like my soul –
The God-representative on earth.

5

Here and now
I must feel that at every moment,
Out of His infinite Bounty,
My Lord Supreme is breathing me
Into His Heart.

6

I plead with God
To give me a little more time.
God says, "No, My child, no!
Here and now."

7

To my greatest delight,
Here and now
I unmistakably see
That God is coming toward me,
Unannounced and
   unescorted.

8

Here and now
I must realise
That every human being
Is endowed with the capacity
To be a towering lighthouse
In the darkness-night
Of the present-day world.

9

Here and now
I must develop the capacity
To see that each human being
Is a bridge-builder
Between the inner
 aspiration-heart
And the outer dedication-life.

10

Here and now,
And not hereafter –
This must be the code
Of my life.

11

Not hereafter,
But Here and now,
This loftiest realisation
Has dawned on me:
To lose is to gain.
I lost my puny self
Only to find my Universal Self.

12

Here and now
I must realise that love of God
Is my only religion,
My only spirituality
And
My only enlightenment.

13

Here and now
I learn from God
That He has reserved something
Very special
For each and every human being.
Therefore,
I must not covet.
I must not regret.
I must not object.
I must not reject.

14

Here and now
I must take my God-manifestation
And
God-satisfaction-responsibilities
Most seriously.

15

Here and now
I am determined to invoke
God's Blessings
To usher in the blissful dawn
Of world peace.

16

Here and now
I must develop
My inseparable friendship
With sleepless vigilance
And
Dauntless concentration.

17

If we really want world peace
To blossom on earth,
Then we needs must value
The supreme necessity
Of spiritual survival.
No delay.
No hereafter.
Here and now.

18

I know, scores of times
I have broken
My peace-offering-promises
To the world at large.
Here and now
I resume my promise,
And this time
My ceaseless love for humanity
And
My adamantine will-power
Are bound to succeed.

19

Here and now
My soul urges
All world-peace-dreamers
And world-peace-seekers
To participate in,
And not just watch,
God's Light and
   Delight-Manifestation
On earth.

20

Here and now
Let each and every human being
Immediately respond to
God's secret and sacred
Beckoning Enthusiasm
And Encouragement-Smile.

21

Here and now
I must realise
That my unconditional surrender
To God's Will
Is the most indispensable part
Of my pleasing God.

22

Here and now
I must realise
That my God-disobedience
Is my
Immediate and immeasurable
Aspiration-heart-failure.

23

Here and now
My breath must learn
How to breathe
The breath of the world.

24

Here and now
My heart shall learn
How to love
The heart of the world.

25

Here and now
My life must learn
How to become
The life of the world.

26

My God-aspiration-thrill,
My God-dedication-thrill
And
My God-manifestation-thrill
Are ever new and never old.
This is what I have come to learn
Here and now.

27

Here and now
My solemn promise
To myself:
No more desire-slavery.

28

Here and now
I shall live my life
Between my desire-banishment
And my God-attachment.

29

Not what I want
But what I must do
For God-satisfaction
Is the wisdom-light
Of Here and now.

30

We are deeply in love
With the beauty
Of God the creation.
We must be deeply in love
With the duty
Of God the Creator as well –
Right from today,
Here and now.

31

Here and now
I have decided to offer
Only one prayer:
My Lord, do make me the lover,
Server and devourer
Of the golden dust of Your Feet.

32

Here and now
The miracle of miracles:
A cute smile of my eyes
Has brought God down
From the Ultimate Beyond.

33

I never knew that my heart's
Fleeting tears
Had such tremendous power.
Here and now I clearly see
They have brought down
God Himself
With His everlasting Smiles.

34

I love God.
God loves me.
This is not a new realisation,
But Here and now
I unmistakably see
That we two have
No separate existence.

35

As I love God,
Even so, He needs me.
As God loves me,
Even so, I need Him.
But Here and now
I see a slight difference:
His Love and Need
Are unconditional.
So far, mine are not!

36

Here and now
I must discover my way
To God's Nectar-flooded Feet
For my God-realisation.

37

Here and now
I must be fully determined
To prayerfully and soulfully
  accept
All God-given
Challenge-opportunities —
And never run away.

38

Here and now
I must dissociate myself
From the destruction-breath
Of ignorance-night.

39

Here and now
I must realise
That my heart's aspiration-thrill
Is ever new
And never grows old.

40

Here and now
An unconditional surrender-life
Is the indispensable part
Of a seeker's life
To please God in His own Way.

41

Here and now
My aspiration-heart must hasten
To the beckoning Call
Of my Lord Beloved Supreme.

42

Here and now
I have come to realise
That it is the same God
Who plays the role
Of God the Creator-Vision
And
God the creation-manifestation.

43

Here and now
I must seek to know
What God's Priorities
Truly are.

44

Here and now
My heart must become
The rainbow-beauty
In the vastness-blue
Of enthusiasm-sky.

45

Here and now
A seeker has to realise
That nothing can be
More illumining and fulfilling
In his life
Than his sleepless and breathless
God-obedience.

46

Here and now
God tells me that He does not want
His Power-Feet
To govern my thoughts,
But He wants His
   Sweetness-Heart
To embrace and lead and guide
My will.

47

Here and now
I am challenging
My shameless long-lasting
Self-doubt-waves.

48

Here and now
I do not have the doubting mind
That curves and swerves,
But I do have the aspiring heart
That glows and flows.

49

Here and now
My Lord Beloved Supreme
Is telling me
That my new beginning
Is my new winning.

50

Here and now
I have come to realise
That no human being
Can ever go beyond
God's Compassion-Eye-Circle.

51

Here and now
I must turn my life into
A God-devotion-heart-fragrance.

52

Here and now
My Absolute Lord Supreme
Takes away from me my
   mind-rock
And gives me His Heart-Diamond
In return.

53

Here and now
I am resolved to keep
My God-gratitude-heart-door
Open at all hours.

54

Here and now
I unmistakably see
That the world-temptation-ocean
Has no shore.

55

Here and now
I clearly see
That God has come down
All the way from Heaven
To earth
To receive a cute smile
From my heart.

56

Here and now
I must worship my Lord's Feet
With my streaming heart-tears.

57

Here and now
I must claim my Lord Supreme
As my own, very own.

58

Here and now
I must realise that
There is no such thing
As a part-time God-seeker,
God-dreamer and God-lover.

59

Here and now
I must realise that my God-love
Without my God-faith
Is no love at all.

60

Here and now
I have realised that everything else
Will fail me in the end,
Save and except
My God-devotion-heart.

61

Here and now
God tells me that my relationship
With Him
Has to be always personal,
Private and confidential.

62

Here and now
I am telling God that
　His Commands
Are my only satisfaction-
　fulfilments.

63

Here and now
I must disappear
From the world's view
To remain only in the Heart
Of my Absolute Supreme.

64

Here and now
I must make friends
With the flower-beauty
Of my blossoming heart.

65

Here and now
God wants His Heart to be
The Home
Of my aspiration-cries.

66

Here and now
May my aspiration-dreams
Make my life a faith-citadel.

67

Here and now
I must make my aspiration-heart
My life's most prized possession.

68

Here and now
My soul wants to spotlight
All my
Surrender-life-stage-
　performances.

69

Here and now
God wants me to approach Him
With the sweetness-innocence
Of a child.

70

Here and now
I must never allow my mind
To be plagued
By countless doubts.

71

Here and now
God wants me to forget
All my faults.
He wants me to remember only
My God-gratitude-heart.

72

God tells me,
"Here and now!"
I tell God,
"Please, please give me
A little more time."

73

Here and now
I want my life to be
In between
My aspiration-ascent
And
God's Satisfaction-Descent.

74

Here and now
May God's Compassion-
 Nectar-Eye
Engulf my aspiration-
 heart-tears.

75

Here and now
I clearly see
That God's Compassion-Heart
Accomplishes everything
For me.

76

Here and now
My gratitude-heart-tears
And smiles
Are the most exciting things
For God.

77

Here and now
I clearly see that God
Does not want anybody to guard
The aspiration-flames
Of my heart-shrine.
He Himself wants to do it.

78

Here and now
May the beauty and divinity
Of faith
Surround my life all the time.

79

Who will write God's Biography
Here and now?
Not my aspiration-heart,
Not my service-life,
But my gratitude-breath-tears.

HERE AND NOW

80

Here and now
I have come to realise
That my surrender to God's Will
Has no problem left to solve.

81

Here and now
I must see that God's Love
Reverberates
In my God-oneness-heart.

82

Here and now
I must make a solemn promise
To myself
To listen to God's daily Broadcast.

83

Here and now
I must not only enjoy
But become
The nectar-dust of God's Feet.

84

Here and now
I must start marching
Towards my own heart-home.

85

Here and now
I realise that Eternity
Is too short
For me to please God
In His own Way.

86

Here and now
I unmistakably see
That each new peace nation
Is a new
God-satisfaction-blossom.

87

Here and now
God embraces my surrender-heart
And commands me
To go forward, to fly upward
And to dive inward.

88

Here and now
God and I are saying
The same thing to each other:
"Do not forget me."

89

Here and now
I need only one thing:
God's Absolute Will.

90

Here and now
I must come to realise
That my unconditional
  God-surrender
Succeeds
When everything else fails.

91

Here and now
I want my gratitude-heart
To prayerfully devour
God's Compassion-Eye,
God's Forgiveness-Heart
And His All.

92

Here and now
I clearly see that
God may play hide-and-seek
With my love and devotion,
But never
With my complete surrender.

93

Here and now
My sole promise to God
Is to fulfil
God's each and every Dream.

94

Here and now
My heart must develop
A keen interest in everything
That is of God,
And my life must develop
A keen interest in everything
That is for God.

95

Here and now
I must increase, and ever increase,
The beauty
Of my God-sincerity-mind
And the fragrance
Of my God-purity-heart.

96

Here and now
I have come to realise that
Surrender means a hungry heart
For the nectar-dust of God's Feet.

97

Here and now
I have discovered
My sleepless and breathless
Love-devotion-surrender:
The only way to cure
All God's headaches.

98

Here and now
My supreme discovery:
When my heart is all soulfulness,
God is God's Fulness-Embrace.

99

Here and now
I must command my mind
To unlearn
All its doubt-suspicion-
　jungle-stories.

100

Here and now
I say to my Lord Supreme:
I can establish
My sleepless and breathless
God-oneness.
My Lord Supreme says to me:
"You have already done it,
My child."

101

Here and now
I have come to learn that
My God-readiness,
God-willingness
And God-eagerness
Are God's immediate neighbours.

102

Here and now,
By virtue of my prayer-life
And my meditation-heart,
I shall get the best view
Of my Lord's Feet.

103

Here and now
God tells me to remember
Only one thing:
He is never too busy for me
Or for anybody on earth.

104

Here and now
No, not even an iota
Of God-disobedience
Has any place
In my spiritual life.

105

Here and now
God tells me that
The heart-gardens
Of the God-seekers
Are His most favourite places
To vacation.

106

Here and now
I clearly see that God's
Compassion-Forgiveness-Days
Have Eternity's Life.

107

Here and now
I have come to realise that
God-manifestation
Is not a one-mile run,
But Eternity's ever-increasing
   miles.

108

Here and now
If I make my heart
An ever-transcending flame
For God-realisation,
Then God alone will wipe the
   tears
Of my long, very long,
Unaspiring years.

109

Here and now
I must become
A sleepless God-adoration-mind,
God-devotion-heart
And God-dedication-life.

110

Here and now
I have discovered
That my life is in between
My weeping heart
And
God's forgiving Heart.

111

Here and now
I have warned the desire-worlds
To stop running
After me.

112

Here and now
I have made a solemn promise
To myself,
That although it is
An endlessly long voyage
From my puny self
To God's boundless Self,
I shall, without fail, complete it.

113

Here and now
I am all determination
To bravely tear asunder
The iron curtain
Of ignorance-night.

114

Here and now
God tells me that
He loves my aspiration-cries
And devotion-throbs
Infinitely more
Than I can ever imagine.

115

Here and now
I have taken a solemn oath
That I shall not jump into
The God-disobedience-
　calamity-whirlpool,
Never!

116

Here and now
I am being cradled
By God's unconditional Grace
And His omnipotent Will.

117

Here and now
I want to become
The ever-blossoming beauty
Of a silence-sea-heart.

118

Here and now
I promise to become
A ceaseless
God-victory
Messenger-boy.

119

Here and now
God wants me to strike
My life's transformation-gong
And play
My heart's nectar-flute.

120

Here and now
My latest discovery:
When I do not soulfully pray
And do not self-givingly meditate,
I helplessly find myself
In a crowded, noisy
And utterly godless mind-subway.

121

Here and now
My new discovery:
Sweet is my Lord's Eye,
Sweeter is my Lord's Heart,
Sweetest is the dust
Of my Lord's Feet.

122

Every day
God blesses me
With His own Motto:
"Here and now."

123

Here and now
I have just cancelled
My desire-land-journey.

124

Here and now
I must conquer my mind's
Frustration-exasperations.

125

Here and now
I have made a solemn promise:
I shall never, never enter
Into my mind's
God-disobedience-country.

126

Here and now
I must love and serve
God the Supreme Guest
Devotedly, soulfully, self-givingly
And sleeplessly.

127

Here and now
I have come to realise
That from God's Compassion-Eye
Every human being has
His own infallible origin.

128

Here and now
I unmistakably feel
That God's Desire-Heart
To please mankind
Is infinitely stronger
Than mankind's desire-heart
To please God.

129

Here and now
My God-worshipping heart-tears
Must reach God's Golden Shore
Of the ever-transcending Beyond.

130

Here and now
I must offer
All my heart's aspiration-tears
And
All my life's gratitude-smiles
To my Absolute Lord Supreme.

131

Here and now
I must keep
A soulful and prayerful eye
On all God's
World-transformation-actions.

132

Here and now
With my God-devotion-tears
I must row my life-boat
To God's Nectar-Heart-Harbour.

133

Here and now
I have come to learn
That God's Compassion
Is my only heart-compass.

134

Here and now
I ask God:
My Lord,
Where can I find You?
"My child,
Inside My Blessing-Eye-Smiles."

135

Here and now
God asks me:
"My child,
Where can I find you?"
My Lord,
Inside my gratitude-heart-tears.

136

Here and now
God asks me
To come out of my mind's
Insecurity-cave
And show Him my heart's
Most powerful
Light-delight sea-waves.

137

Here and now
I have come to learn that
Only at God's choice Hour
The mind retires for good
And the heart aspires
Throughout Eternity.

138

Here and now
My soul wants me
To put an end to humanity's
Widespread inner
　peace-starvation.

139

Here and now
God tells me never to enjoy
Prayer and meditation-holidays
If I want to remain
A choice soldier of His
For His full manifestation
On earth.

140

Here and now
God kindles in me
Limitless aspiration-heart-flames
To clasp His Divinity's Feet.

141

Here and now
When I give God my possessions:
Devotion-tears,
God gives me His Possessions:
Nectar-Embraces.

142

Here and now
I have thrown my open heart
Into God's
Compassion-flooded Eye.

143

Here and now
My sleepless God-obedience
Has conquered
All my inner enemies.
To name a few –
Pride, insecurity, fear and doubt.

144

Here and now
God tells me that it is quite easy
To satisfy and please Him.
He advises me to take every day
Just a few aspiration-steps,
Dedication-steps
And devotion-steps
Towards my ultimate Goal:
His universal Fulfilment.

145

Here and now
God tells me:
"Cry not like a beggar
For your own liberation.
Smile and strive,
And strive and smile
Like a hero supreme
For My complete manifestation
Here on earth."

146

Here and now
I must terminate
My long-standing friendship
With ignorance-night.

147

Here and now
I must become
A fathomless
God-faith-reservoir.

148

Here and now
I must resolve
To take each and every day
As a God-service-day.

149

Here and now
My crying breath
And streaming tears
Must enter into
God's Heart-Room.

150

Here and now
I must totally break
My ego-horn
Into millions of pieces.

151

Here and now
I must push myself
Most powerfully
To reach a new
God-satisfaction-height.

152

Here and now
I must dauntlessly stop
Impossibility
From blocking my Godward way.

153

Here and now
I must offer
My gratitude-heart-present
To God.

154

Here and now
I must end all my
Desire-tiger-attacks.

155

Here and now
I have come to realise
That only when I end
My pride-exhibit
God will begin
His Pride-Parade.
What for?
Just to bless and crown me.

156

Here and now
I give God what I have:
My weeping heart.
And God gives me what He is:
His Smiling Eye.

157

Here and now
God tells me
That I can turn my head
Away from Him
If I want to.
But He will never allow me
To turn my heart
Away from Him.

158

Here and now
All the desire-worlds
Have ceased
Running after me.

159

Here and now
I have come to learn
That everything of mine
God loves,
But He loves
My devotion-heart-throbs
Infinitely more.

160

Here and now
I must cast aside
The tears
Of my unaspiring days.

161

Here and now
God tells me
That He can never be too busy
For His Heart-bound children.

162

Here and now
God makes my God-
   realisation-hope
Stronger
And my God-manifestation-
   promise
Clearer.

163

Here and now
I must claim God's ambrosial Feet
As my own,
Very own.

164

Here and now
God is telling me
That He will before long
Visit my heart-temple.
I must keep it
Absolutely immaculate.

165

Here and now
My heart's aspiration-surge
Is carrying me
To God's Heart-Garden.

166

Here and now
I have come to realise
That my surrender to God's Will
Is the only one-way street
To perpetual happiness.

167

Here and now
I must develop
A sky-blue vastness-heart
To embrace all humanity
To manifest God's Will
On earth.

168

Here and now
The human in me
Must bathe every day
In God's Forgiveness-Heart-Sea.

169

Here and now
My human life must take shelter
Under God's Forgiveness-Tree.

170

Here and now
God is blessing me
With thunderous applause
For my self-doubt-conquest.

171

Here and now
I must start obeying
The dictates
Of my Pilot Supreme.

172

Here and now
I must become
A concentration-mind-seeker.

173

Here and now
I must become
A meditation-heart-builder.

174

Here and now
I must become
A dedication-life-enjoyer.

175

Here and now
I myself must become
A problem-solution-warrior.

176

Here and now
I must develop the eagerness
To feel desperate urgency
To fulfil God's Will
Every single day.

177

Here and now
I must develop
The eagerness-capacity
To faithfully follow God's Will
All-where, always.

178

Here and now
I must capsize
My world-conquering
Ambition-boat.

179

Here and now
I have come to learn
That God wants me
To transform my limitations
Into God-satisfaction-perfections
And not demolish them
   altogether.

180

Here and now
With my soul's indomitable will
I shall flood my heart
With inner sunshine.

181

Here and now
I have come to realise
The difference between
My mind and my heart:
My mind delights in
   ignoring God;
My heart delights in seeking God.

182

Here and now
I must develop
An intense eagerness
To feel my God-realisation
As a pressing necessity.

183

Here and now
I must devour
The nectar-harvest
Of my God-realisation-soul.

184

Here and now
My mind must bloom
And
My heart must blossom
In the depths of soundless silence.

185

Here and now
To my greatest joy
I see the Power-Sun
Of the Beyond
Shining upon me.

186

Here and now
I must become
The perfect satisfaction
Of God's
Full manifestation-examination
On earth.

187

Here and now
My soul is commanding me
To climb up
My soul's ever-transcending pole.

188

Here and now
My Lord's solemn Promise:
Before long He will carry me over
All the anxiety-worry-seas.

189

Here and now
God is telling me
That He will always reserve
A sunny place
For my cheerful face.

190

Here and now
Finally I have realised
That my heart needs
Only one power to realise God:
Gratitude,
Abundant gratitude,
Gratitude infinite.

191

Here and now
I clearly see
That there are many roads
To arrive at the Goal,
But the absolutely shortest road
Is the heart-road.

192

Here and now
God tells me
That He never fails to perform
His special Task every day:
He watches me
And He catches me
Just before I fall.

193

Here and now
God tells me that I must believe
In His Sincerity
When He tells me that He has
Implicit Faith in my ability.

194

Here and now
I must inspire
The hero-warrior-souls
On earth
Not to retire.

195

Here and now
My tears must cry and cry
So that I can fly
In my Beloved Lord's Heart-Sky.

196

Here and now
I have come to realise
That there is only
One safe addiction:
My God-devotion-addiction.

197

Here and now
I clearly see the difference
Between me and my God:
I love flattery
From the beginning to the end.
God loves mastery
From the beginning to the end.

198

Here and now
On the strength
Of my heart's climbing cries,
I shall enjoy
The Beauty and Fragrance
Of Heaven.

199

Here and now
God tells me
To ignore my mind
When it belittles
My heart-capacity.

200

Here and now
God tells me
To embrace my heart,
For my heart self-givingly
Worships God.

201

Here and now
God wants only one thing:
Reconciliation between
My doubting mind
And
My strangling vital.

202

Here and now
God tells my body: "Get up!"
My vital: "Stand up!"
My mind: "Grow up!"
My heart: "Look up!"
And my life: "Cheer up!"

203

Here and now
I must go forward,
Pleasing God
With every sure step.

204

Here and now
I must silence
My ego-mind-boxer
And
My ego-vital-wrestler.

205

Here and now
I must end the length and breadth
Of my
Ignorance-stupidity-capacities.

206

Here and now
I want to be
A God-listening ear
And
A God-pleasing heart.

207

Here and now
God tells me
That if I want to proclaim
His supreme Victory,
Then I must make my friendship
With patience solid.

208

Here and now
I must start feeding myself
With God's
Compassion-Eye-Beauty
And with God's
Forgiveness-Heart-Fragrance.

209

Here and now
No more
The mind-fantasy-world.
More, ever more,
The God-intimacy-world.

210

Here and now
I have come to realise
That each divine thought
Is an earth-awakening
And a God-Victory-ringing bell.

211

Here and now
I am enjoying two things –
Secret and sacred God-whispers
And
Open and unreserved God-cheers.

Notes to *Here and Now*

1-20. 30 May 2000, Canadian Parliament, Parliament Hill, Ottawa, Canada.
21-35. 15 June 2000, US Capitol Office Building, Washington, DC, USA.
36-55. 25 July 2000, Landmark Community Centre, Port Washington, New York, USA.
56-88. 10 September 2000, Harvard University, Cambridge, Massachusetts, USA.
89-122. 23 September 2000, Molson Centre, Montreal, Canada.
123-132. 7 October 2000, Old Pine Street Church, Philadelphia, Pennsylvania, USA.
133-162. 21 October 2000, Xcel Energy Centre, St Paul, Minnesota, USA.
163-202. 30 October 2000, Reykjavik University Theatre, Reykjavik, Iceland.
203-211. 1 November 2000, King's College, Cambridge University, Cambridge, England.

PART XLII

IF I COULD START MY LIFE ONCE MORE

IF I COULD START MY LIFE ONCE MORE

1

If I could start my life
Once more,
Every day I would become
A new aspiration-heart-blossom.

2

If I could start my life
Once more,
I would shed only
God-manifesting tears.

3

If I could start my life
Once more,
I would devotedly place
All my incapacities
At the Feet of my Lord Supreme.

4

If I could start my life
Once more,
I would definitely not long
For my desire-fulfilment.

5

If I could start my life
Once more,
I would never ignore
My Lord's sorrowful Tears.

6

If I could start my life
Once more,
I would not allow my vital
To torture my life.

7

If I could start my life
Once more,
I would not allow my mind
To torture my heart.

8

If I could start my life
Once more,
I would study the divinity-course
In humanity's heart.

9

If I could start my life
Once more,
I would not accept any defeat
In the battlefield of my life.

10

If I could start my life
Once more,
I would never miss
God-Invitation-Hours.

11

If I could start my life
Once more,
I would every day become
A new morning rose
In the garden of the universe.

12

If I could start my life
Once more,
I would never surrender
To ignorance-shackles.

13

If I could start my life
Once more,
I would not waste even
A fleeting moment
On the way
To God's Heart-Home.

14

If I could start my life
Once more,
I would remember
That all the mind-tours
Are a sheer waste of time.

15

If I could start my life
Once more,
I would have only
Indomitable faith
And not fractured faith
In God.

16

If I could start my life
Once more,
I would enjoy only
The silence-breath
Of my God-aspiration-ecstasy.

17

If I could start my life
Once more,
I would every day bathe
In God-Fragrance-Sea.

18

If I could start my life
Once more,
I would not allow myself
To be blinded
By insecurity-jealousy-
    impurity-fog.

IF I COULD START MY LIFE ONCE MORE

19

If I could start my life
Once more,
I would every day take shelter
Under patience-tree.

20

If I could start my life
Once more,
I would remember that
My earth-heart-planet
Is as beautiful
As all the Heaven-born planets.

21

If I could start my life
Once more,
I would not take
Perfection-achievement
As an impossible task.

22

If I could start my life
Once more,
I myself would boldly capsize
My God-dissatisfaction-
   mind-boat.

23

If I could start my life
Once more,
I would every day sail
My God-satisfaction-heart-boat.

24

If I could start my life
Once more,
I would unmistakably abandon
My earth-bound mind
On doubt-torture-doorstep.

25

If I could start my life
Once more,
I would look anything undivine
Straight in the eye.

26

If I could start my life
Once more,
I would never visit
God-ingratitude-human beings.

27

If I could start my life
Once more,
I would be extremely proud
Of God's Thunderbolt-Command.

28

If I could start my life
Once more,
I would not fail
In offering regularly
My progress-life-reports
To my Lord Supreme.

29

If I could start my life
Once more,
I would not become reconciled
To my fate,
But I would be my fate-conqueror.

30

If I could start my life
Once more,
I would not accept any complaint
From my mind.

31

If I could start my life
Once more,
I would not find fault
With any human being,
Either consciously
Or even unconsciously.

32

If I could start
My life once more,
I would have equanimity
As my name
To brave the buffets of life.

33

If I could start my life
Once more,
My life would lead a caravan
Of God-manifestation-deeds
On earth.

34

If I could start my life
Once more,
I would be seriously in love
With God-manifestation-victories.

35

If I could start my life
Once more,
I would not accept a Master
Who would not scold me
   ruthlessly
Every day.

36

If I could start my life
Once more,
I would not allow doubt-
   fear-spears
To kill
My aspiration-heart-
   progress-deer.

37

If I could start my life
Once more,
I would depend only
On God-reliance,
And never on self-reliance.

38

If I could start my life
Once more,
I would try not to be
A peace-maker
But a peace-lover.

39

If I could start my life
Once more,
I would have a heart
To be claimed
Only by God's Affection-Heart.

40

If I could start my life
Once more,
Sleeplessly my heart would throb
With God-devotion-waves.

41

If I could start my life
Once more,
I would remain under
My soul-domination.

42

If I could start my life
Once more,
I would not have,
Even for a single day,
God-forgetting uncomely
   thoughts.

43

If I could start my life
Once more,
I would never allow myself
To be under the thumb
Of temptation.

44

If I could start my life
Once more,
I would never allow myself
To be in the company
Of those who droop and drowse
In the spiritual life.

45

If I could start my life
Once more,
I would not allow myself
To suffer from
Ignorance-shackle-nights.

46

If I could start my life
Once more,
I would only live in the lands
Of inspiration, aspiration
And dedication.

47

If I could start my life
Once more,
I would not even out of curiosity
Take a ride
Through the mind-jungle.

48

If I could start my life
Once more,
Every day I would fly
On the most beautiful
God-devotion-wings.

49

If I could start my life
Once more,
Even for a fleeting second
I would not open any
God-disobedience-gate.

50

If I could start my life
Once more,
I would make the heart
Extremely popular
And the mind
Extremely unpopular.

51

If I could start my life
Once more,
Even in my dreams
I would not touch
The self-doubt-tree.

IF I COULD START MY LIFE ONCE MORE

52

If I could start my life
Once more,
I would not care to know
The depth of the sea
But only care for
The depth of my heart.

53

If I could start my life
Once more,
I would not try to understand
God's Grace,
But I would become
God's Grace itself.

54

If I could start my life
Once more,
I would have a prayer-life
And meditation-heart
To span all distances.

55

If I could start my life
Once more,
I would say and do everything
From my heart of love.

56

If I could start my life
Once more,
I would take God-obedience
As my choicest determination.

57

If I could start my life
Once more,
I would take God's Presence
In my heart
As my only Home.

58

If I could start my life
Once more,
I would sing only God-Glories
To remain always in tune
With God's Heart.

59

If I could start my life
Once more,
I would live not for worldly
    acclaim,
But to proclaim God's Victory
On earth.

60

If I could start my life
Once more,
I would see how far
I could go ahead,
Instead of looking back.

61

If I could start my life
Once more,
I would make
My mind's obedience,
My heart's love
And my life's surrender
An inseparable trio.

62

If I could start my life
Once more,
I would carefully walk in peace
All the time
To keep in step
With my Lord Supreme.

63

If I could start my life
Once more,
I would not long for
God-explanation
Or God-expectation,
But I would long only for
God-satisfaction.

64

If I could start my life
Once more,
I would never blow
Self-doubt and God-doubt-horns.

65

If I could start my life
Once more,
Every day I would soulfully attend
My Lord's open question time.

66

If I could start my life
Once more,
I would not allow
Expectation-frustration
To prevail in my life.

67

If I could start my life
Once more,
I would always avail myself
Of my Lord's
Compassion-Abundance.

68

If I could start my life
Once more,
Every day I would try to feel
My Lord's Compassion-
  Protection-Feet.

69

If I could start my life
Once more,
I would never allow myself
To fall into
The chasm of depression.

70

If I could start my life
Once more,
I would always find myself caught
In my Lord's
Compassion-Illumination-
  Heart-Home.

PART XLIII

MY LIFE'S EVERY DAY HOPE-BLOSSOMS AND PROMISE-TREES

MY LIFE'S EVERY DAY HOPE-BLOSSOMS AND PROMISE-TREES

1

Every day
I am on strike
Against my mind-boss.

2

Every day
I enjoy sailing
With my heart-boatman.

3

Every day
God and I have
Private conversations
At least for seven hours
Inside God's Soul-Room.

4

Every day
I fly with my soul-bird
Towards Heaven,
No traffic at all.

5

Every day
I give my body, vital and mind
An ultimatum:
Either be all for God
Or be totally out of my sight.

6

Every day
God tells me,
"My son, what I need from you
Are heart-essentials,
Not mind-credentials."

7

Every day
God receives from my vital
A disobedience-tornado.

8

Every day
God receives from my heart
An obedience-sea.

9

Every day
I am
My God-dependence.

10

Every day
God is
God-Embrace.

11

Every day
I do not know
Why and how I suffer
From the heavy rain of sorrow.

12

Every day
I realise that I live
In my mind-hesitation-limitation.

13

Every day
Early in the morning
I take the train to go
From my Lord's Hope-Station
To His Promise-Station.

14

Every day
I go to participate
In the self-doubt-prevention club.

15

Every day
I vehemently deny
My short-lived
Satisfaction-possession.

16

Every day
I am a new self-disciplined
Determination-dynamo.

17

Every day
I aim at a higher goal
With each God-aspiring breath.

18

Every day
I put my sad misfortune
To happy and good use.

19

Every day
I try to remain a perfect stranger
To attachment-parasite.

20

Every day
I learn and teach
And learn and teach
At God-awareness-school.

21

Every day
I tell God,
"How can I live my life
Where Your Heart is not?"

22

Every day
God wants me to enjoy
The unparalleled fragrance
Of my forgiveness-heart.

23

Every day
I beg God for power.
He gives me light instead.

24

Every day
I beg God for superiority.
He gives me humility instead.

25

Every day
God replaces
My world-conquest-thought
With self-conquest-will.

26

Every day
God tells me that
My inner peace
And my inner freedom
Do not depend
On my outer circumstances.

27

Every day
God tells me that I do not need
A painful experience
To increase my God-devotion.
What I need is a sleepless
God-awareness-heart.

28

Every day
I find myself
In the streaming tears
Of my heart
And in the beaming smiles
Of my soul.

29

Every day
I thank God
For having one thing:
Obedience-eagerness.

30

Every day
I thank God
For not having one thing:
Disobedience-ruthlessness.

31

Every day
God tells me that
To sow love in the heart
Is to reap peace in the life.

32

Every day
God tells me
My God-dedication
Is my God-union.

33

Every day
God prevents me from visiting
The mind-doubt-factory.

34

Every day
God wants me to spend
At least four hours
In my soul-company.

35

Every day
I break my desire-toys
With tremendous pride.

36

Every day
I take God's Presence in my heart
As my life's present to mankind.

37

Every day
My mind tells me
My soul is a foreigner,
Therefore not to trust my soul.

38

Every day
My heart-telescope sees God,
No matter how far away He is.

39

Every day
My God-obedience equals
My God-satisfaction.

MY LIFE'S EVERY DAY HOPE-BLOSSOMS AND PROMISE-TREES

40

Every day
God tells me that
My God-surrender
Has the capacity
To make up for lost time
In my spiritual journey.

41

Every day
God asks me to challenge
My life's imperfection-enemies.

42

Every day
It is becoming clearer to me
That disobedience is the root,
Destruction is the tree.

43

Every day
I sadden God's Heart
By not leaving the desire-land.

44

Every day
I sadden my Lord's Heart
By listening to the advice
Of my desire-mind.

45

Every day
I get
God-Heart-Umbrella-Protection
For the asking.

46

Every day
God's Compassion-Heart
Awakens me
And God's Justice-Eye
Illumines me.

47

Every day
I monopolise God's Love.
Yet God's Compassion-Ocean
Remains infinite.

48

Every day
I apply my adamantine will
Against my life-pressure.

49

Every day
A life of pleasure
Is emptying my heart's
Beauty-fragrance-treasure.

50

Every day
God unconditionally helps me
To bring to the fore
My heart-delight.

51

Every day
God tells me
If I want to bind my heart-joy,
Then I shall blind my life totally.

52

Every day
I must deeply value
My world-detachment-hours.

53

Every day
My desire-mind rushes
To a nowhere-destination-land.

54

Every day
God's Greatness-Height
Fascinates my eyes.

55

Every day
God's Goodness-Depth
Liberates my mind.

56

Every day
I please God by revolting
Against my mind-government.

57

Every day
God tells me the real miracle
Is not walking on water,
But loving the heart
Of each and every human being.

58

Every day
I act like a real fool
By living in my mind-cage
And not in my heart-palace.

59

Every day
I realise that my insecurity
Is not only endless,
But utterly senseless.

MY LIFE'S EVERY DAY HOPE-BLOSSOMS AND PROMISE-TREES

60

Every day
God takes special pride
In my secret and sacred
God-fulfilment-wishes.

61

Every day
I shall promptly do
My God-service
And never put it on hold.

62

Every day
I shall expand the horizon
Of my God-loving heart.

63

Every day
I shall surprise my Lord Supreme
With something new.

64

Every day
I shall accompany
My deep meditation
To my heart-temple.

65

Every day
The human in me says:
"I pray and pray,
And God delays and delays."

66

Every day
The divine in me says:
"God's Grace is at once
My inspiration-sky
And my aspiration-sun."

67

Every day
There can be a new way
To touch God's Feet
And love God's Heart.

68

Every day
I need nothing and I need nobody
But You only, my Lord, You.

69

Every day
My mind pressures God
And
My heart treasures God.

70

Every day
I need only one thing:
A one-pointed devotion-heart.

PART XLIV

MY MASTER

MY MASTER

Section one – My Master

1

My heart dies
The moment it sees
My Master's sadness-tears.

2

My heart sings, plays
And dances
In ecstasy supreme
When it sees my Master's
Gladness-smiles.

3

Time salutes and stops
When my Master proudly
   expresses
His love, affection, sweetness
And fondness for me.

4

Every morning
My Master helps my heart
Wake up
With his heart's sunrise-beauty.

5

My Master cautioned me
And warned me
Of the tragic descent
Of my disobedience-life.

6

O my impurity-mind,
Do not whine!
O my insecurity-heart,
Do not cry!
Behold, our Master,
With his compassion-flooded eye,
Is fast approaching us.

7

When the Master appears,
He immediately says
To my frustration-mind,
   vital and body:
"Stop!
Enough of your stupidity-pride!"

He then says to my heart:
"Enjoy no more ignorance-sleep!
I want you to accept
Some of my
World-transformation-
   responsibilities."

8

The Master appears and says:
"I am sure this time
My iron rod will work,
Since up until now
My sweetness-flute
Has sadly failed."

9

My Master does not come alone.
He carries with him
His heart-home
So that his children
Do not wander any more
Inside their mind-jungles.

10

Master, Master,
What is the difference
Between my faith in you
And your faith in me?

"My child, your faith in me
Depends on your sweet
Hope-fulfilment by me.
My faith in you
Entirely depends on
Your heart's love-strength
And
Your life's surrender-length."

11

Master, Master, over the years
I have given you so many things.
It seems to me that you have
   shown me
No sense of appreciation.
Master, this time I have
Two very special gifts for you.
I am sure you will enjoy them.

"My child, tell me, tell me.
I am all eagerness."

Master, this time I shall give you
My gratitude-heart
And my surrender-life-beauty-
   fountains.

12

Master, Master, please tell me
How you love me
More than I love you.

"My child,
Your heart needs repair.
Leave it with me just for an hour.
I will do the needful."

Section two – A God-realised Soul

13

A God-realised Soul
Is
Divinity's Lion-Prince
But
Humanity's donkey-slave.

14

The Soul of a God-realised Person
Tries with God
And
The Heart of a God-realised
Person
Cries with God
For the transformation
Of humanity.

15

A God-realised Soul
Is at once
God's Responsibility-Partner
And
Man's responsibility-
   frustration-reservoir.

16

A God-realised Person
Is
Ninety-nine per cent
   underestimated
And
One hundred per cent
   misunderstood
By the elephant-ignorance-pride
Of humanity.

17

A God-realised Person
Receives two gifts
From humanity:
Crucifixion-torture
From the desire-world
And
Glorification-rapture
From the aspiration-world.

18

The silence of the inner world
Tells the God-realised Soul:
"Wake up! Tarry not! Hurry up!
Run up and down
While serving God
Inside the heart of humanity."

The sound of the outer world
Tells the God-realised Soul:
"Shut up! Shut up!
Stay not here!
Pack up!
Go elsewhere!
Not here, not here!"

19

The immortal Motto
Of a God-realised Soul:
Tomorrow's Dawn never begins.
Yesterday's Night never ends.

20

A God-realised Person
Is at once
Humanity's thunder-kick-
   football-sufferer
And
Divinity's Bowling-Ball-
   Winner-Dreamer.

21

A God-realised Soul
Swims in the sea
Of Divinity's Tears
And
Drowns in the ocean
Of humanity's frowns.

22

Humanity does not need
A God-realised Soul
Because
He is not useful in
   humanity's eyes.

Divinity opens Heaven's Door
For a God-realised Soul
Only after He has accomplished
His supreme Task on earth.

23

Divinity
Encourages a God-realised Soul
In His God-Manifestation-
   Hunger
By thunderous clapping.

Humanity
Discourages a God-realised Soul
In His God-Manifestation-
   Hunger
By ferocious slapping.

24

The Heart of a God-realised Soul
Blossoms inside
God's Immortality-flooded Smile.

The Life of a God-realised Soul
Dies inside
Humanity's jealousy-dragon-eye.

25

A God-realised Soul
Does not know how to
Tarnish and punish.

He only knows how to
Cry and try, again and again,
To see Divinity's Sun
In humanity's sky.

26

CONSOLATION PRIZE

Finally, the Absolute Supreme
Tells a God-realised Soul:
"My child,
You are My own
Eternity's Vision-Eye
And
You are My own
Immortality's Reality-Heart."

Section three – Mine is a God-Dream

27

Mine is a God-Dream
That can never
Be shattered.

28

Mine is a God-Dream
That can never
Be even shaken.

29

Mine is a God-Dream
That never loses
My God-appointment book.

30

Mine is a God-Dream
That tells me
That my heart's aspiration
Is nothing other than
My life's recreation.

31

Mine is a God-Dream
That embodies only
The mountain-silence-peace.

32

Mine is a God-Dream
That only knows
My heart's rising aspiration-sun
And never
My heart's setting aspiration-sun.

33

Mine is a God-Dream
That is always
Empty of doubt-poison.

34

Mine is a God-Dream
That is always
Triumphant over
My earthly human fate.

35

Mine is a God-Dream
That tells me
That it is not our sadness
But our selflessness
That makes us very special
To God.

36

Mine is a God-Dream
That is, indeed,
My passport to God's
Celestial Country Home.

37

Mine is a God-Dream
That does not allow
My God-manifestation
Heart-song
To remain unsung.

38

Mine is a God-Dream
That always finds
My Lord Beloved Supreme
Available
Inside my heart-home.

39

Mine is a God-Dream
That bravely swims across
The ocean of impossibilities.

PART XLV

TO-DAY IS THE DAY

TO-DAY IS THE DAY

1

To-day is the day
Of my life's
Moment-to-moment
Dedication.

2

To-day is the day
Of my heart's
Moment-to-moment
Aspiration.

3

To-day is the day
Of my mind's
Moment-to-moment
Enthusiasm.

4

To-day is the day
Of my vital's
Moment-to-moment
Dynamism.

5

To-day is the day
Of my body's
Moment-to-moment
Sacrifice.

6

To-day is the day
My heart-plants
Must thrive
On my God-gratitude-tears.

7

To-day is the day
That I must turn
My self-confidence
Into
My God-reliance.

8

To-day is the day
That I must sing
All my God-devotion-songs
With every tick of life's clock.

9

To-day is the day
That my soulful gratitude
Will grow into
God's Sweetness-Smile.

10

To-day is the day
Of my registration
For three supreme courses:
Ceaseless God-obedience,
Sleepless God-manifestation
And
Breathless God-satisfaction.

11

To-day is the day
God is telling me
That no real God-seeker
Can ever afford
To take time off.

12

To-day is the day
That I must tear down
All my mind-doubt-walls
With my heart's adamantine
God-faith-hammer.

13

To-day is the day
That I must bring back
My child-heart-tears
And
My child-eye-smiles
To conquer God's Heart.

14

To-day is the day
That I must help my heart
To come back home
From my mind's exile-tyranny.

15

To-day is the day
That I must muster
All eagerness
To see the full blossoming
Of my inner sun.

16

To-day is the day
Of the total obliteration
Of my ego-mind-life.

17

To-day is the day
Of my complete preparation
For the ever-transcending
God-realisation-journey.

18

To-day is the day
That God has blessed me
With the heart
That will grow younger
Every day.

19

To-day is the day
Of God's Promise
To show me
The uncrowded road
To His Palace.

20

To-day is the day
Of God's Request to me
To join Him in scattering
Peace-dream-seeds
With His every Breath
All over the world.

21

To-day is the day
That God's Compassion-Eye
Has promised to bless me
With a jasmine-sweet
Devotion-heart.

22

To-day is the day
That God is urging me
To climb up
To the topmost branch
Of His Compassion-Tree.

23

To-day is the day
That my earth-heart
Desperately needs
Heaven's peace-breath.

24

To-day is the day
God has asked me
To tell ignorance-night
That it will have to get used
To my regular and permanent
Absence.

25

To-day is the day
That my heart's
Enthusiasm-river
Shall break through
All untold obstacles.

26

To-day is the day
That God is begging me
To charm and gladden Him
With my heart's
Ever-increasing smiles.

27

To-day is the day
That God wants me
To become His Vision's
Full manifestation-champion-
   hero.

28

To-day is the day
That I must clearly
And perfectly sweep
My mind-path.

29

To-day is the day
That God is telling me
My God-realisation-life
Has His Eternity's Breath.

30

To-day is the day
That each thought of mine
Must arrive
At its God-Destination-Home.

31

To-day is the day
Of God's heralding
My unconditional
God-surrender-life.

32

To-day is the day
I have come to learn
That God secretly
And sacredly records
All my
God-manifestation-promises.

33

To-day is the day
God has decided
To teach my heart
His own
Nectar-flooded Heart-Songs.

34

To-day is the day
That I shall not,
Even for a fleeting moment,
Step into the messy puddles
Of life.

35

To-day is the day
God is telling me
That each moment of my life
Is a new fulfilment-promise
Of His Vision here on earth.

36

To-day is the day
God is telling me
To claim unreservedly
His Eternity, Infinity
And Immortality
As my own, very own.

37

To-day is the day
That my complete
God-satisfaction-dream
Begins.

38

To-day is the day
God has promised to carry
My gratitude-heart-tears
Wherever He goes.

39

To-day is the day
That I am seeing for the first time
My unconditional
God-surrender-life
Nestled in God's own Elysian Lap.

40

To-day is the day
God is telling me
That I shall be able
To understand my Master
Only after
My God-realisation.

41

To-day is the day
God is telling me
My Master's heart
Is His inner Choice
And
My Master's life
Is His outer Voice.

42

To-day is the day
God is asking me
To constantly breathe
World-peace-dreams,
Like my Master.

43

To-day is the day
God is telling me
That definitely there shall
   come a day
When this world of ours
Will be ready
For real spiritual Masters –
His direct representatives
Here on earth.

44

To-day is the day
I have come to realise
The supreme truth:
The Forgiveness-Sun
Of my Absolute Lord Beloved
   Supreme
Never sets.

45

To-day is the day
God wants me to offer Him
My ceaselessly complaining mind
And receive from Him
His endlessly forgiving Heart.

46

To-day is the day
That God wants to proudly watch
The perfect union
Of
My heart's streaming tears
And
His Heart's beaming Smiles.

47

To-day is the day
God wants to hear
Only my heart-songs
And not my mind-stories.

48

To-day is the day
God wants to strike
My God-manifestation-
   Victory-drums.

49

To-day is the day
God wants me to slow down
And, before long, to stop
My life-journey on the
   desire-road.

50

To-day is the day
God wants me to speed up
And, before long,
To drive the fastest
Until I have reached
My Immortality's
  Destination-Home.

51

To-day is the day
God has decided
To stop examining
My heart's
Sincerity-flooded tears.

52

To-day is the day
God has decided
To examine every day
My mind's
Insincerity-inundated smiles.

53

To-day is the day
I have decided to send
My devotion-letters to God
With my gratitude-heart-tears.

54

To-day is the day
God has severely scolded me
For standing for such a long time
Outside His Heart-Door.

55

To-day is the day
God has completely destroyed
My desire-jungles,
So that I can look at Him
And drink deep the Beauty
Of His Compassion-Eye
At my sweet will.

56

To-day is the day
God has changed my prayer
From
"Give me!"
To
"Take me!"

57

To-day is the day
God has shown me
That my mind's pride-balloon
Is shockingly empty of God.

58

To-day is the day
God has firmly closed
My two world-doubting eyes.

59

To-day is the day
God has proudly opened
My world-embracing heart.

60

To-day is the day
God has sternly halted
My ignorance-indulgence-
   walking life.

61

To-day is the day
I have seen the Beauty
Of God's Face,
I have smelled the Fragrance
Of God's Heart
And I have won
God's Oneness-Partnership.

62

To-day is the day
God wants me to sit beside Him
On His Golden Throne
And not in front of Him.

63

To-day is the day
God has told me
That my heart-tears
Are infinitely more powerful
Than His Justice-Light.

64

To-day is the day
That the tears of my heart
Are singing and dancing
With the smiles of my soul.

65

To-day is the day
God has come to me
With His unconditional Heart's
Compassion-Eye.

66

To-day is the day
That I soulfully asked God,
"My Lord,
Who am I?"
God's proud Answer is:
"My child,
Who are you not?"

67

To-day is the day
God has promised me
A perpetual
Aspiration-heart-bloom.

68

To-day is the day
I have given God
An affection-drop
From my heart,
And He, in return,
Has given me
A Fondness-Ocean
From His Heart.

69

To-day is the day
God has blessingfully granted
My gratitude-heart-tears
A permanent home:
His own Heart-Home.

70

To-day is the day
I have given God
The thorns of my desire-life
And
The roses of my aspiration-heart.
He has gladly and equally
Accepted them.

"My child,
Since the beginning of
   My creation,
I have been claiming you
As My own, very own.
What is wrong with you?
Can you not also do the same?"

My Lord,
I certainly can.
I am doing it.

"My child,
You have done it.
You have done it.
You have done it."

PART XLV

THE STREET BEGGAR

THE STREET BEGGAR

1

The final journey,
No, no!
A million times!

2

An ever-blossoming voyage,
Yes, yes!
A billion times!

3

When things go wrong,
God gives us the opportunity
To run towards Him more
　speedily
And more self-givingly
To have joy in His smiling
Heart-Garden.

4

If I find God
Inside a tiny drop,
Then, immediately,
God the Ocean
Becomes mine.

5

Adversity
Purifies the mind
And strengthens the heart.

6

Who is educated?
Not he who has read
Countless books,
But he who is fed
By God's Compassion-flooded
　Heart.

7

When we pray on our knees,
God the Tree,
With flower-beauty
And fruit-nourishment,
Bends.

8

We give so much importance
To the blackness of our mind.

9

We have no time to pay attention
To the whiteness of our heart.

10

Love Light more.
Night is bound
To disappear.

11

The mind knows
How to dictate me.

12

The heart knows
How to elevate me.

13

When we look at life,
It frightens us.
When we look into life,
It surrenders.

14

The depression-mountain
Blightens the mind.

15

The humour-fountain
Lightens the mind.

16

The most important thing in life
Is not possession
But transformation.

17

Slow down, slow down,
If you really need
God's golden Crown.

18

My eyes love
To see beauty.

19

My heart loves
To become Beauty,
God-Beauty.

20

Battlefield-victory
Does not last.

21

Heart-field-victory
Forever lasts.

22

We are such fools.
We want to know what life has
And not what life is.

23

The human in us
Works to live.

24

The divine in us
Lives to work,
God's Work.

25

God will share with us
His almighty Will-Power
If we dare to control
The inhuman in us.

26

Work-retirement
Must not be
Life-retirement.

27

The doctor knows
How to create fear.

28

The Master knows
How to blossom cheer.

29

Life begins
Not when we think of time,
But when we become
The Lord of time.

30

Faith is the medicine
For the mind-malady.

31

Love is the vitamin
For the life-comedy.

32

Leadership sinks.
Friendship sails.

33

The blunders of the past
Must be kept behind us
And not ahead of us.

34

Do not continue to fret.
Try to forget.
Happiness guaranteed!

35

There are countless exercises.
The most difficult exercise
Is self-giving.

36

Why not say it?
God is all yours.

37

Why not do it?
Touch and remain
At God's Feet.

38

The Compassion-Eye
Descends unconditionally.

39

The aspiration-heart
Ascends swiftly.

40

The heartiest smile
Is
The strongest power.

41

We strengthen
The difficult people
By thinking of them.

42

We disarm
The difficult people
By placing them
At the Feet of God.

43

Until God's unconditional Grace
Descends,
I must be responsible
For my own fate.

44

A strange request:
God, give me
What You have.

45

A spontaneous request:
God, take me
And my all.

46

The outer loneliness
Needs friends
And acquaintances.

47

The inner loneliness
Needs only God
And nobody else.

48

God wants me to live
Not on borrowed time.

49

God wants me to live
Inside
His hallowed Eternity.

50

Aspiration says:
"I shall do it."

51

Dedication says:
"I am doing it."

52

Surrender says:
"I have already done it."

53

Happiness is not
An outer fruit.

54

Happiness is
An inner seed.

55

The human artist
Paints
The outer world.

56

The divine artist
Dreams
Of the inner world.

57

God sleeplessly tells me
That He wants to be
The prisoner of my love.

58

The God who tells me
To pray
Is the same God who asks me
To take time to play.

59

Life
Is not a series
Of disappointments.

60

Life
Is a daily
God-appointment.

61

Future
Is not darkness.

62

Future
Is God-oneness.

63

I do not want
My life
To go my way.

64

I am choosing,
Once and for all,
One way:
God's Way.

65

There is only one race:
The masked God-Face.

66

For me,
Nothing can be sweeter
And purer
Than my God-starvation-heart.

67

Success is
Dollar-power.

68

Progress is
God-Shower.

69

God frequently comes
To my heart-emptiness.

70

God never comes
To my mind-loneliness.

71

The mind's constant question:
Why?

72

The heart's immediate answer:
Why not?

73

Yesterday
God cried for me.
He cried for my perfection.

74

Today
I am crying for God.
I am crying for God's Satisfaction.

75

From tomorrow,
Smilingly,
God and I will live
Only for each other.

76

When I keep my eyes closed
And pray,
I feel that God is for me.

77

When I keep my eyes half-open
And meditate,
I am absolutely certain
That I am all for God.

78

Prayer
Is the life-seed.

79

Meditation
Is the life-plant.

80

Contemplation is the life-tree
That produces
Flower-beauty-enjoyment
And
Fruit-nourishment-satisfaction.

81

Final earth-departure
Has no extension.

82

God wants me
To count His Smiles first.
Only then
Will He count my tears.

83

Gratitude-virtue
Is yet
An unborn reality.

84

Disobedience
Is not the humiliation
Of the Master.

85

Disobedience
Is the self-annihilation
Of the disciple.

86

God's immediate Choice
Is the heart that bleeds
For humanity's smiles.

87

The mind
Is the usual
Cloud-lover.

88

The heart
Is the spontaneous
Star-enjoyer.

89

Perfection
Is the sleepless
Self-examination.

90

Satisfaction
Is the breathless
God-invocation.

91

God pleads with me:
"My child,
Be true to yourself!"

92

We must pay attention
To our imperfections –
If not, sooner than at once
They will multiply.

93

A thought-minus mind
Is
A soul-plus will.

94

When I love God,
I let things happen
In God's Way.

95

When I love myself,
I make things happen
In my way.

96

The mind-thorn
Is
Extremely dangerous.

97

The heart-rose
Is
Supremely precious.

98

God tells me
That my half world-dedication
Equals
My full God-aspiration.

99

God tells me repeatedly
Not to take His Work away.
His Work is to change the world,
And my work
Is to love the world.

100

Each smile
Is the beauty
Of a new heart.

101

Each tear
Is the fragrance
Of a new life.

102

God wants me
To complete
My illumination-task.

103

God does not want me
To compete
With the rest of the world
In the battlefield of life.

104

With each hope
I walk
Towards God's Palace.

105

With each promise
God runs
Towards my heart-temple.

106

Patience, patience, patience!
Patience
Is the ultimate victory.

107

Everybody hates darkness,
But how many are willing
To invoke Light?

108

If you are great,
That means
You know how to talk.

109

If you are good,
That means
You know how to listen.

110

If you are perfect,
That means your silence-sound
Is the answer.

111

The life that has no tears
Cannot near God.

112

You say that the world
Is full of wrong forces.
Unfortunately,
Your own mighty contribution
Cannot remain unnoticed.

113

The eyes can see the world,
But the heart alone
Can become the world.

114

Do not stop
Being an all-lover.
Do not stoop
To being a supremacy-hunger.

115

Man's mind
Builds houses.
God's Heart
Makes homes.

116

Today's street beggar
Shall become tomorrow
The keeper
Of God's Heart-Door.

APPENDIX

FOREWORDS TO FIRST EDITIONS

Forword to *My soul is free*

The poems in this volume were offered by Sri Chinmoy during meetings and meditation sessions held in 1988.

Forword to *A heart of oneness-peace*

Sri Chinmoy offered the poems in this book during Peace Concerts in the United States, Canada, Europe, Australia and New Zealand from February to July 1989.

Forword to *The Moment I please God in God's own Way*

The following prayers were offered by Sri Chinmoy in New York during February and March 2000 and recited turn by turn by various girls' and boys' groups.

Forword to *Here and Now*

The following poems on the theme "Here and Now" were written by Sri Chinmoy during the six-month period from 29 May to 1 November 2000. He recited many of them at various Peace Concerts in America and abroad during this time.

BIBLIOGRAPHY

SRI CHINMOY:

— *Disobedience, time is up!*, New York, Agni Press, 1994.
Suggested citation key: DT

— *Matter and spirit*, New York, Agni Press, 1993.
Suggested citation key: MTS

— *My perfection-promise to God*, New York, Agni Press, 1993.
Suggested citation key: PPG

— *I am my life's God-hunger-heart, part 1,* New York, Agni Press, 1994.
Suggested citation key: GHH

— *I am my life's God-hunger-heart, part 2,* New York, Agni Press, 1994.
Suggested citation key: GHH

— *I am my life's God-hunger-heart, part 3,* New York, Agni Press, 1994.
Suggested citation key: GHH

— *I am my life's God-hunger-heart, part 4,* New York, Agni Press, 1994.
Suggested citation key: GHH.

— *Fast, faster, fastest progress*, New York, Agni Press, 1994.
Suggested citation key: FFF

— *God's Compassion-Eye and my happiness-heart*, New York, Agni Press, 1994.
Suggested citation key: GCE

— *My life's sixty-three heart-blossoms*, New York, Agni Press, 1994.
Suggested citation key: LHB

— *My soul is free*, New York, Agni Press, 1994.
Suggested citation key: MSF

— *No return on my God-Destination Road*, New York, Agni Press, 1994.
Suggested citation key: NRG

— *Command from God the Justice, Whisper from God the Compassion*, New York, Agni Press, 1994.
Suggested citation key: CGJ

— *God's Heart I desire, God's Feet I choose*, New York, Agni Press, 1994.
Suggested citation key: GHF

— *Take your God-search seriously,* New York, Agni Press, 1994.
Suggested citation key: GSS

— *Heaven's ecstasy-flames,* New York, Agni Press, 1994.
Suggested citation key: HEF

— *Idleness: the loneliest existence in the entire world,* New York, Agni Press, 1994.
Suggested citation key: IL

— *Impurity: the mad elephant mental asylum,* New York, Agni Press, 1994.
Suggested citation key: IME

— *My jealousy is my madness-burden,* New York, Agni Press, 1994.
Suggested citation key: JMB

— *No unreachable goal,* New York, Agni Press, 1994.
Suggested citation key: NUG

— *Say a final farewell to your mind's bondage-life,* New York, Agni Press, 1994.
Suggested citation key: SFF

— *Success-jumps, progress-songs,* New York, Agni Press, 1994.
Suggested citation key: SJS

— *Peace: God's Heart-Home, part 1,* New York, Agni Press, 1995.
Suggested citation key: PGH-1

— *Peace: God's Heart-Home, part 2,* New York, Agni Press, 1995.
Suggested citation key: PGH-2

— *My evening descends,* New York, Agni Press, 1996.
Suggested citation key: ED

— *My morning begins,* New York, Agni Press, 1996.
Suggested citation key: MMB

— *Power and love,* New York, Agni Press, 1996.
Suggested citation key: PL

— *Science and nature,* New York, Agni Press, 1996.
Suggested citation key: SN

– *A true disciple,* New York, Agni Press, 1998.
Suggested citation key: TD

– *I climb up, I fall down,* New York, Agni Press, 1998.
Suggested citation key: CUF

– *The difference between God and me,* New York, Agni Press, 1998.
Suggested citation key: DFM

– *God's Greatness and God's Goodness,* New York, Agni Press, 1998.
Suggested citation key: GG

– *I am flying and flying and flying,* New York, Agni Press, 1998.
Suggested citation key: IFF

– *Retirement not granted,* New York, Agni Press, 1998.
Suggested citation key: RNG

– *A heart of oneness-peace,* New York, Agni Press, 1999.
Suggested citation key: HOP

– *God was simply shocked,* New York, Agni Press, 1999.
Suggested citation key: GWS

– *My Lord reads my letters,* New York, Agni Press, 1999.
Suggested citation key: LRL

– *The difference between a false Master and a true Master,* New York, Agni Press, 1999.
Suggested citation key: DFM

– *Two divine qualities: confidence and sincerity,* New York, Agni Press, 1999.
Suggested citation key: TDQ

– *Emperor-smiles. Orphan-tears,* New York, Agni Press, 2000.
Suggested citation key: ES

– *The moment I please God in God's own Way,* New York, Agni Press, 2000.
Suggested citation key: MIP

– *My Sunrise-Heart, part 1,* New York, Agni Press, 2000.
Suggested citation key: MSH

– *Yes, I can! I certainly can!!,* New York, Agni Press, 2000.
Suggested citation key: YIC

– *Great people and good people,* New York, Agni Press, 2001.
Suggested citation key: GP

– *Here and now,* New York, Agni Press, 2001.
Suggested citation key: HN

– *If I could start my life once more,* New York, Agni Press, 2001.
Suggested citation key: ICS

– *My life's every day hope-blossoms and promise-trees,* New York, Agni Press, 2001.
Suggested citation key: MLE

– *My Master,* New York, Agni Press, 2001.
Suggested citation key: MM

— *To-day is the day,* New York, Agni Press, 2001.
Suggested citation key: TID

— *The street beggar,* New York, Agni Press, 2003.
Suggested citation key: STB

POSTFACE

Publishing principles

This edition of *The works of Sri Chinmoy* aims to obey the Author's wish: scrupulous fidelity to his original words, use of typographical style by him selected, specific spelling choices, end placement of any editorial content (i.e. not written by Sri Chinmoy himself), particular treatment of some personal nouns in special cases, etc.

Textual accuracy

The text of this edition has been checked to ensure faithful accuracy to the originals. Although much effort has been put in proofreading and comparing different versions of the text, this print may still present a few lingering errors.

The publisher would be grateful to be apprised of any mistypes, possibly with scan of the original page where the text is different. Please use original books only, specifying the year of publication.

Acknowledgements

Our deepest gratitude to Sri Chinmoy. His living presence can be felt breathing throughout his writings. It is a privilege to be involved with his works, in any form.

Sri Chinmoy Canon

We could not use better words than Professor Lambert's, who kindly offered the name Sri Chinmoy Canon:

> «By defining Sri Chinmoy's first editions as editio princeps we chose to follow classical scholarship criteria, not because we consider Sri Chinmoy's work antique, but because we believe it is among the few post ‹classical antiquity› works to rightly deserve to be considered a classicus, designating by that term superiority, authority and perfection.
>
> «The monumental work Sri Chinmoy is offering to mankind is awe-inspiring and supremely pre-eminent in proportions and quality. It is manifest that Sri Chinmoy's work — which we feel right to call The Sri Chinmoy Canon — will be of profound help and source of enlightenment to anyone seeking a higher wisdom, truth and reality supreme.»

[Translated from French by M.G.S.]

TABLE OF CONTENTS

Disobedience, time is up!	13
Matter and spirit	23
My perfection-promise to God	33
I am my life's God-hunger-heart	41
Fast, faster, fastest progress	71
God's Compassion-Eye and my happiness-heart	85
My life's sixty-three heart-blossoms	99
My soul is free	109
No return on my God-Destination Road	121
Command from God the Justice, Whisper from God the Compassion	129
God's Heart I desire, God's Feet I choose	139
Take your God-search seriously	147
Heaven's ecstasy-flames	157
Idleness: the loneliest existence in the entire world	167
Impurity: the mad elephant mental asylum	177
My jealousy is my madness-burden	187
No unreachable goal	195
Say a final farewell to your mind's bondage-life	205
Success-jumps, progress-songs	213
Peace: God's Heart-Home	223
My evening descends	247
My morning begins	299
Power and love	349
Science and nature	359
A true disciple	367
I climb up, I fall down	377
The difference between God and me	387
God's Greatness and God's Goodness	403
I am flying and flying and flying	413
Retirement not granted	423
A heart of oneness-peace	429
God was simply shocked	445
My Lord reads my letters	455
The difference between a false Master and a true Master	477
Two divine qualities: confidence and sincerity	489

Emperor-smiles. Orphan-tears	499
The moment I please God in God's own Way	509
My Sunrise-Heart, part 1	527
Yes, I can! I certainly can!!	543
Great people and good people	559
Here and now	573
If I could start my life once more	603
My life's every day hope-blossoms and promise-trees	615
My Master	625
To-day is the day	633
The street beggar	645
Appendix	659
Forewords to first editions	661
Bibliography	665
Postface	671
Table of contents	675

www.ingramcontent.com/pod-product-compliance
Lightning Source LLC
Chambersburg PA
CBHW030110240426
43661CB00031B/1357/J